SEAPORTS AND SEAPORT TERMINALS

Geography

Editor

PROFESSOR W. G. EAST

Professor Emeritus of Geography
in the University of London

SEAPORTS AND
SEAPORT TERMINALS

James Bird
B.A., Ph.D., A.M.Inst.T.

*Professor of Geography
in the University of Southampton*

HUTCHINSON UNIVERSITY LIBRARY
LONDON

HUTCHINSON & CO (*Publishers*) LTD
178–202 Great Portland Street, London W1

London Melbourne Sydney Auckland
Wellington Johannesburg Cape Town
and agencies throughout the world

First published 1971

*The cover of the paperback edition shows container
cargo ships loading and unloading at Port Elizabeth,
New Jersey. By courtesy of the Port of New York
Authority*

© James Bird 1971

*This book has been set in Times type, printed in Great Britain
on smooth wove paper by Anchor Press, and
bound by Wm. Brendon, both of Tiptree, Essex*

ISBN 0 09 107340 5 (cased)
0 09 107341 3 (paper)

TO MY WIFE

Every ultimate fact is but
the first of a new series and
every general law a particular
fact of some more general law
presently to disclose itself.
Ralph Waldo Emerson

CONTENTS

MAPS AND DIAGRAMS

PREFACE

The main objective of this book has been to draw forth from seaport study such useful generalisations as can be made, using real-life cases as illustrative examples. To carry out this task an army of references has been marshalled and is presented for review, not to daunt the reader but to aid him in following up a point, perhaps raised here in over-compressed form. If you love ships and the sea, you may be disappointed to see vessels sail in and out of the ports as rather blurred silhouettes. For once, you encounter an author who is determined to make seaports the stars of the show. That this is a rather rare aim is surprising when one considers the importance of seaports to national and international economies. One of the reasons for this curious state of affairs is that a seaport is a functional meeting place not only of many trades but also of many professions, and he who would probe deeply into the one subject of seaport functioning must also probe widely—hence the ranks of references comprise very varied recruits indeed. On some particular aspects of seaport functioning the number of references is already of flood proportions. In answer to the oft-repeated query, 'Have you any literature on containers?', the Secretary-General of the International Cargo Handling Coordination Association (ICHCA) is inclined to reply: 'Send a container, and we will fill it.' The required dimensions of this particular container will soon rise from 20 ft ISO standard to the standard length of 40 ft.

This book was produced in 1971 and will date quickly or slowly according to the rate of particular seaport developments. But it has been written with this contingency in mind, so that the reader who knows of subsequent long- or short-term trends can consider the conclusions of this book against the background of what has actually happened. It may be reassuring to realise that in such a developing subject the reader always has this advantage over an author imprisoned in his pages. However, it is psychologically very satisfying to write on a subject that has a rising curve of interest which it is hoped this book does nothing to flatten.

The study could not have been undertaken without the detailed work produced within the industry itself and by students in universities and institutes, some of whom may not have been primarily concerned with seaports as such, yet who have provided valuable insights on the subject of their functioning. I should particularly like to thank Dr G. A. Theel, Director of the Institute of Maritime Economics, Bremen, who with his multi-lingual staff made me so welcome and helped as guides through the Bremen treasure-house of seaport and shipping literature. The officers of the British National Ports Council were very helpful in making available many references including their commissioned consultancy reports. I should also like to thank those correspondents in seaports all over the world who did their best to answer questions which at the time must have seemed bizarre or bald without the context in which the answers were intended to be set. The publishers and the editor of the series deserve a special medal for patience; at times it must have seemed that these ports would never appear over the horizon.

All the maps and diagrams were prepared in the Cartographic Unit here in the Department of Geography at Southampton, under the supervision of the Senior Experimental Officer and Chief Draughtsman, Mr A. S. Burn, A.M.Inst.T. To him and to my secretary, Mrs R. Flint, I extend my gratitude for their skill in dealing with difficult MSS.

Lastly, and most important, a world-wide survey of ports in a brief compass is bound to contain errors of emphasis and of fact, despite attempts to be as objective and accurate as possible. The author would be most grateful if readers in a position to improve the text on either count would dispatch cargoes of information to improve the quality per unit of weight of this particular export from Southampton.

Department of Geography   J.H.B.
University of Southampton
September 1970

INTRODUCTION:

THE SEAPORT AS MODERN TRANSPORT NODE

The modern major seaport has both cargo berths served by inland transport and deep-water terminals serving port industries, and this duality has been emphasised in the title of this book. A seaport is best defined in terms of its function as a place where each-way exchanges between land and sea transport regularly take place. Regularity of function cannot usually be achieved in exposed water sites, and today it is axiomatic that a successful commercial seaport is equipped with harbour properties, which may be natural but are usually artificially enhanced. Encyclopaedias and other works of reference abound with descriptions of 'fine natural harbours', very often resulting from the eustatic rise of sea-level since the last ice age as it impinged upon an area of considerable relief—fringing coral around a submerged volcanic cone (atoll), a drowned deep valley (ria harbour), or flooded glaciated valley (fiord). Attractive as such places appear on atlas maps, only rarely do their deep and sheltered waters form the prime desideratum for the location of a major multi-functional port. Consider the following equations:

$$C_i \propto V_i - A\frac{j}{n}$$

$$A\frac{j}{n} \propto (L,S,I)\frac{j}{n}$$

Putting this into words it can be said that the commercial importance (C) of a given port (i) is proportional to the amount of import and export cargo (V) in the port's hinterland minus the cargo (A) that could pass through the port but which is attracted to a rival port (j) or ports (n). The dimensions of this cargo attracted to rival ports $\left(A\dfrac{j}{n}\right)$ is proportional to the extent of the superiority of their land transport (L), the superiority of their number and type of sailings (S), and the superiority of their institutional factors, allowing that adjective to cover trading and financial practices, including special transport rates and governmental intervention. The word 'harbour' finds no place in such equations. Indeed, a British committee on port terminology found that

the words port and harbour have become interchangeable. . . . For convenience, port is used hereafter in this report. (*Report on Port Charges Terminology*, 1969, 4)

and 'harbour' referring to a concept separate from 'port' is not used again in this book.

There is a major twofold classification of cargoes handled by ports: bulk cargo and break-bulk cargo. Bulk cargo is essentially homogeneous, without packing, usually consisting of fuel or raw materials, and has been subject to the economies of scale in transport by ever larger bulk carriers. Such enormous consignments of cargo, often in instalments of 100,000 tons and more, are destined for storage in the port area immediately on landing and are then processed in some way in giant tidewater industries. At present, only crude oil can economically be transported in large quantities a long distance inland, and even then it is via a fixed pipeline link to the refining industry. The industrial function of ports has grown not only because of the availability of these deliveries of huge cargo instalments but also because large-scale industry needs wide flat sites, not too distant from home markets yet able to export overseas. The liberalisation of world trade has enabled industries in developed countries to rely on distant sources of fuel and raw materials, a trend particularly emphasised by the shift from coal to oil (L. H. Klaassen and N. Vanhove, 1970, 2). The giant long-voyaging ship services this industrial implantation in deep water alongside wide areas of flat land, often reclaimed downstream of the older-established areas of ports.

Break-bulk cargo used to be described as 'general cargo', an unsatisfactory term since it had a specific reference to heterogeneous dry cargo, packed in small lots, such as foods or high value per unit of weight raw materials or manufactured products, and all generally bound for many consignees. Many of these cargoes pass right through a port since their high value per unit of weight enables them to be transported economically by both rail and road. Uneconomic factors enter into play if such cargoes are delayed through slow transhipment methods in ports. A. S. Svendsen (1958, 101) once pointed out that conventional cargo liners may spend as little as 20–25% of their time at sea, and further that three-quarters of the time in port was 'dead time' for week-ends, holidays, and non-working hours in cases where ports worked a five-day week and one eight-hour shift per day (*The Turn-around Time of Ships*, 1967, 3). Such delays convert the ship into a highly expensive floating warehouse, thus adding to the cost of transport. The various forms of 'through' transport by unit cargo methods have revolutionised the conventional ways of handling break-bulk cargo package by package.

This simple twofold classification of cargoes introduces two concepts of cargo-handling in seaports. There are those cargoes that move 'through' a seaport considered as a gateway; and there are those that are delivered at deep-water specialised terminals for immediate storage and, most often, for first processing in the port area. The opening proposition returns: the modern seaport has within it functions which cause it to act as a sea 'port' or gateway, overseas or inland, and functions which cause it to act as a sea terminal.

Measuring the port

Bulk and break-bulk cargo make up the total tonnage passing through the port, and this dimension forms a convenient measure of port size, though passenger movements have to be handled differently. It must also be remembered that the higher value per unit of weight of break-bulk cargo probably brings more revenue to the port which like other transport organisations is well alive to the possibilities of charging what the traffic will bear. Break-bulk cargo movements are generally more difficult to organise, even when arranged in unit loads, because they must be shipped and collected to and from many different places. Students of seaports often undertake origin and destination studies to reveal significant port measures. Tonnages measured at the port are more meaningful if bulk and break-bulk cargoes are distinguished, though in practice this causes difficulties of data assignment. It is usually easier and a step in the right direction if fuels are separately totalled. Although tonnage handled is the most frequently used measure of port size, it does have disadvantages, but then so do all the available criteria (Table 1). Sometimes it is possible to combine two or more criteria to arrive at a more meaningful comparative picture when ports are arranged in league tables (J. Bird, 1968, 1–6; for types of port statistics and some problems of interpretation see A. S. Svendsen, 1958, 105–25). A most important aspect of port size is the datum against which it

TABLE 1

CRITERIA FOR ASSESSING COMPARATIVE SIZES OF PORTS

Criteria	Main disadvantage
Berthing accommodation for ships Capacity for cargo handling	} May not be fully used by vessels trading regularly
Depth of port approaches Depth of accommodation for ships	} Ports which can accommodate the largest ships are not necessarily the largest ports
Weight of cargoes landed and shipped	Raw material and fuel-handling ports over-'weighted'
Value of cargoes landed and shipped	Fluctuates with rise and fall of prices
Net registered tonnage of shipping entering	Vessels may arrive with partly-loaded cargoes or in ballast

is measured or compared, and this is also the case when measuring the hinterlands of ports or their forelands overseas. Some of the problems attendant on these exercises are discussed at length in this book, but this introduction to the subject may be illustrated with the type of approach involved when making more meaningful the progression of the tonnage through-put of a single port arranged in an annual time series. P. J. Rimmer, 1966, measured such an individual time series against the total cargo handled in a national unit in which the port is located. An economic unit could also be employed as the 'universe'. Suppose port X had 3·7% of the total tonnage handled in its national unit in 1950, and 5·6% in 1961, an increase of concentration of 1·9%. This concentration can be translated into absolute terms by

calculating the difference between the actual tonnage of a port in 1961 and hypothetical figures showing what the tonnage would have been if the port had grown at the national rate between 1950 and 1961. The formulae for calculating the difference between the actual and hypothetical tonnage are:

(1) $H_p = X_p \, YNZ \div XNZ$
(2) $Y_p - H_p =$ comparative gain or loss
$H_p =$ hypothetical tonnage of port
$X_p =$ tonnage of port in initial year
$XNZ =$ tonnage of New Zealand [the universe in question] in initial year
$YNZ =$ tonnage of New Zealand ports in terminal year
$Y_p =$ tonnage of port in terminal year

(loc. cit., 2–3)

The 'Cleveland' effect—ports as weighted median locations

A simplified sequence of events is now put forward: growth of demand; growth of supply to meet the demand; ships are built to service the links of the trade; ports arise at the boundary (the economic interface) between sea and land transport to marry them together. As the sea carriers are usually much larger than those on land, port engineers have their biggest problems in satisfying ship requirements. The location of a port is almost by definition of its function to be seen as eccentric to the land area in which it is situated, although this eccentricity is often reduced by siting ports at heads of inland navigations, a site that becomes less easy to sustain as ships grow larger. Seaports often have flourishing industries, although they may be sited midway between the raw materials and fuel supplies, or between centres of primary production and major consumer markets. For shorthand this may be called the 'Cleveland' effect, since the lakeside steelmaking port of Cleveland, Ohio, occupies such a midway location between Superior iron ore and Pennsylvania coal; and also, rather nicely in order to drive the point home, the discovery of iron ore in the Cleveland Hills of Yorkshire in 1850 pulled the iron industry to the port site of the Ironmasters' district of the then new town of Middlesbrough and away from the coking coal of west Durham (J. Bird, 1963, 67). Such a midway position can have a sound economic basis founded on transport costs, as W. Alonso, 1964, 86–8, has shown for a one-material, one-market concern. In Fig. 1 the top curve represents total transport costs, and is the sum of the two curves below it.

... if the plant is located at M, the costs will be $e+f+g+h$; if it is located at B, the costs will be $a+b+g+h$; and if it is located at C, they will be $a+b+c+d$. (loc. cit., 87)

The costs at B, the port, are represented as being the same as at the production centre (M) and the market (C)—the three low points on the top curve. A location anywhere else adds another transhipment cost. Of course, transport rates vary, but they may do so to give the port location an even greater advantage, especially if through commercial and industrial success it becomes an important market in its own right, as has been the case with so many of the great world port-city metropolises. This is also why so much of the world's steel produced from ore by fuel power is made in port locations off the coking coalfields and often thousands of miles away from the sources of iron ore.

These ideas of minimum total transport costs can be translated on to a map using techniques derived from classical location theory.

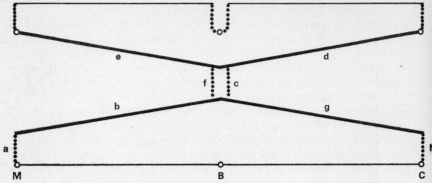

Fig. 1 Three possible locations for minimum transport costs: production centre, market, and port

M is a production centre; B a port; and C a market. a indicates port loading and unloading costs; b sea transport costs, M to B; c inland transport loading costs at B and unloading costs at C; d inland transport costs; e the cost of moving the finished product from M to B; f the loading and unloading costs in ports; g the cost of moving the product from B to C; and h the costs of loading and unloading the inland transport. The total of the two curves appears at the top of the diagram. For further explanation see text.

Source: W. Alonso, 1964, 87.

Since many university departments of geography run whole lecture courses on the development and elaboration of this subject, such a wide topic can receive only the minimum of treatment here, allowing cartographic application of theory to illuminate the advantages of port location for industry. Classical location theory derives from A. Weber, 1909, with notable refinements and extensions by E. M. Hoover, 1948, and W. Isard, 1956, and a fundamental basis is minimum transport costs. The pull of the port due to the minimisation of transport costs can be demonstrated on a map by the devices of isovectures (or isotims) and isodapanes. An isovecture is a line joining places having equal component transport costs, and an isodapane is a line joining points with the same total transport costs.

The first example comes from O. Lindberg, 1953. In Fig. 2 (top)

Fig. 2 The pull of the port

H is a port, and A an inland centre; a and b refer to rivers. The thick lines are isodapanes, lines joining places with the same total transport costs, comprising relevant totals of the values of iso-vectures (thinner lines), joining places with equal component transport costs. For further explanation see text.

Source: O. Lindberg, 1953, 31–2.

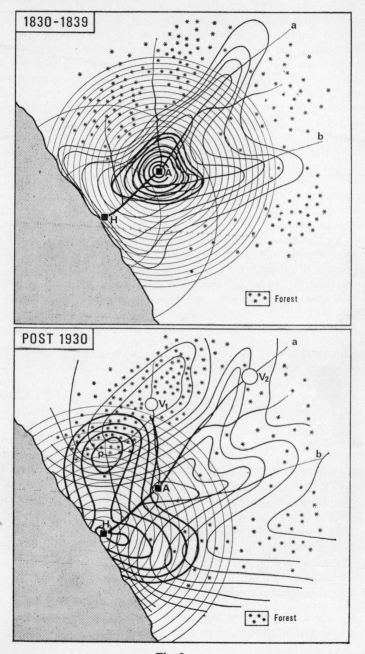

Fig. 2

there are three sets of isovectures. The first emanate from the inland centre *A*, source of straw and rags, raw material for the Swedish paper industry at the hand-mill stage in the second quarter of the nineteenth century. The isovectures are elongated by the cheapness of river transport along rivers *a* and *b*. The isovectures representing costs of transport of finished paper increase outwards in all directions from the main consumption centre *A*. It is assumed that only a small quantity is exported, so that the isovectures are much wider apart around port *H* than inland centre *A*. The resultant isodapanes (heavy lines) clearly favour inland centre *A*. From 1930 a constrasted picture is manifest. The raw material for the paper industry is now the forest so that isovectures are thinly distributed over the woodland and cluster together in inhabited areas. The seaport *H* has increased in importance, since paper is exported and fuel must be imported. The most important source of power is at harnessed waterfalls V_1 and V_2. But since water power can be cheaply transported to the chosen site, the mill can be located away from the power source at the points of minimum total transport costs at *p* or the seaport *H*. An example using actual transport costs is given by O. Lindberg (p. 39) where it can be seen that the isodapanes have low values at ports.

A second example is given by J. A. Quinn, 1943. In Fig. 3 figures in brackets indicate per mile costs of transport to or from each location per 500 units of finished products. *A*, *B*, and *C* are locations of raw materials; *P* is a source of power; and *M* and *N* are the markets. It is assumed that unit transport costs to market are 50 per unit of distance. The optimum location for an industry with the indicated relative transport costs, using such raw materials and power, is at *M*. If a coastline is added to J. A. Quinn's diagram ($C-C_1$), such that the industry also exports overseas (arrow), then the weighted median and optimum location of the port *M*, which will have provided a market through its associated urban population in the first place, will be reinforced for that industry. The weighted median location could be defined as the site where half the transport costs are balanced in all directions along relevant routes. Since transport costs are unequal, relative to the different inputs, the weighted median locations may well be eccentric to the distribution of the inputs and the markets, as in the case of Fig. 3. If industries depend on large amounts of seaborne imported inputs, or seek to add overseas export sales, there will be an increased weighting for the eccentric locations occupied by seaports.

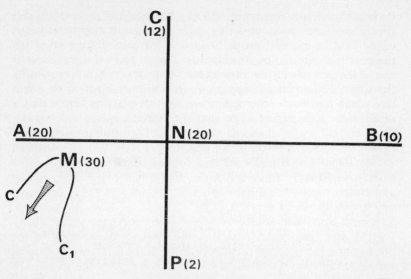

Fig. 3 The weighted median location
For explanation see text.
Source: after J. A. Quinn, 1943, 155.

The gateway concept

The student of ports is quite accustomed to the eccentric position of
the port city with reference to the hinterland served. A proposition
could be made that port location is not an aberrant case in urban
geography but can provide valuable insights into the laws governing
spatial organisation. Consider the simple case of a country with a
small peninsular appendage. A regional centre, R, is likely to arise
in the middle of the shoulder by which the peninsula is joined to the
main body of the country—a location where the settlement can act
as ambassador for the peninsula to the rest of the country and
through which all links to and from the peninsula can be focussed.
The only likely rivals to such a location are coastal port sites which
might pull R off the geometric centre of the peninsular shoulder.

Imagine next a provincial boundary existing across the peninsular
shoulder. The city, R, offset from the geometric centre of the peninsula, may yet be central to a service area lying on either side of the
provincial boundary. Now allow the provincial boundary to become
a coast. The peninsula becomes an island in which PR, a port city,
is, of course, still situated off the centre of the island. But as far as

its port function is concerned, *PR* can be regarded as serving a discontinuous total space consisting of the contiguous hinterland in the island and the overseas areas, or forelands (see p. 126), with which the port is connected by its shipping. Again, this total service area can be thought of as lying athwart the boundary, now represented by the coast. These remarks apply only to the port function of *PR*, a city which has many other functions. Some equations below merely repeat these ideas, using a few simple assumptions.

Let the area served by $R=P+M$
P is the area served (functions $\times$ area) in the peninsula
M is the area served (functions $\times$ area) on the mainland
$P=M$

Let the total space served by $PR=I+F_1 \ldots F_n$
I is the area served by the port function in the island
$F_1 \ldots F_n$ are the areas served by the port overseas
$I=F_1 \ldots F_n$ (when the sum of functions $\times$ area is performed and the trade is balanced)

Let the number of forelands be four and all of equal importance
Let R and PR have the same total functional importance
Let the port function account for one-quarter of *PR*'s total functions
Then

$$I=\frac{P}{8}$$

$$F_1=\frac{P}{32}$$

$\frac{P}{8}$ is to be taken not as meaning that the port hinterland in the island is only one-eighth the size of the city service area in the peninsula, but that the port function represents one-eighth of the functional importance of the city over the entire service area of similar extent. The other 'eighth' must be spread out over the forelands overseas to meet the assumption that the port function accounts for one-quarter of the port city's total functions. In real life the $\frac{P}{32}$ functions overseas are discharged by four overseas ports, if each foreland is assumed to have one port. But under conditions of balanced trade these ports dispatch trade from their hinterlands to *PR*, increasing its port function for the island hinterland by $4 \times \frac{P}{32}$, if the trade is balanced. Thus

$$I = \frac{P}{8} + \frac{4P}{32}$$

meeting the assumption that the port function accounts for one-quarter of PR's total functions.

A regional centre is likely to have a service area the shape of which narrows towards settlements of a higher order. For reasons which will be discussed in the chapter on hinterlands (p. 133 ff.), a successful port is likely to have a hinterland shape that widens inland. However, the dominant direction of trade is also important. Vancouver's hinterland for Far East imports into Canada extends much further east than it does for European imports (R. Robinson, 1967, 53–4). These ideas can perhaps be summed up by saying that the gateway function of settlements can pull them off centre of the areas they serve—the gateway concept. This would certainly apply to ports which are gateways by definition and often sited off centre *force majeure*, since deep-water ships often cannot penetrate to the heart of densely populated areas. These seem to be the major distortions introduced by transport into the idea of settlements at the centre of service areas of a size proportional to settlement size and rank ('central place theory', see p. 132). The gateway concept needs more testing in the real world. One way of doing this is to go back to a point in time to postulate how networks might develop between settlements, leading to a selective growth of the settlements subsequently. The generated model patterns can then be compared with what actually happened (K. J. Kansky, 1963, used Sicily as an example). W. R. Black, 1967, experimented in generating the railway network of southern Maine from 1840. He found that the most important hypotheses were (1) nearness to the point at which the network began; (2) a gravity model formulation (see below, p. 136 ff.); and (3) closeness of route link orientation with regional orientation. In a region with important overseas trading links, regional orientation is channelled through relatively few coastal locations. One can then imagine the implications for the development of nodes and routes in the transport network of the hinterland—leading back to the idea of spatial organisation based on geometrically 'eccentric centres'.

Countries with shapes that narrow towards coasts, or which possess low coastal length/area ratios (centripetal coastlines) are likely to have port concentration; whereas countries that have high coastal length/area ratios, such as peninsulas and islands (centrifugal coastlines), may find themselves equipped with many ports, with difficult problems of selection if port concentration is demanded by the technology of the day and by economic groupings that come to transcend national boundaries in common markets or free trade areas. However, length of coastline is not deterministically related to the availability of port sites. A gateway location, a port site, is not to be thought of as something intrinsically possessed by a given location, for these are qualities imposed on places by man. And man's actions are not determined by the environment (physical and social) but by what he thinks the environment determines him to do, given the knowledge that he has at any one particular time.

The proclaimed impulse and the ports ahead

For many major ports it is now impossible to determine the reasons for the original foundation. It is important to remember that the location of ports is due not to the direct influence of any inherent qualities of land and water sites, but to the way in which such sites were assessed by the founders. Australia provides fascinating details of port foundation because the original decision-makers had to give explicit reasons to their superiors in London. The general areas of choice for the first Australian seaports, now the Australian state capitals, depended on the following major considerations: (1) the question of desirable isolation (Sydney, Hobart, and Brisbane) or, in the case of the free settlement of Adelaide, isolation from the contamination of convict colonies; (2) centrality to potential agricultural areas not fully explored at the time of foundation (Perth–Fremantle, Adelaide, and Melbourne); and (3) a desire to forestall the French or other nations (Hobart, Perth). Once this general area of choice was decided upon, local questions of site overrode any question of centrality with regard to an area the settlement might dominate. Yet all these capitals do dominate the population distribution of their respective states today and are the major seaports. The following alternative deductions seem possible: either the founders made no mistakes in foreseeing future population and seaport potentialities of sites, or that some other factor has been at work. To assume that the founders made no mistakes is to assume that they knew the qualities of all the other sites in the area, and this can be demonstrated not to be the case (J. Bird, 1968, 29). Even though mistakes were therefore distinctly possible, none of the capitals, once founded, was ever moved.

From the beginning, however, the capital sites were endowed with opportunities to act as commodity markets and financial exchanges since they were seaports or close to seaports. As each was the capital of a territory, however little known that territory might be, each became also the seat of the market of ideas, of political influence, and of power, first through the presence of the Governor alone, and later via colonial and state legislatures. To have a regular market, of whatever kind, presupposes the publishing or proclamation of a set of rules and regulations. The proclamation which establishes the legal basis of the market, using 'market' to cover all the circumstances developed above, is the great impulse converting a primitive site of a pioneer settlement into the recognised site for a regional centre. 'Proclaim' appears to be the right word because it means that a decision is made openly, solemnly, and publicly, and all these conditions are necessary if geographical momentum is to be given the greatest impetus. In British and American law the word 'proclaim' is used only of notices by an administrative or executive officer. A founder may choose the site for a settlement, but it is a proclamation of some kind that founds the regional centre and puts 'centrality' on a legal and secure basis. No port can operate without some formally proclaimed legal status. Such a proclamation in its earliest form will have led to the foundation of the port and its current legal expression allows the port function to continue.

A fascinating particular example of the 'proclaimed impulse' at work comes from Canada. In 1927 F. Palmer, later Sir Frederick Palmer, produced a report to the Canadian Government in which he recommended that Churchill should be the major port on Hudson Bay and not Nelson. The decision had to be based on a number of major considerations: (1) cost of construction, including the extra 140 km of railway to Churchill (yet the total cost of Nelson was estimated to be twice as much as Churchill); (2) maintenance cost (greater at Nelson); (3) relative shelter for ships (better at Churchill); (4) room for expansion (about equal); and (5) relative length of ice-free seasons (no conclusive evidence). The Canadian Government accepted the report which favoured Churchill, and this acceptance was the proclaimed impulse that established the modern port. For the purposes of argument, let us suppose that the relative lengths of the ice-free season were a critical factor in the choice between Churchill and Nelson (Supposition A). In detail, let it be supposed that if the shipping season was twenty days shorter at Churchill, this would more than nullify the cost advantages over Nelson (Supposition A_1). Now in 1927 'the evidence regarding ice conditions at both ports is vague and inconclusive, and no satisfactory or reliable decision can be given in regard thereto' (F. Palmer,

7)*.* But in 1965 the evidence was forthcoming. Break up of ice occurs on the Churchill river an average of 27 days later than on the Hayes River at Nelson (D. K. Mackay and J. R. Mackay, 1965, 11). Supposition A_1 would then require the principal Hudson Bay port to be at Nelson, but this would not happen (even if Supposition A_1 was correct and it is not, remember) because the proclaimed impulse in 1927 gave 38 years of geographical momentum to Churchill before the ice evidence was available. Geographical momentum is 'The tendency of places with established installations and services to maintain or increase their importance after the conditions originally determining their establishment have appreciably altered' (British Association Geographical Glossary Committee, *Geographical Journal,* **118**, 1952, 346).

Having defined the port, measured it, exposed its fascinating median location, and having gone back to the beginning to proclaim it, the introduction is over.

A voyage now begins through seaport literature. The plan of the book is to sail up the port approaches, see the port at work, survey its inland and overseas links, and finally look at the problems of the port planner, particularly as he peers from the present into the future. With regret, the important associated subjects of naval architecture, ship operation, shipbuilding, and the fishing industry have been omitted.* The remaining agenda seems quite wide enough, using a wide-angle lens, with interpolated narrow-focus shots on a variety of different contributory subjects. The difficulty of such a study technique merely adds to the spell of the subject and the pull of the port.

A note on references

Every source consulted in preparing the text has been included so that the reference lists at the end of each chapter might provide a basic bibliography for the subject in question. At this early stage the reader might like to be aware of eight on-going sources of information: the first four are useful for up-to-date factual information on ports; and the last four always contain articles of interest, although there are of course many journals in this second category.

Jane's Freight Containers (annual), P. Finlay (Ed.), London: Sampson Low, Marston.
Large Tankers and World Bulk Carriers (annual), Oslo: Fearnley and Egers.

* The reader is referred to two publications based on recent study: A. D. Couper, *The Geography of Sea Transport,* a forthcoming companion volume in the Hutchinson University Library; and *Report of the Committee of Inquiry into Shipping* [Rochdale Report] (1970) London: HMSO, Cmnd. 4337.

Port Dues, Charges and Accommodation (annual), London: Philip.
Ports of the World (annual), London: Benn.
Containerisation International (1967 to date), London: National Magazine Co.
Dock and Harbour Authority [The] (1921–, monthly), London: Foxlow.
Index of Technical Publications Issued by ICHCA [International Cargo Handling Coordination Association] (1952–), London: ICHCA.
Research and Technical Bulletin (1966 to date), London: National Ports Council.

Three less accessible sources are: *Seewirtschaft: Beitrage zur ökonomischen Entwicklung in Seehafen und Seeschiffart*, L. L. V. Jolmes, G. Braun, W. Klugmann, and W. Schroder (Eds.), Hamburg: Okis, 1966, a series of wide-ranging essays on both shipping and seaports; *Research on Ports: a Study of World Wide Thought, Study, Research and Development*, London: Martech Consultants, 1964 [unpublished]; and the many reports published by the US Maritime Cargo Transportation Conference set up in 1953.

Finally, interesting speculations about the future, particularly the possible developments of ships, are contained in *Ship/Shore 1980: a Survey of Technological and Other Developments that may affect the Movement of Goods across the Interface between Sea and Land within the next 12 Years*. Prepared by: Study Group with representatives from British Ship Research Association, Dock and Harbour Authorities' Association, Ministry of Technology, National Physical Laboratory, and National Ports Council, London: National Ports Council, 1968. Reviewed by R. O. Goss in The technological future of seaports, *Research and Technical Bulletin*, 5, 1969, 244–7, London: National Ports Council.

Alonso, W. (1964) Location theory, *Regional Development and Planning*, J. Friedmann and W. Alonso (Eds.), 78–106. Cambridge, Mass.: MIT.
Bird, J. (1963) *The Major Seaports of the United Kingdom*. London: Hutchinson.
——(1968) *Seaport Gateways of Australia*. London: Oxford University Press.
Black, W. R. (1967) Growth of the railway network of Maine: a multivariate approach, *Discussion Papers*, 5. University of Iowa, Department of Geography.
Hoover, E. M. (1948) *The Location of Economic Activity*. New York: McGraw-Hill.
Isard, W. (1956) *Location and Space-Economy*. New York: Wiley, 1956.
Kansky, K. J. (1963) Structure of transport networks: relationships between network geometry and regional characteristics, *Research Papers*, 84. University of Chicago, Department of Geography.

Klaassen, L. H., and Vanhove, N. (1970) *Macro-economic Evaluation of Port Investments*. Paper delivered at Semaine de Bruges, April. Bruges: College of Europe.

Lindberg, O. (1953) An economic-geographical study of the localisation of the Swedish paper industry, *Geografiska Annaler*, **35**, 28–40.

Mackay, D. J., and Mackay, J. R. (1965) Historical records of freeze-up and break-up on the Churchill and Hayes Rivers, *Geographical Bulletin*, **7**, 7–16.

Palmer, F. (1927) *Report to the Canadian Government on the Selection of a Terminal Port for the Hudson Bay Railway*. London, 1927.

Philbrick, A. K. (1927) Principles of areal functional organisation in regional human geography, *Economic Geography*, **33**, 299–336.

Quinn, J. A. (1943) The hypothesis of the median location, *American Sociological Review*, **8**, 148–56.

Report on Port Charges Terminology (1969) London: Joint Committee on Port Terminology of the National Ports Council and the Dock and Harbour Authorities' Association, First Report.

Rimmer, P. J. (1966) The status of ports—a method of comparative evaluation, *The Dock and Harbour Authority*, **47**, 2–7.

Robinson, R. (1967) *Spatial Patterns of Port-linked Flows: General Cargo Imports through the Port of Vancouver*. University of British Columbia, Department of Geography. Mimeographed.

Svendsen, A. S. (1958) *Sea Transport and Shipping Economics*. Bremen: Institut für Schiffahrtsforschung.

Turn-around Time of Ships in Port [The] (1967). New York: United Nations ST/ECA/97. Mimeographed.

Weber, A. (1909) *Theory of the Location of Industries* [in German] (1928); edited and translated into English by C. J. Friedrich. Chicago: University of Chicago Press.

I

PORT APPROACHES

The mariner approaching a port might be forgiven for sometimes imagining that his destination is in the most awkward location—up a twisting creek, through a narrow breach, or on a lee shore. Commercial ports are not sited for the convenience of sailors, and even the old harbours of refuge were located for ships on voyages between ports sited with other considerations in mind. To understand these locational considerations, the bifocal vision of the urban geographer must be borrowed. The site of a town is taken by urban geographers to be the actual area occupied by the buildings and includes the relief and geological structure of the immediate surroundings. This is a view of location only in its vertical component, down to the rocks beneath, and as such concentrates on something solid and static. The situation of a town, on the other hand, is taken to mean the aspects of location turned towards the area served by the town—its umland (see p. 125)—and these areal connections will have to be traced over wider dimensions as the town increases in size, causing it to occupy a larger site and extend its urban influence. Thus 'situation' refers to a horizontal component and the dynamic links with other locations. These same considerations apply to ports, but the concepts of water site and water situation must be added. The usual name for the water site is, of course, the harbour, but the introduction showed that this term cannot easily be extended to cover all the components of the water site of a modern port. The concept of water situation comprehends the location of the port in relation to the bands of shipping lanes across the seas and oceans, and also to the approach channels of these water links—the subject of this chapter.

The length of a port approach is dependent on the size of the ship. A small vessel will be able to head towards the inner berths of the port, whereas a mammoth tanker could be deemed to begin her approach much further out and probably be able to berth at only the most seaward terminals in the port. Ideal port approaches are of course deep and sheltered, but these ideal characteristics are found infrequently in the natural approaches to major commercial ports. The reasons are not difficult to seek. Deep water offshore implies a steeply plunging land surface which might be expected to rise steeply out of the water. Shelter implies the windbreaks of country with high altitude. Combine these two implications and it can be seen that the deepest and most sheltered waters appear in fiords which are always surrounded by high mountains out of which they have been gouged by glaciers on their way to the sea. But fiorded mountains do not support the dense urban populations which large commercial ports exist to serve.

Fortunately, a sequence of events has given rise to favourable natural port approaches in many parts of the world. Since the last ice age the sea-level has oscillated, but the net movement has been a rise of the order of 100 m. This post-glacial eustatic, or world-wide, rise has been due to the release of water formerly locked up in glaciers, just as a significant warming-up of world climate from today would release more water from the polar ice-caps with, of course, progressively disastrous effect on ports and coastal cities. Coastal relief forms, including river estuaries, carved by the agents of erosion during the low sea-levels of the last ice age in those areas which were ice free, would have their forms 'drowned' by about 100 m. Of course, this is an extra dimension to be added to those forms carved by ice itself in the fiords already mentioned. But a corrective is necessary to this oversimplified picture, since it would manifestly be too sweeping to suggest that 100 m have been added to all coastal depths since the last ice age. This would be to ignore the differential movement of the land due to crustal disturbances; also the agents of erosion and deposition have been at work to produce the present micro-relief of underwater deeps and shoals. Nevertheless, it is still possible to detect drowned forms; the most common of these is the drowned estuary, for which the Spanish word *ria* is used. A ria is a drowned estuary eroded by a river in a coastal zone where land relief is measured in hundreds of metres rather than in tens. As in the case of fiords, depths plunge quickly offshore and rise quickly back from the shore, but not so precipitously nor so high as in the glaciated mountains. The type area for this form is in north-western Spain, although perhaps the easiest type-identification on small-scale atlas maps is to be found in south-western Ireland. Brest, San Francisco and Sydney are some of the famous ports which have harbours originally carved by inter-glacial rivers and drowned post-glacially. The detail of the depths in such harbours is due to the reworking of sediments by estuary currents, in a push-pull effect if the tidal range is great. The deepest part of the estuary is often to be found where the bed is swept clean by fast-flowing currents in the narrower parts of the ria where stream velocities are increased. This augments the ability of the bottom current to transport material, perhaps to deposit it in wider areas of the ria, either downstream or upstream by tidal inflow.

Drowned estuaries, which may scarcely qualify as fully-developed rias, occur on coasts of low relief, with consequently less deep pre-glacial dissection by rivers. Nevertheless, their drowned portions may provide deep-water approaches or are capable of being dredged, for their sides and bottoms consist only of loose post-glacial infilling. Such drowned estuaries are particularly exemplified in north-west Europe: Thames, Humber, Weser, and Elbe. North-west Europe also offers the example of a drowned delta, on which three major ports have been sited, Amsterdam, Rotterdam, and Antwerp, though subsequent silting by the Rhine has necessitated the re-cutting of channels to the sea. On some coasts the build-up of material, by rivers in deltas and by wave action in offshore bars and spits, appears to override the eustatic rise. Such constructional forms have posed great difficulties for port engineers because of the necessity of finding a silt-free approach to firm land. Today such disadvantages are mitigated by the efficiency of dredging technology and by the consequent ability to mould such soft material into deep dredged channels with wide flat areas artificially built up with dredged spoil to give really spacious sites for the back-up areas of port terminals. However, even when a deep channel has been provided, either by eustatic rise or by an artificial cut, through coastal dunes and inconvenient solid rock bars due to the disposition of offshore geological structures, in many cases that is not the end of the approach difficulties. Material may be drifted into the deep channel by forces at work upon the coastline, and, more especially, further out beyond the breaker zone.

Terminology of coastal current systems has been established by F. P. Shepard and D. L. Inman, 1950, and these and other related terms have been collated by J. C. Ingle, 1966. The four principal zones where there is water movement along the coast are the swash zone, the surf zone, the breaker zone, and beyond the breaker zone. This last area is the most important when considering port approaches because the other three zones cover shallow water, by definition. Indeed, on a steep shore the swash and surf zone may not be present at all. If a port entrance has to be constructed across these inner zones, perhaps based on an interruption to them caused by a rip current making a breach in an offshore bar, then the artificially deepened entrance has to be totally protected from the forces at work in these zones—waves, breakers, and longshore currents—or ships will be unable to navigate in the near shore currents which will rapidly silt up the dredged channel. Moles will have to be thrown out to interrupt these processes.

Seaward of the breaker zone, alongshore movement of material impelled by the coastal current has been observed at depths of 100 m (D. G. Moore, 1963). The direction of the coastal current is usually a function of the prevailing wind direction and the angle of incidence with the coast. This direction can be modified or even reversed if the predominant wind comes from another quarter in storms, and also where there is a strong tidal oscillation. In shallow water the movement of water shape induced by tidal forces is transformed into a physical movement of water in ebb and flood currents, and these certainly have power to move bottom material. Model studies have indicated that the net movement of bottom material seaward of the breaker zone is consistently shoreward—another unfortunate circumstance for the port engineer (J. C. Ingle, 1966, 106). This net movement masks the fact that it is the larger grains that are moved onshore, whereas the finer material may even move offshore—a sorting of material appears to take place, but in such directions that it is of little practical assistance to the designer of a navigational channel across such a zone. In protecting a cutting across such a coastal current, a mole is often thrown out from the shore, in the absence of a convenient headland. This structure is designed to cut across the inner zones of the coastal current, with the possible result that there is a build-up of material on the windward side of the breakwater. This material may eventually work round the head of the mole and into the channel unless the structure is thrust so far out into deep water that the supply of abundant coarse material is cut off. In that case there may be a build-up of sediment on the updrift side. P. Bruun, 1968, describes a now frequently used bypassing technique in which the updrift sediment is dredged and deposited on the eroded downdrift side. Collection of sediment is aided and concentrated by depressed weirs and sediment traps. This technique obviously works in the same direction as the natural littoral drift process.

Channels must also be constructed by creative, or capital, dredging, so that big ships can come close inshore, across bays, and penetrate up rivers. Thereafter the depths must be preserved by maintenance dredging. This may have to be a continual operation, even by night and day in those port entrances under the severest attack from the depositional forces.

Ports and ships' dimensions

This section begins with the truism that the increasing size of ships makes demands that port engineers struggle to fulfil. The chief reason for this is that a new ship can be conceived on the drawing board and then be a sailing fact within two years. Major port developments may take five years to complete, yet they ought to be ready before the coming into service of the generation of ships for which they are designed. The naval architect does not have absolute freedom in choosing the size of his vessel because the larger she becomes the fewer are the ports and terminals that can accept her. Meanwhile, the port engineer struggles with difficult physical sites where land and water meet, perhaps beset by high-ranging tides; exposure to wind and swell; or particular hazards like consolidated dune bars, volcanic dykes, and coral reefs. The relation between ports and ships' dimensions needs to be analysed into several components: the technical reasons for extra depth between a keel; the basic reasons for increasing ship size, and this includes other dimensions besides draught; and the historic increase in ship size, making a distinction between break-bulk ships and bulk carriers, with the trends of the former being carried on by container vessels.

The Permanent International Association of Navigation Congresses, 1961, recommended that the depth of port approaches in protected waters should be the summer salt water draught of the design vessel plus 1·5 to 2·5 m. When a vessel enters brackish or fresh water, her draught increases by an order of $2\frac{1}{2}\%$ due to decrease in the density of the water. Entering shallow water the ship produces bigger waves relative to velocity, and she tends to squat in the water. This is because of the average decrease in the water surface along the profile of the ship in shallow water, and this squat effect increases if the vessel departs from the centre line of the channel. Although the squat may be less than 1 m in most cases, it must be calculated because all the components of draught must reach the right total or the ship may ground. At port entrances, pitching, or scend, and rolling must be taken into account; 3 to 4 m is usually allowed for this. Vessels are often trimmed so that they set down at the stern by 0·3 to 0·6 m in order to improve steering ability. Finally, an additional safety margin of 0·6 to 1·2 m is necessary in case of temporary obstructions in the channel, such as a sunken log which a ship's propeller might encounter. Of course, tide effects give periodic

B

increases in depth availability, but the faster turn-round of all types of vessel makes waiting for the tide increasingly irksome and against the effective employment of the capital represented by the modern ship (D. Hay, 1968).

The basic reason for increasing size of vessel has been the law of increasing returns applied to sea carriage: increasing size of vessel has not resulted in corresponding increase in capital invested, in fuel costs, and crew, repair, and maintenance costs. Cost of building ships per dead-weight ton fall dramatically with increase of size. But at present mild steel is the only material meeting the requirement for ship construction of great strength and toughness combined with cheapness. It has been estimated that the upper limit of steel ship construction will be reached when buckling and deflection of structures are caused by the lack of stiffness in mild steel (Y. Watanabe, 1965, 191). Steels of more than 60 kg per sq mm raise costs, and it remains to be seen whether this cost parameter will affect the general parameter of increasing returns with increasing vessel size. The tonnage at which a single screw must be replaced by twin screws will also have an effect on cost curves against ship size.

The historic increase in ship size may be demonstrated by considering the dimensions of typical dry cargo liners in this century. Here the discussion will need to distinguish between break-bulk and bulk ships.

TABLE 2

DEVELOPMENT IN CONVENTIONAL CARGO LINER DESIGN

Ship	Built	Tons (gross)	Length (m)	Beam (m)	Draught (summer) (m)	Bale capacity	Service speed (knots)
Laomedon	1912	6,490	140	15·0	8·26	11,341	12
Agamemnon	1929	7,829	146	18·0	8·55	12,806	14½
Anchises	1947	7,634	149	18·4	8·54	13,445	15½
Menelaus	1957	8,539	151	19·9	8·82	14,228	16¾
Glenlyon	1962	11,918	166	23·0	9·14	16,337	20

Source: Sir Stewart MacTier, 1964.

Draught of these vessels did not increase dramatically. Increases in bale capacity have been achieved by increases in length and particularly in beam. The savings in draught relative to capacity have been effected by lighter materials used in construction and the practice of welding, rather than riveting which was prevalent before the Second World War. Increased speed has resulted from increased efficiency of engines and the fact that a flush-welded hull has a 15% less resistance to motion than a riveted hull. The *Glenlyon* of Table 2 is a typical C4 class ship (US Maritime Commission classification), and to cater for the growth of such vessels, it seemed sensible for port authorities to allow for a length of up to 185 m and a draught of up to 10·5 m. The reason why this class of ship did not increase in size dramatically is that a doubling of cargo capacity would merely have doubled the time in port. Increasing returns could be effected only if the savings in ton/mile costs were not offset by proportionally longer turn-rounds in port. This obstacle was overcome by the container ship.

Significantly, container ship size is usually indicated by the number of container units that the vessel can carry. This is of course only a shorthand indication of the vessel's size. The reasons for the concentration on container carrying capacity are twofold: the number of containers per vessel is a prime factor in the back-up area, or hard-standing necessary adjacent to the berth; and this is often the most difficult dimension for the port to fulfil. Secondly, there have been no dramatic increases in other dimensions given in Table 2 by ships in the middle range of container ships (carrying 900 containers); for example, one launched in 1968 had a length of 189 m, a beam of 23·8 m, and a maximum draught of 9·75 m. The largest container ships in the early 1970s are expected to draw 10·65 m. Most ports will therefore find it necessary to provide 12·2 m minimum depths in their approaches, but this figure has already been exceeded in order to cope with bulk vessels. It may therefore merely be necessary to provide a deep-water spur from the bulk carrier approach to the container berth. This task may be in fact much less onerous than finding the 5–8 hectares alongside the dredged berth—the area dimensions necessary being dependent upon the method of container storage.

Among the bulk carriers, the oil-tanker growth has consistently outstripped the forecasts of experts. A Japanese expert writing in 1965 (Y. Watanabe) predicted that vessels built by current methods would reach a maximum of 200,000 tons deadweight. By 1967 the *Idemitsu Maru* of 209,000 tons had shown the law of increasing returns to apply by operating on the Persian Gulf–Japan route. Compared with a 80,000-ton tanker there is a saving of 38% in transport costs; and savings of 59% compared with transport by a 40,000-ton tanker. A 200,000-ton tanker draws 17·9 m and the 300,000-ton tankers servicing the Bantry Bay terminal in a southwest Ireland ria require 30·4 m, and are unable to enter the North Sea.

Many of the current class of tankers in the range 200,000–250,000 tons deadweight were ordered as a result of the closure of the Suez Canal. Although such vessels operate at 25 % less per ton-mile on the Persian Gulf–Europe route compared with a 75,000-ton vessel, theoretically using the canal both ways, the larger ships have been specifically designed to travel in ballast through the canal when it is reopened, assuming the fairway is dredged to 16·1 m. This one-way canal passage saves another 10 % per ton miles for a 250,000-ton vessel compared with the two-way Cape round voyage. The canal closure may have caused a leap upward of average tanker size, yet it has also acted as a partial stabiliser, except for tankers operating to terminals located 'off the refinery market', sometimes in fiord or ria harbours like Bantry Bay, and sometimes offshore. The numbers of 300,000-ton plus vessels will increase, but, of course, with increasing size, the number of the world's shipyards able to build such vessels decreases. Many Japanese shipyard docks in which vessels are built and floated, rather than being launched from a slipway, cannot accommodate vessels larger than 300,000 tons. The Panama Canal cannot take vessels in excess of about 60,000 tons deadweight, and most continental shelf areas are closed to 300,000-ton vessels drawing 24·9 m or more. These areas include the English Channel, the southern part of the North Sea, the Baltic, large areas of the White Sea, the approaches to the Black Sea, the approaches to New York and to the ports of the River Plate. This leads to the conclusion that the largest vessels in the world are the first true ocean vessels since they have outgrown the limiting depths of the seas above the continental shelf.

Nevertheless, for bulk carriers average length and beam have increased proportionately more than the summer draught (E. Hunter and T. B. Wilson, 1969, Chart 1); and flexibility of operation of the larger vessels may be increased by partial loading and unloading. Although extra costs of transhipment are involved, these can be traded off against

the lower freight costs of the larger shipment during the long sea haul and result in lower overall delivered cost per ton of cargo at the final reception points. (loc. cit., 194)

This is particularly significant when it is realised that larger vessels obtain a greater reduction in draught for the same proportionate reduction of load than smaller vessels of the same type. Port authorities ought to offer inducements for partial loading by basing relevant tariffs on draught rather than net registered tonnage; and, incidentally, such a tariff could embrace a surcharge for those deep-draughted vessels that may have necessitated an expensive approach channel (ibid., 195).

E. Hunter and T. B. Wilson, 1969, 196–7, also conveniently sum up the limiting tidal measurements for different shipping trades: entry to a dock—mean high-water neaps (most unfavourable high tide); for a prolonged stay at a tidal berth—mean low-water springs (most unfavourable low tide); packet* ports, where ships are scheduled round the clock—mean low-water springs (most unfavour-

TABLE 3

FACTORS DETERMINING SHIP SIZE

Factors leading to larger optimal ship sizes	Notes
Increasing profitability	This is the principal factor; profitability must be considered in the light of total cost, and not just those that are direct costs for ship operators
Lower costs per ton of cargo	Ship operating costs only considered (see text above)
The longer the routes	Ship operating costs then form larger proportion of total costs
The faster the turn-round	Big ships have higher daily costs than small ones
The lower the extra payment for working overtime in port	Overtime is needed to speed turn-round
The lower the manual effort of cargo-handling	Manual labour productivity falls in overtime periods
The lower the cost of mechanising cargo-handling	The faster the replacement of manual labour
The lower the cost of providing cargo storage	Bigger ships need bigger cargo build-ups in port
The lower the value of goods per unit of weight	Cargo build-ups stored in port have to be financed by payment of interest charges *ad valorem*
The higher the annual cargo flow	Increases the service frequency of bigger ships reducing cargo storage duration
The higher the level of seamen's earnings	Above 25,000 tons deadweight, crew numbers do not increase and ships become progressively less labour intensive

Source: based on R. O. Goss, 1970, 5–10.

* Originally, the boat maintained for carrying the 'packet' of State papers and shortened to packet-boat early in the seventeenth century, see J. Evelyn's *Diary*, 'packet boate', 11 October 1641.

able state of tide in the port approaches). The limitation of low-water springs at tidal berths can be circumvented by pocket dredging at the berth, or by the provision of higher capacity discharging or loading equipment, so that the ship is quickly lightened.

R. O. Goss (1970; see also R. O. Goss and C. D. Jones, 1970) has attempted to comprehend the factors affecting optimum ship size. The factors and notes within Table 3 attempt to summarise the qualitative part of his argument, although there are obvious drawbacks to such compression. As far as ports are concerned, two points may be noted. The increasing size of break-bulk cargo ships is for some years hence likely to be contained within the port dimensions already provided for bulk cargo vessels (in the matter of port approaches) and already provided for conventional break-bulk vessels in the matter of quay depths, but not in respect of quayside lifts or upland areas. Secondly, as far as bulk carriers are concerned, an important limiting factor on increasing ship size is the fact that the larger the vessel, the fewer are the port approaches that can accommodate her, so that many factors leading to an increasing size of bulk carriers focus on the question of dredging.

Dredging

Discussion of this topic will involve the process by which a port is extended seawards or on to a flood-plain and estuarine marshes raised above spring tides (*Dredging*, 1968, a symposium of eleven papers with good bibliographical references). Dredging implies spoil availability, so that dredging and reclamation are often two parts of the same process. Whereas harbour and river deepening have been carried out for centuries, dredging of the seabed approaches to ports is very recent. An important breakthrough in dredging technique occurred in the nineteenth century, and credit for the use of the first specially designed trailing hopper dredger using suction techniques goes to the US Corps of Engineers which used such vessels to deepen Charleston Harbour in 1890 and the Gedney Channel of New York. The latter was lowered 76 cm down to 8·2 m along its entire length as early as 1885. The advantage of suction dredgers is that they can steam ahead while at work, and require no anchors, so they are no obstacle to other shipping. In 1876 G. F. Lyster, engineer to the Mersey Docks and Harbour Board, had seen a static suction dredger at work in the River Loire and subsequently tried to use such a centrifugal pump dredger in the Liverpool Docks, but the material to be removed was too light. Centrifugal pumps had been invented in the early nineteenth century and demonstrated for dredging purposes at the Paris Exhibition of 1867. Centrifugal pump dredging uses the principle of the water turbine in reverse, and could become efficient only with the development of the steam turbine, and therefore not until after 1880. Suction alone cannot be used where heavy clay, hard coral, or rock bars occur. But these may be dealt with by a rock-cutting suction dredger with a pipe of 65–70 cm diameter, perhaps after underwater blasting has reduced the rock to manageable fragments. The use of trailer hopper suction dredgers predominates over paternoster bucket dredgers for two sets of reasons —one hydraulic, the other economic.

A long-recognised principle in dredging port approaches is that it is more effective to deepen a channel gradually over the entire length desired, than to bite out separate holes down to the required depth, but only in limited areas at a time (*Dredging*, 1968, 33). The suction dredger works to the first principle, while the bucket dredger is less mobile, cannot operate in swell conditions, and is much less seaworthy. If waves become higher than one metre, the mooring of barges is difficult; and the grab dredger needs mud barges in which to dump spoil. The cost of moving bucket dredgers from one harbour to another is much greater than for the modern trailer suction dredger which is a sea-going vessel. Port authorities have tended to invest in bucket dredgers for work in sheltered parts of harbours at

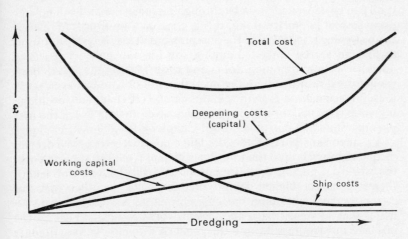

Fig. 4 Basic economics of dredging

The increased working capital cost with larger ships includes increased interest charges on larger amounts of goods in the shipping pipeline.

Source: R. O. Goss in *Dredging*, 1968, 23.

specific and perhaps recurring shoal areas; but contract dredging companies tend to rely on a fleet of mobile suction dredgers.

Many books and articles quote a supposed 'dredging law' which normally reads as follows; the cost of dredging varies in relation to the cube of the increase in depth. Such a statement may have some use in drawing attention to the possible steep increases of cost in gaining a few extra centimetres in a difficult channel. But the generalisation is falsely based on the physical properties of channels rather than upon the economic difficulties of dredging them. In estimating the cost of deepening a channel, the dredging contractor must take many considerations into account. First, and most obvious, there is the actual depth compared with the required depth. The nature of the rock is relevant, ranging from material that first may necessitate using a clam dredge, underwater blasting, and then rock-cutting before suction comes into play. At the other extreme, fine silt, soft clay or sand can be sucked up in one operation. The angle of rest of the seabed material will determine the top width of the channel to be dredged in order to obtain effective bottom width. The boundary slopes may be as gentle as 1:40 for sloppy mud, but the extra cost of dredging fine materials on this score is of little significance compared with the extra operations in dredging hard rock that may stand with a vertical face. Disposal of spoil is another important item. If the spoil can be deposited close by through a pipeline, which can now be up to several kilometres long, this is cheaper than transferring spoil to a sea-going hopper barge for dumping out at sea. It may be difficult to find an agreed seabed dumping site for an appliance that can open her bottom-dumping doors and drop 18,000 tons at a time. A spoil ground near the dredging operation not only reduces costs, but if useful reclamation is achieved, this can be offset against the dredging costs. Discussion of the economics of dredging considered as a port investment is postponed until Chapter 8 (p. 206 ff.).

An important part of the dredging contract price results from getting the vessel on to the job. Ports distant from the main bases of the world's dredging fleets in Europe and the United States must therefore expect higher capital dredging bills—another cost disadvantage for developing nations. One large dredging group estimates that its vessels have an efficient work-load of only 50%. The idle time includes repairs, and this is a larger item in the case of rockcutters and bucket dredgers—yet another disadvantage of the latter compared with trailer suction vessels. Perhaps the very first dredging of the open sea was undertaken in 1962 by the Esso Petroleum Company in order to enable fully-laden tankers drawing 14·3 m to reach the oil terminal of the Fawley refinery on Southampton Water.

Safe passage of such vessels requires an approach depth of 17 m, but the tidal conditions in the port approaches make up such depths if the channel is dredged down to 13·7 m minimum. In Southampton Water no problems were encountered, the waters are sheltered, and the spoil was removed by bucket dredger. But it was also necessary to dredge a channel 2,500 m long across the Nab Shoal of the English Channel, eight kilometres due east of the eastern extremity of the Isle of Wight. Here the least depth was only 11·9 m. Fortunately, the bed of the sea in this location is composed of gravel and sand, being the former bed of the 'Solent River', drowned traces of which survive as the straits between the Isle of Wight and the mainland. At first the seabed dredging efficiency was only 50%, large quantities of spoil running back into the channel. But when the work was one-third completed, the north-going tidal stream helped to scour out debris, and the channel has proved to be largely self-maintaining. At the time of writing, the largest seabed dredging operation is the extension of Europort into the North Sea with dredging of the approaches to Rotterdam's New Waterway (Fig. 5).

Such seabed dredging takes place where a slight amendment of the continental shelf permits vessels to approach port sites which have been considerably dredged in areas protected naturally or artificially from seabed longshore drifting. The artificial protection is usually a solid mound breakwater thrown out like an arm against sand choking a port entrance. In bay and estuary dredging the problem is often localised on an area called a bar. This rarely consists of rock but is more usually a shoal where currents wane so that their loads of silt are dropped in the same area. This loss of velocity may be due to a widening in current cross-section, at an estuary mouth for example; or it may occur where salt tidal currents lose their energy in penetrating upstream. These flood streams are known as salt wedges (J. B. Hinwood, 1964), and form a bottom layer of higher density than the river because of their salinity. They may flow upstream for a considerable distance, before being turned and swept back to the sea in the ebb flow. Very little mixing takes place between the salt and fresh water. Where the current is slowed, deposition takes place, and this may be several miles upstream from the sea. An underwater bar may also be formed of the deposits of an ebb current of a river which slows down and spreads out on meeting denser sea water. The supreme effect of this is of course a delta when built up in seas with low tidal ranges. Flood channels eroded by currents of flood tides in waters of decreasing depth have the characteristic of shoaling towards the land; whereas ebb currents shoal seawards. There is therefore often a bar or sill between them, especially in view of the fact

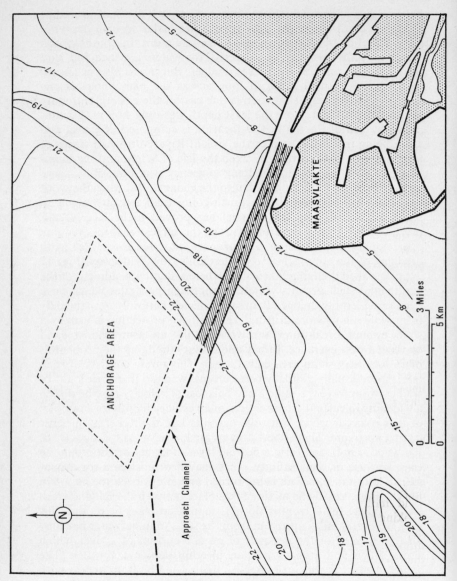

Fig. 5 Dredging and reclamation: Rotterdam–Europoort

Sea contours in metres. The original shoreline was a spit within the triangular area of reclaimed land (stipple) north of the entrance, once the site of the original hook (or spit) of Holland.

that the flood- and ebb-channels are often offset from each other, separated by what is known as the Fe-cell line (R. Maddrell, 1970, 53). A chief reason for this is a marked difference in salinity, and the salt wedge may still penetrate the estuary in one area when the ebb has begun to run in another part. Dredging often has the task of effecting a forced marriage between these two types of offset channel. Sometimes this enforced junction has to be aided by a training wall where the principle is to confine the cross-section of the current's activities so that they will naturally scour and thereby maintain the dredged channel. The same principle is at work in erecting training walls for dredged rivers. The Columbia River gives a good example of dredging in a meandering river with associated training works (Fig. 6). Problems arise at the crossing bar where the flood stage of the river greatly increases the river's cross-section (cf. sections *A–A* and *B–B* with *C–C*); and materials picked up by the faster currents at the side of the river are deposited on the bar.

W. A. Price and M. P. Kendrick (*Dredging*, 1968, 32–6) have pointed out the dangers of over-dredging a channel, particularly where the supply of material is almost unlimited. In many cases this replacement material may be more difficult to dredge because it is finer and more cohesive than the original.

... the equilibrium channel-depth in silt appears to be less than in sand ... the shear-force (which is proportional to current-velocity near the bed) needs to be higher to initiate the movement of particles of silt than it does to set more granular material in motion. Thus a channel in silt will continue to shoal until the depth has been reduced (and therefore the average current-velocity increased) to the point at which the shear-force is enough to initiate bed-movement.

Another suggestion this time as to why a dredged cut tends to fill with finer material, is that once the current-velocities on a tide have exceeded the values needed to lift fine sediments off the bed, then the current can transport these finer particles further and faster than it can carry coarser grains. They are therefore more readily available for deposition when deeper water is encountered, as over the dredged cut. (op. cit., 34)

Solid rock may certainly be encountered in port approaches and its removal may require an operation of capital dredging, perhaps to unlock an otherwise deep bay or estuary. Underwater blasting is then necessary prior to suction, and a special case is the Lindö method. This was first evolved in 1957 in constructing the Lindö Canal entrance to the Port of Norrköping, Sweden (J. Magnius, 1963). An overburden of 3·65 m, consisting of clay and sand cemented by morainic debris, was drilled by a pipe with an annular cutting head. A steel drill runs through the pipe, and both are forced through the overburden 1·25 m into the rock by powerful jetting. The rock drill then takes over and drills the hole in the rock for the blasting charge. When drilling is finished, plastic pipes are forced through the drill pipe so that explosives can be placed in position. This method soon spread to other ports in Sweden, particularly to Lulea. It was later used in the confined harbour of Genoa where excavation was needed in the westward extension between an airport and a shipyard. In this particular operation the essential saving was that the Lindö method could be undertaken entirely from the surface without the necessity of divers placing the charges—a very slow process.

Removal of rock is a once-for-all-time process. More common problems are those recurring shoals which are due to the slowing down of tidal or river currents. In dredging such areas three fundamental principles may be recalled: dredge a channel gradually along the entire length on an alignment so that currents will assist in keeping it largely self-maintaining; make sure that the cross-section is uniform or widens gradually, with sufficient contraction to maintain the velocity of the current, erecting training walls if absolutely necessary; and protect the channels from coastal current deposition by some form of by-pass embankment, or solid-fill pier.

Port entrances

The plan pattern of two almost-embracing moles thrust out into the sea is very common on the coasts of the world. In the days of sailing ships the protected water often became known as a harbour of refuge. On a coast without natural indentations, moles may be necessary to carve a port out of the sea. Sometimes the thickened root of a breakwater provides opportunity for deep-water berths. These have the disadvantage of confined and cul-de-sac landward connections compared with land-backed wharves, although this would not be a disadvantage for an oil terminal; and by definition the whole of the berth must be expensively built into the sea in a relatively exposed site. Whether the protective breakwaters shelter

---

Fig. 6 Dredging and river training: Columbia and Willamette Rivers

This particular example comes from the Columbia River between Vancouver and Portland (US). The crossing bar between concave (in plan) banks is dredged and the spoil placed in new-shore areas behind training works designed to narrow the cross-section and increase velocity. This pattern replaces the earlier method illustrated when it was thought best to remove the spoil altogether from the river, but thereby increasing the cross-section.

Source: S. K. Eisiminger, 1963, 329.

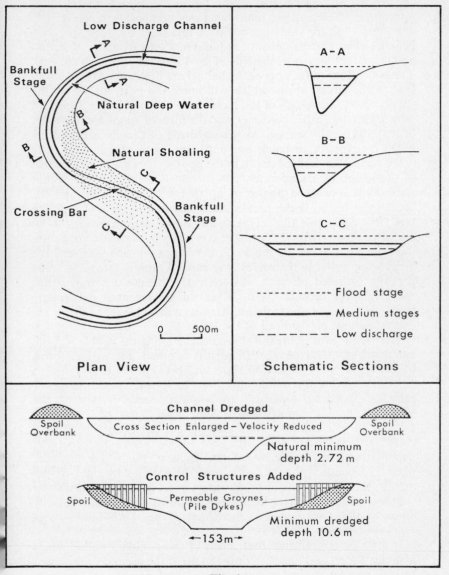

Low Discharge Channel

Bankfull Stage

Natural Deep Water

Natural Shoaling

Crossing Bar

Bankfull Stage

0   500m

Plan View

A–A

B–B

C–C

----------- Flood stage

——————— Medium stages

— — — — — Low discharge

Schematic Sections

Channel Dredged

Cross Section Enlarged – Velocity Reduced

Spoil Overbank

Spoil Overbank

Natural minimum depth 2.72 m

Control Structures Added

Spoil

Permeable Groynes (Pile Dykes)

Spoil

Minimum dredged depth 10.6 m

←153m→

Fig. 6

the whole port, just some of the berths, or merely the seaward
approaches, they have two main functions: to provide shelter against
wind and swell for ships navigating a relatively confined approach
channel where currents must be reduced to a velocity below $3\frac{1}{2}$ knots;
and to prevent longshore drifting of sand into the approach channel.
The dimensions of the approach channel are determined by the forecast of the largest vessel which will enter the port, known as the
design vessel. The length of the moles is determined by the approach
dimensions, the seabed contours, and the form of longshore transport
of material on the seabed. As a rough rule of thumb, breakwaters
might be expected to reach out until the depth of water off their
heads equals the dredged depth in the approach. Sometimes the zone
of deposition of a sand-laden ebb-current is displaced into deeper
water as it spreads at angles of up to twelve degrees beyond the
breakwater heads. If the breakwaters narrow together towards the
land, this may cause the height of any advancing wave front to be
increased. Wave refraction induces convexity in the wave front since
the ends are retarded by the shallower water on each side near the
breakwater walls; so the waves may expand rapidly into wave traps
possibly provided on each side near the breakwater roots, thus
reducing surge between them. If seabed movement is dominantly
from one direction, the mole on that side will be longer to throw the
coastal current off the head of the lee mole.

The oldest form of breakwater construction is the rubble mound,
and this is still the type most frequently adopted. The various forms
of revetment and cross-section allow such breakwaters to be suited to
particular wave and ground conditions. In Japan, caissons alone, or
caissons topped by stonework are employed since, in general, the
seas around that country are quieter than those of north-west
Europe. In such calmer waters the seas are not thrown back by a
closed structure. An open structure allows waves to penetrate,
annihilating their energy by internal friction. But where Japanese
ports experience typhoons, with wave heights up to eight or ten
metres, the foundations of breakwaters must go down to twelve or
thirteen metres, material being moved down to a depth roughly
equal to the wave height (*Proceedings of the Fifth International
Harbour Congress*, 1968, 69).

It must be remembered that much of these mighty undertakings
is under water, and one sees only the tip of the mound surmounted
by the parapet against storm waves. Developments at Ijmuiden,
Netherlands, illustrate many of the above points. The entrance to the
Port of Ijmuiden had to be enlarged because of the new tankers
coming into service from 1958 onwards, and these design vessels

demanded a depth of 14·5 m in the approach channel and a wider area in which to manœuvre. A tanker can enter between the moles at 16 knots and yet come to a halt at a safe distance from the lock gates at the entrance to the North Sea Canal. Placing heavy rubble-mound breakwaters on the sandy seabed of the North Sea demands great care. Willow mattresses were first placed in position to prevent tidal scour undermining the stonework which had to be placed in position very accurately. At Ijmuiden a special radar network threw

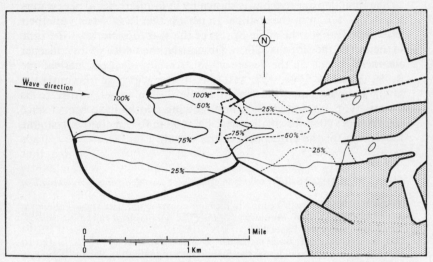

Fig. 7 Port entrance: Ijmuiden, Netherlands

Pecked lines are lines of equal wave height, expressed in percentages of the wave height in front of the entrance mouth before the west-ward extension was built. Solid lines show the transformed pattern of wave penetration in the enlarged entrance. The assumed wave direction is shown, and the assumed wave period is 9½ sec.

Source: compiled from J. J. Vinjé, 1966, 5.

an electronic grid over the entire working area, and stone could be dropped to a positional accuracy of less than 1 m; this enabled work to go on during periods of poor visibility which incidentally coincide with calm working conditions. Stone had to be imported from Belgium, and was most cheaply transported by sea-going dumper barges. It is difficult to imagine the vast quantities involved: 1½ million tons of stone and 600,000 tons of gravel. Cranes on self-elevating pontoons did the final shaping and covering with asphaltic concrete. This was the first time that cranes resting directly on the seabed had been used in breakwater construction. The channel thus protected was dredged to permit free passage of vessels drawing 13·7 m and was constructed to a point eight kilometres off the coast where the natural seabed depth equalled the depth in the dredged channel—16 m. The spoil was rinsed and transported to the Amsterdam port area in order to consolidate and raise polderland sites for industrial development—the familiar story of dredging being linked with reclamation.

The Ijmuiden approach was shown by hydraulic tests to necessitate a width of 170 m in the channel to permit two 80,000-ton vessels to pass. Allowing for the angle of rest of the seabed material, the width at the top of the slope is 300 m. Obviously, the width of an entrance channel depends on the design vessel. An empirical law derived by R. R. Minikin, 1963, 157, states that the width of the entrance channel should equal the length of the design vessel, while A. D. Quinn, 1961, 92, stated that the following widths have been found satisfactory: 90 m for small ports; 120–150 m for medium ports; and 150–250 m for the large ports of the world.

Abbott, M. R. (1960) Salinity effects in estuaries, *Journal of Marine Research*, **18**, 2, 101–11.

Bruun, P. (1968) Shore protection in harbour construction with special reference to littoral drift shores, *Proceedings of the Fifth International Harbour Congress*, 2–8 June. Antwerp. Paper 1.3.

Chapon, J. (1967–8) *Travaux maritimes*. 2 vols. Paris: Eyrolles.

Dredging (1968) Proceedings of the Symposium organised by the Institution of Civil Engineers, 18 October.

Eisiminger, S. K. (1963) Widening and deepening the Columbia and Willamette Rivers, *The Dock and Harbour Authority*, **43**, 327–9.

Goss, R. O. (1970) *The Size of Ships*. Paper delivered at Semaine de Bruges, April. Bruges: College of Europe.

——and Jones, C. D. (1970) The economics of size in dry bulk carriers, *BOT 1970*. London: HMSO.

Hammond, R. (1969) *Modern Dredging Practice*. London: Muller, 1969.

Hay, D. (1968) Harbour entrances, channels and turning basins, *The Dock and Harbour Authority*, **48**, 269–76.

Hinwood, J. B. (1964) Estuarine salt wedges, *The Dock and Harbour Authority*, **45**, 79–82.

Hunter, E., and Wilson, T. B. (1969) The increasing size of tankers, bulk carriers and containerships with some implications for port facilities, *Research and Technical Bulletin*, **5**, 186–224, London National Ports Council.

Ingle, J. C. (1966) *The Movement of Beach Sand: an Analysis using Fluorescent Grains*. New York: Elsevier.

Inglis, Sir Claude, and Allen, F. H. (1957) The regimen of the Thames Estuary as affected by currents, salinities, and river flow, *Proceedings of the Institution of Civil Engineers*, **7**, 827–78.

Ippen, A. T. (Ed.) (1966) *Estuary and Coastline Hydrodynamics*. New York: McGraw-Hill.

Lutgens, R. (1967) Die grosstanker-schiffahrt, *Schiff und Hafen*. Hamburg: University, Institute of Geography and Economics.

MacTier, Sir Stewart (1964) Some aspects of cargo handling in the deep-sea liner trades, *The Dock and Harbour Authority*, **45**, 12–14.

Maddrell, R. (1970) Evolution of the Outer Thames Estuary, *The Dock and Harbour Authority*, **51**, 52–6.

Magnius, J. (1963) The Port of Norrköping and the Lindö Canal, *The Dock and Harbour Authority*, **44**, 206–12.

Miniken, R. R. (1963) *Winds, Waves and Maritime Structures*. London: Griffin.

Moore, D. G. (1963) Geological observations from the bathyscaphe *Trieste* near the edge of the continental shelf off San Diego, California, *Bulletin of the Geological Society of California*, **74**, 1057–62.

Permanent International Association of Navigation Congresses (1961) *Report on Proceedings of the 20th International Congress*. Baltimore.

Price, W. A., and Kendrick, M. P. (1963) Field and model investigation into the reasons for siltation in the Mersey estuary, *Proceedings of the Institution of Civil Engineers*, **24**, 473–517.

Proceedings of the Fifth International Harbour Congress (1968) 2–8 June, Antwerp.

Quinn, A. D. (1961) *Design and Construction of Ports and Marine Structures*. New York: McGraw-Hill.

Radway, E. R., and Perfrement, D. (1968) Berthing accommodation for large ore carriers, *Proceedings of the Fifth International Harbour Congress*, 2–8 June, Antwerp. Paper 2.6.

Shepard, F. P., and Inman, D. L. (1950) Nearshore water related to bottom topography and wave refraction, *Transactions of the American Geophysical Union*, **31**, 196–212.

Vinjé, J. J. (1966) Modelonderzoek van de havenmond van Ijmuiden, *Land and Water*, **10**, 24–32.

Watanabe, Y. (1965) How big will ships become? *The World in 1984*, **1**, 190–5. Harmondsworth: Penguin.

2

PORT INSTALLATIONS AND THROUGH-PUT

The installations of a port can be divided into two broad categories. First, there are port infrastructures designed to steepen the junction between land and water and to join that junction with landward communication, the whole being protected from the instability of the ground and the range of the tide if necessary. Secondly, port super-structures are concerned with aiding movements of cargoes to and from ships across that prime junction between water and land. Installation superstructures are sited in the back-up area of each berth. The total of the back-up areas is the upland of the port, the cargo-handling and cargo-manœuvring area back from the quays up to the port perimeter, which may be a customs fence or simply the boundary between port and non-port land uses. In order that ships drawing 10 m or more shall come alongside a solid stable surface connected with the mainland, considerable amendment of the land-water perimeter is generally necessary. T-head jetties can extend out to deep water, or canals can lead deep water far inland. The peri-meter can also be extended by artificial peninsulas or embayments, and then more ships can be berthed within a given lineal distance of the coast or land-water boundary in an estuary or delta. There are some ports where little engineering work has been carried out; here ships must anchor in a natural roadstead with goods transferred to and from the shore by lighters or other craft. There are also some ports where there are no superstructures for assisting cargo transfer on shore. But usually some equipment is provided first to assist and per-haps later to replace the equipment carried by the ship herself—usually known as ship's gear. The objective in providing such loading and discharging equipment is to reduce a ship's turn-round time in port by increasing cargo through-put across the perimeter—whatever that may be: quay, jetty, or perhaps open beach and river bank.

In the past great increases in through-put would have resulted only in flows faster than could be dispersed or collected by land transport. Running through this chapter is the recurring theme of increasing the specialised functions and through-put of port installations. Common user facilities for all comers are declining in favour of specially designed berths and terminals. These terminals are the subject of the next chapter, while in this section concentration is placed on the form of the installations and the way their functions are evolving towards that specialisation.

Provision of marginal quays

In the days of small sailing ships, vessels were designed to go aground at low water in the port. They sat on the layer* (of mud) adjacent to the strand where cargoes were unloaded on the worn-down surface of the land. It must have become apparent very early that if a cut or hithe was made at this land-water junction, the strand could be raised above a layer covered with more water at low tide, and thus made able to accept larger vessels. Fig. 8b deduces how subsequent reclamation of the layer on either side of a hithe combined with piling may have given rise to the forerunners of the present site and shape of Queenhithe, London.

The distinction between the amendment of the land-water junction and jetties built out from the shore remains valid to this day. Below are quoted the introductory remarks of W. H. Little, 1961, opening an informal discussion on the construction of quays and jetties at the British Institution of Civil Engineers in 1961.

. . . Quays will be taken as being parallel to the land line and Jetties as 'jutting' out from the land. As such, jetties are unlikely to retain earth and therefore most likely to be open piled structures but they can sometimes be solid either as blockwork or large buoyant boxes floated out, sunk and filled.

Quays are more likely to retain earth by mass concrete, blockwork caissons or steel sheet piling but can often be open piled work over the slope of a bank.

In the 1970s a typical berth might consist of a quay length of 224 m (735 ft) or more, with a shed, if provided, not less than 30 m from the string-piece. (For a comprehensive review of transit sheds, see *Port*

---

* Adopted here as a general term, apparently first used in a Swansea record of 1555, and referred to in an Act of 1796 when the Glamorganshire Canal was to be extended to the 'Lower Layer' south of Cardiff.

a)

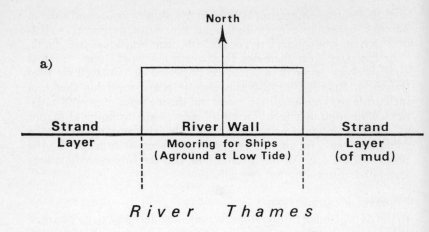

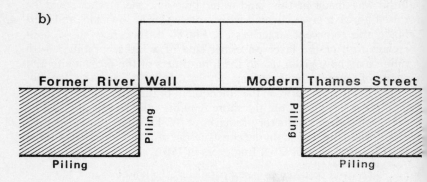

Fig. 8 A port dating from the ninth century: Queenhithe, London

(a) Schematic deduction from a charter referring to Queenhithe, on the left bank of the Thames in the City of London in A.D. 899 (then Æ deredys Hyde).

(b) Reclamation of layer (diagonal ruling) to give hithe with piled perimeter, still observable in modern London.

Sources (for Charter): MS Lambeth, 1212, p. 321; and R. Twysden, *Historiae Anglicanae*, X, A.D. 1652, p. 2218. Quoted in J. M. Kemble, *Codex Diplomaticus Aevi Saxonici*, V, 1847, Document 1074, pp. 141–2; and Sir Walter de Gray Birch, *Cartularium Saxonicum*, 2, London: Whiting, 1887, 220–1.

Structures, etc., 1969, ch. 5.) There should be rail tracks at the apron and at the rear of the shed, with provisions for the installation of a shore-based gantry crane built into the foundations of the wharf structure. There should be at least six hectares of open hardstanding in the back-up area. Such a berth would be capable of handling conventional break-bulk, container, or bulk cargoes, or a mixture of them (F. Fontanella, 1967, 37); but the fundamental structure is the quay wall. Fig. 9 presents the main types of quay construction which are of course treated in detail by the specialist engineering literature. Solid quays provide a cushion of water between themselves and the berthing ship, and they therefore need no expensive fendering and little general maintenance. The drawback with this method is usually one of high capital cost (F. A. Greaves and P. R. Robinson, 1955). Instead of timber pilings, steel or concrete piles are now used. Any timber construction is likely to wear out differentially, a grave disadvantage. Concrete particularly began to replace timber when the cost of on-site formwork was eliminated by prefabrication both for piles and for caissons. Thus quays and piers in timber are everywhere obsolescent, not only for the reasons outlined above but also because they cannot support the weight of modern requirements in superstructures.

It is dangerous to generalise about which engineering design is most economical for quay construction. Site conditions vary considerably. There now appears a general tendency for monoliths and concrete walls placed in the wet to be more expensive than sheet pile walls, but they may be very useful methods in difficult sites, and this may be a factor in raising the costs of the examples on which this generalisation is based (*Port Structures*, etc., 1969, Figs. 3.2–3.9 inclusive).

The most economical structures are those in which the most ingenuity has been used to meet the particular site conditions. Standard designs to meet various conditions are not economic. Moreover, the cost of quay structures is so high that it would be false economy to attempt to reduce design costs by limiting the scope of design studies. . . .

Maintenance costs of quay structures are not high and the savings which can be achieved in initial capital cost are much more important. The lowest cost structure will not necessarily be the one with the shortest life (idem, p. 34).

Entrance locks to quays in impounded wet docks have usually been provided when the tidal range exceeded five metres. This is because wet docks are generally less costly than tidal basins or open berths, given such a range. In the latter cases there is the additional cost of constructing stronger quay walls to withstand variations in pressure between high and low tides. Moreover, the saving on lock gates and machinery was more than offset by the capital cost of the greater depth required for the basin and its foundations. The task of dredging was infinitely greater in a tidal basin compared with an enclosed dock. Thus where an entrance lock could serve a number of berths, this proved to be the best engineering practice. However, the coming of the beamy container ship, too wide for many existing entrance locks, and demanding a quick turn-round, without delays due to locking and unlocking, has swung the balance of advantage to tidal marginal quays and to those ports with low tidal ranges. Examples of recent lock entrances are: Antwerp, $500 \times 57 \times 17.50$ m; and Le Havre, $400 \times 62 \times 17$ m.

TABLE 4

CAPITAL COST OF A CONVENTIONAL QUAY BERTH IN AN
ENCLOSED DOCK

	Per cent of total
Share of cost of enclosed dock system	32
Quay (200 m) with road and rail access	39
Transit shed (130 m by 50 m)	10
Quay cranes and tracks	11
Other engineering works	8

Source: *A Study of Port Operations*, 1967, 7, based on a variety of examples.

The figures given in Table 4 are already historic, as far as container operations are concerned, in that they refer to a quay with a covered transit shed, but it is interesting to observe that the cost of the quay

Fig.9 Main types of quay construction

Solid types:
(a) bulkhead with sheet-pile cells;
(b) sheet-pile bulkhead, supported by tie rods;
(c) sheet-pile bulkhead supported by batter piles;
(d) gravity wall of precast concrete blocks;
(e) caisson, or monolith.

Open type:
(f) piles, with or without relieving platform, indicated here by fill.

Pattern of stipple indicates coarseness of fill, and horizontal ruling represents original ground.

Sources: A. D. Quinn, 1961, 230 ff., and *Port Structures*, etc., 1969, 17 ff.

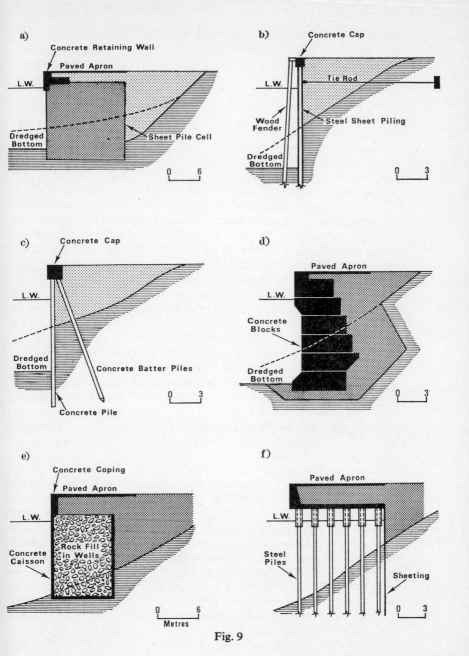

a) Concrete Retaining Wall
Paved Apron
L.W.
Dredged Bottom
Sheet Pile Cell
0   6

b) Concrete Cap
L.W.
Tie Rod
Wood Fender
Steel Sheet Piling
Dredged Bottom
0   3

c) Concrete Cap
L.W.
Dredged Bottom
Concrete Batter Piles
Concrete Pile
0   3

d) Paved Apron
L.W.
Concrete Blocks
Dredged Bottom
0   3

e) Concrete Coping
Paved Apron
L.W.
Concrete Caisson
Rock Fill in Wells
0   6
Metres

f) Paved Apron
L.W.
Steel Piles
Sheeting
0   3

Fig. 9

itself is only about 40 % of the total cost and that almost 30 % of the cost is due to superstructure costs.

Installation superstructures

Specialised cargoes implied specialised handling on the waterfront from very early days. Winches and pulleys and spouts for loading by gravity at staiths were very common at many ports particularly for loading coal, including bunkers. Until shortly after the last war, the dominant types of quay installation for dealing with break-bulk cargo were the level-luffing quayside crane, particularly in Europe, and cargo beams used with ship's gear in the US (burtoning). 'Level luffing' means that the crane jib can be raised or lowered (luffing) without altering the height of the load, and this can be done with the crane swinging. Ship's gear generally consists of a pair of cargo booms for each hatch. One boom is stayed over the offshore side of the hatch opening and the other is positioned over the quay. The cargo is suspended on a link attached to both hoisting lines and thus can be moved vertically or horizontally; one derrick lifts the cargo whilst the other exerts a side pull to move each set or individual load or cargo quaywards. An extension of this married gear or 'union purchase' is when one of the derricks is replaced by a cargo mast attached to a shed on the quayside, with the cargo landed on the quay between the burtoning mast and the ship's derrick. This is sometimes called the housefall system, and its main advantage is that the quay-based equipment is very light and can be employed on light quay structures which would not support quayside cranes. Also where there are narrow aprons on quays, there may not be room for quayside cranes.

Both these circumstances imply timber jetties which as has been shown are obsolescent infrastructures. US ports are likely to move direct from the housefall method to container cranes. But the ship's gear versus quay cranes controversy has been well summed up by E. S. Tooth, 1958, who believed that expensive quay cranes place emphasis on speed of handling whereas systems using ships' gear have the attraction of cheap capital cost. R. B. Oram, 1965, ascribed most of the cargo-handling differences to 'the custom of the port'—one continues in the way one has started since 'it has always been done that way', until revolution overturns tradition. The methods described above are being superseded by unit-load handling because they involve several disadvantages. First, there are three movements: hoist out of ship's hold, swing, and deposit on quay (and the reverse for exports). Secondly, the methods involve unloading small sets of cargo at a time, generally less than five tons. While these are being unloaded, they receive no protection from the weather. Another appliance is needed on the quay, a man's shoulder, a trolley, a fork-lift truck, or a mobile crane in order to pile the load under covered accommodation awaiting the next inland movement. The goods must be tallied, because each set is made up impromptu in the hold, and the only method of totalling it is to count the loads as they come on to the quay, often mixed up to different consignees, each with individual bills of lading and other necessary documents. At each movement there may be spillage of the load; pilferage may occur; and so individual cargoes have to be securely packed to be protected from such hazards as they may encounter consonant with their liability to damage and value per unit of weight. This is a summary of the disadvantages of the unloading of 'general cargo' in small lots. 'General cargo' is a vague term for a class of goods distinguished from the discharge of instalments of totally homogeneous cargo—bulk cargo. Henceforth, 'general cargo' will be called 'break-bulk' cargo in this book.

Indivisible loads of more than 20 tons can be described as heavy lifts as far as ports are concerned. The normal quayside crane capacity is up to five tons. Sometimes two cranes can be rigged together to provide a yo-yo lift within the range of their combined lifting power. The commonest heavy lifts in break-bulk cargo are: individual items that weigh more than five tons because they consist of complex machinery assemblies that are too complicated to be put together on delivery; unpacked road vehicles, including buses; unpacked tractors and earth-moving machinery; and locomotives. But major ports must be able to cope with much larger loads, up to 400 tons. Hammerhead cranes on quaysides of up to 200-ton capacity necessitate the ship moving to that berth to receive the load. Much more flexible and common are heavy duty floating cranes. The number of heavy loads is increasing, particularly 'transformers, steel castings, generating station boilers, heat exchangers for nuclear power stations and reaction vessels for the chemical industry' (*Report of the Committee of Inquiry into the Major Ports of Great Britain*, 1962, para 344). A forecast indicates that the number of heavy indivisible loads above 90 tons will increase in Great Britain by one-third in the period 1968–72 from 187 to about 250, of which some 60% will be for export (calculated from *Working Party*, etc., 1970, Tables 2, 3, 4, and 5). Such great loads exceed the gauge and height restrictions of the railways, and when due for export must be brought to the ship by road, or coastwise vessel. Heavy lift roll-on vessels are particularly useful. To some extent the heavy lifting appliances attract their own business, since the loads are drawn to them perforce. But too few heavy loading appliances result in very long and inconvenient journeys by road. The problem is therefore eminently suited to be considered in the context of regional or national planning.

The operation of port installations—labour and through-put

Until this century the operation of port installations was everywhere labour-intensive, but with the increase of specialised quayage and the change to mechanical handling even for break-bulk cargo, the demand for labour on the waterfront is decreasing. The Woodward Report of 1967 in Australia (*General Report of the Stevedoring Industry Conference*, Appendix G) estimated that the 22,000 Australian waterfront workers would see their number reduced by half in the ten years from the mid 1960s—'an entirely novel redundancy situation not so far faced by any Australian industry'. In developed countries this redundancy danger is not easy to avoid without labour strikes. The problem is even more acute in developing countries where labour is cheap, so that there is less incentive to invest in costly machinery, particularly if the port has a monopoly over a hinterland.

Where mechanisation of ports is proceeding apace, labour is more organised, and there is some divergence in port practices from country to country due to different legislation and trade union organisation, but this section scarcely descends into such detail that national differences become important. Waterfront labour history is a large subject in every maritime nation, and much of the source material is to be found in government reports. All over the world the waterfront worker has tended to be strike-prone, and the interruption to the flow of goods has precipitated many an official enquiry. Most of the fundamental problems of port labour are common to all developed maritime countries, and attempted solutions in particular countries are here merely used to illustrate the general points.

In a world-wide survey C. Kerr and A. Siegel, 1954, have shown that among workers over the whole range of employment, dock workers share with seamen and miners the greatest propensities for strike action. The authors concluded that these three classes of workers had the following features in common. The labour force is in 'isolated masses', a 'race apart', detached from the employer as well as from the community. The possibility of protest by leaving to take another job is reduced because these three industries do not in general equip a worker with skills easily transferred into other industries. Thirdly, there is little occupational stratification so that the workers tend to be closely-knit communities where grievances can quickly spread 'horizontally'. Fourthly, the work is often relatively unpleasant and physically demanding, and this encourages the recruitment of tough and forceful workers. The strike-prone industry is therefore one that segregates large numbers of persons who have relatively unpleasant jobs of a similar character. From this it will be seen that increased mechanisation of cargo-handling attacks 'strike-proneness' in three ways: it will give workers differential skills causing a stratification within the labour force; these skills will be of use if the worker wishes to transfer to another industry; and mechanisation will take much of the physical effort out of dock work. It is significant that men permanently employed at specialised terminals by industrial firms rarely go on strike.

A rather particular difficulty besetting the waterfront is the irregularity of the work-load. Ships are delayed by storms or 'Acts of God', there are peaks and troughs in particular trades due to irregularity of demand, erection of tariff or tax barriers, political discriminations, the seasonal surpluses of agriculture, and the ice-bound season of high-latitude ports. As a result the port labour force has tended to be on a casual basis, *ad hoc* as the demand arose. If men are employed from a labour pool by different employers as need arises, their loyalty to an employer is weak, and their solidarity with each other may be strong. It is difficult to have pride in the job when unloading and loading ships, since there is little to show for physical effort; indeed, the more efficient the operation the quicker the ship and her cargo disappear altogether. The Devlin Report (*Final Report*, etc. 1966) on British port labour, which, as is usual with such reports, included a good summary of the national history of waterfront labour, asserted that loyalty decreased with higher wages (para 17), though perhaps was on surer ground in saying that 'Casual labour produces a casual attitude' (para 19). At this point it is worth making a distinction between three different basic kinds of port operations: all-comers common user; programmed common user; and programmed tied user. The first applies to a berth that is freely available to all ships that are willing to pay the dues; the second type comprises the berths that are used by a similar class of ship on a regular basis; and the third is where the operator of the terminal also operates the ship, perhaps through an associated company. The first type is everywhere giving way to the other two types, but it is the all-comer common user berth, originally ubiquitous, that gave rise to casual employment.

Casual labour not only produces a casual attitude, it also spawns idiosyncratic practices, called 'customary' by workers and 'restrictive' by employers. In the past these practices have arisen as a form of self-protection by employees who were bid for by employers in an open market. If rigid practices had not arisen, workers would have found themselves at the mercy of those of their colleagues who would have been willing to work the longest hours or otherwise undercut their workmates. Undoubtedly, such labour exploitation occurred in the past, and still occurs today in developing countries. The growth of labour practices is a natural defence against casual employment and an attempt to maintain standardised earnings in circumstances of irregular work-loads and of great variations of the types of work involved, due to the heterogeneous nature of break-bulk cargo. Practices may take the form of agreed time off during work shifts, the agreed method of prolonging a job into the overtime period, or perhaps an agreed late start or early finish to account for journey to work difficulties. Some of these practices when extended into an era of modern labour legislation seem very curious. Even in an advanced country like New Zealand the hours of waterfront work per week were reported in 1964 to be on average as many as 59; yet as much as 50–60% of the time was non-productive '. . . many waterfront workers leave their homes at about 7 o'clock in the morning and return about 10 o'clock in the evening' (*New Zealand and Overseas Trade*, etc., 1964, paras 350 and 358). This seems like a state of affairs current several decades ago in manufacturing industry. In any case it has been deduced that more improvements in through-put rates are achieved by working ships more intensively (say through more gangs per ship) rather than by working longer hours (*A Study of Port Operations*, 1967, 31).

A major landmark in waterfront labour relations was the 'buying the book' agreement on the US Pacific Coast. The Mechanisation and Modernisation Agreement (known as the 'M. & M. Agreement') was signed on 18 October 1960 between the International Long-shoremen's and Warehousemen's Union and the Pacific and Maritime Association of employers. The idea behind this was that the labour practices, enshrined in the labour rule book, were given up in return for $25 million over five years, representing 4½% of the wage bill per annum. $10 million were used to secure a guaranteed wage, while reduction in the labour force due to increased mechanisation was achieved by natural wastage; and $15 million was used for the pension fund. In fact the agreement was limited in scope to sling loads, first place of rest, multiple handling, and manning scales, albeit practices that had particularly impeded mechanisation.

A much wider attempt to 'buy the book' was the British National Directive of 1961 by the National Joint Council for the Port Transport Industry (quoted as Appendix N in *Report of Committee of Inquiry*, etc., 1962). This directive proposed a deal which never came off. The Devlin Committee (*Final Report*, etc., 1965) showed

that the issues and lessons are wider in scope than the British port
scene, and their comments may stand as a fitting conclusion on the
supersedence of casual labour by a specialised labour force using
modern mechanical cargo-handling aids.

The National Directive proposed a quid pro quo on a grand scale.
Had it come off it would have been even more revolutionary than the
West Coast M. & M. Agreement. The latter 'bought the book' for money or
money's worth. The former attempted not only to buy the book, abolishing
all restrictive practices, but to abolish the casual system as well and to pay
for the first with the second. . . .
  We think—with all the benefit of hindsight—that it is possible now to
see why the deal collapsed.
  In the first place there was at the root of it a false assumption. This
was the assumption that decasualisation was a 'grant' or 'benefit' to the
men to be regarded by them as money's worth. In truth management needs
it as much as the men and it soon became apparent that the men would
never regard the 'substantial extra cost' [to the employers] as if it was
money in the pay packet. The assertion of the extreme view that it was a
'grant' [by the employers] led to the counter-assertion of the other extreme
that it was an 'entitlement' [of the workers]. We do not look upon it as
either of these things. It should be looked upon, we think, as a change
which is being forced upon the industry by the need to adapt itself to the
conditions of full employment; and as a change which, while it necessarily
imposes financial obligations on employers, also inevitably results in
certain practices, excusable under a casual system, ipso facto becoming
obsolete. (paras 318 and 319)

Needless to say decasualisation has supervened, and will undoubtedly spread to other countries where casual labour survives for
various reasons. However, even under a casual system, rises in
productivity can be remarkable with mechanical aids, as revealed by
Table 5.
  It would be wrong to correlate these decreasing numbers against
increasing volume of seaborne trade, because much of the increased
tonnage handled passes across specialised terminals where dock
workers play little part in increasing berth through-puts.
  To calculate berth through-puts is to calculate berth productivity;
and to compare the efficiency of berths of different dimensions, productivity can be refined to through-put per lineal unit of quay length,
and the following examples can be quoted, in tons per lineal metre:
German ports, 500, New York, 570, Algiers, 800, and for the larger
berths at Antwerp, 1,200. These figures and the chief factors involved
in this through-put performance ($T(e)$) have been set out by J. G.
Baudelaire, 1966, and summarised in three equations.

TABLE 5

DECLINE IN THE NUMBER OF BRITISH DOCK WORKERS*

	Census of average daily part employment in the London area	Number entered on register of dock workers in the London area	National total on register of dock workers
1921	34,000†	—	—
1924	31,000†	—	—
1925	—	55,000†	—
1931	26,000†	36,000†	—
1938	—	43,000‡	130,000§
1949	—	26,798‖	74,850‖
1955	—	31,448‖	80,577‖
1966	—	20,023¶	45,728¶

* For the distinction between 'dock worker' and other professions and trades in the docks see *Digest of Statistics* (annual), London: National Ports Council Inclusion of all such workers would add about one-third to current figures.
† *New Survey of London Life and Labour*, 1931, London: King, ii, 399–402.
‡ D. L. Munby, *Industry and Planning in Stepney*, 1951, Oxford: University Press, 316.
§ A. H. J. Bown, 1953, Ports and shipping turn-round; causes of delay and suggested remedies, *The Dock and Harbour Authority*, **33**, 264.
‖ Registered labour forces at the last week of each year, National Dock Labour Board Statistical Officer.
¶ *Digest of Statistics*, 1966, vide supra, Table 10.

First equation: $T(e) = \dfrac{No.\ of\ working\ days \times berth\ occupancy\ factor}{Length\ of\ berth}$

Second equation: $T(e) \times l = T(s) \times S + T(r)$
where $T(e)$ = lineal through-put of quays
l = length
$T(s)$ = through-put per unit area of sheds
S = area of the sheds
$T(r)$ = the amount of direct transfer from land or inland barge of lighter conveyance and vice versa

Third equation: $T(s) = \triangle \times \dfrac{365}{D}$

where $\triangle$ = stacking capacity
D = length of time (in days) that goods stay within the perimeter of the berth

A new concept introduced here is the berth occupancy factor

$\left(\dfrac{\text{time ships actually being worked}}{\text{total working time}} \times 100 \right)$, an index of by how much

maximum through-puts are not achieved. This happens because although cost of operating the berth increases with decreased through-put, the total cost of handling cargo includes the cost of the ship's total waiting time which must increase with high berth occupancy factors. Fig. 10a shows that there is an optimum number of berths for a given traffic; Fig. 10b shows that increasing berth occupancy factors cause rising total costs due to cost of delays to ships; and Fig. 10c suggests how port development might be implemented in stages to keep the berth occupancy factor between 70 and 85%. Obviously, the actual most economic berth occupancy factor depends on the type of cargo and the type of carrier. As D. P. Bertlin, 1966, 258, points out, the more expensive the annual costs of the berth relative to the ship (quays, cranes, and transit sheds being used by break-bulk conventional ships in an enclosed dock), the higher should be the berth occupancy factor. Mammoth tankers at relatively cheaply provided oil jetties will use berths less intensively. It is unfortunate that in the former case the costs fall on different organisations: loss of revenue due to low occupancy factors falls on port authorities if they are the providers of the berth; costs caused by delays to ships fall on shipowners (*The Turn-around Time*, etc., 1967, 9). Thus the minimum of joint costs occurs where berths are being operated above minimum cost, if this minimum is based on berth cost alone (Z. Pelcynski, 1964).

A seminal paper on operational research applied to cargo-handling was by R. T. Eddison and D. T. Owen, 1953, with particular reference to iron ore discharge. These authors defined the elements of cost in ore discharge and found that cost per ton declined with: increasing berth occupancy; increasing number of berths in situations of increase in tonnage of ore discharged; and use of 25-ton ore unloaders in place of 10-ton kangaroo cranes. The 1953 figures and graphs are not quoted in detail since very different congestion costs per day must be added on compared with 1953 because of the much greater average size of ore carrier. Turning to a more recent paper, F. G. Culbert and F. C. Leighton, 1963, 3, summed up the five factors involved in the turn-round of ships at a berth: variability of the arrival pattern of land- and sea-based carriers; payload capacity of the carriers; cost of idleness of the carriers; fixed and variable costs of providing the berth; and level of annual through-put and the market value of the material handled. They sum up the position in these words which are a good verbal version of Fig. 10a: 'The basic economic concept to be applied when planning materials handling centres is the balancing of the cost of delays against the cost of providing the service' (23). It should also be apparent that it is not possible to plan port extensions on the principle of merely dividing the estimated port tonnages by the capacity of the installations involved.

Berth through-puts are very amenable to the model approach—'a representation, in algebraic terms, of the significant factors and the relationships between them, which make up the operation being studied' (225, *vide infra*). Three models among several may be cited (*Research and Technical Bulletin*, **5**, 1969, 225–32; and **6**, 285–93. London: National Ports Council), although the parameter levels in any model of this type are likely to vary from port to port with variations in the incidence of costs. It is too early to say that a general model approach has yet been evolved. (D. Singh, 1970, includes a review of operational research simulation models.) The theoretical approach seems to indicate that above 1,200 tons through-put export and import functions ought to be carried on at separate berths, and that intensive working of ships with plenty of storage room on the berth is important in reducing total costs. S. J. Reeves, 1970, describes a model which generates the random arrival of ships (a Poisson random variation*), random ships' service time (according to an Erlang distribution), and the delays due to weather (based on actual records). An Erlang distribution includes a constant K, and as this is increased in value, the Erlang function provides a pattern with increasing uniformity. This is most useful in considering the randomness of ships' service time, less with tankers and other bulk

* Both C. H. Plumlee, 1966, and S. N. Nicolaou, 1967, agree that for 'general cargo ports' (i.e. those serviced by conventional break-bulk ships) the observed pattern of ship arrivals appears to agree with Poisson's law of random distribution.

Fig. 10 Relationship between berth costs, total cargo-handling costs, and berth occupancy

(a) Conditions of constant traffic: the cost of delays to ships falls as more berths are provided, but the minimum total costs occur before the minimum cost of delays to ships.

(b) Conditions of increasing traffic: the cost of berths as a percentage of total costs falls with increasing berth occupancy, but the cost of delays to ships increases. (The case illustrated is applicable to break-bulk ships.)

(c) Conditions of increasing traffic: the port is developed in stages to keep the berth occupancy factor in the preferred range for break-bulk ships.

Source (diagrams only): D. P. Bertlin, 1966, 258.

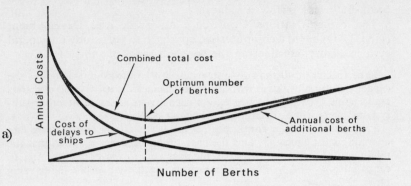

a)

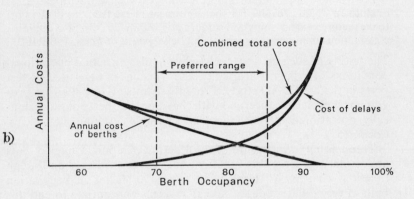

b)

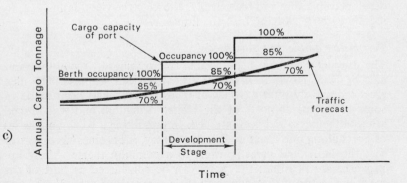

c)

Fig. 10

carriers (higher K values assigned), and highest with conventional break-bulk vessels (low K values).

The United Nations Conference on Trade and Development (UNCTAD) based a computerised approach to port study on general systems theory, considering the port as a series of sub-systems.

The capacity of all the sub-systems cannot be the same and unless the capacity of the sub-system with the lowest capacity is equal to all demands made upon it (which implies excess capacity in all or most other sub-systems) there will be occasional or regular bottlenecks; . . .

The static optimum for a port exists when all the sub-systems are operating most effectively and the operating procedures are such that the minimum total cost (where 'cost' includes cost to the port authority, to cargo interests and to shipping interests) is achieved within the existing physical framework of the port; and . . .

The dynamic optimum for a port is achieved when a growth pattern is established which provides for the adjustment of the facilities of the port to the requirements of ships and cargo, again within the criteria of attaining a continuous minimum cost position. (*Development of Ports*, 1969, 18)

The testing of such an approach is by simulating actual operational conditions of a port. Casablanca and Vancouver were used as test ports in the UNCTAD study. From these tests an optimisation programme is evolved 'concerned with choosing the "best" of the technically, operationally, and economically feasible development policies' (idem, 157).

Through-put is a measure of the function of a port. Quay lay-outs are designed to serve this function, but past forms linger on though functions change. All large ports consist of forms of installation built at very different dates, and so it seems appropriate to end this chapter with a general view of how port installations have been developed spatially and technically, allowing the view, Janus-like, to see the pattern evolving into the future.

Perspective on the *Anyport* model

The *Anyport* model has been used in two volumes by the author and also by B. S. Hoyle in a study of East African seaports. The idea grew inductively after a series of investigations had been made of some of the major ports of the United Kingdom and was refined after all the ports had been studied. In presenting a work on a series of ports along one coast or in one country, it becomes necessary to link the individual investigations to a common theme. Many approaches are possible: the ports can be considered as part of the maritime sector of the economy; their competitive roles in dividing up a common areal hinterland can be assessed; or they can be considered merely as evolving terminal nodes of a country's transport network. The *Anyport* model uses yet another approach—the evolution of the installations of a port. This scheme has a simple merit in that it keeps the focus on the actual port area, but lays itself open to the objection that insufficient attention is paid to the hinterland the port serves, to the foreland served by the ships, or indeed to the development of shipping itself. Obviously, if a model is to be based on port installations, these other factors must be considered in some supplementary way, but the *Anyport* approach is not as restrictive as it may appear at first sight. Developments in the hinterland and in shipping are normally reflected with a greater or lesser time-lag by the provision of new port installations designed to serve them. The converse is not true. Hinterland models (as will be seen in Chapter 5) do not take into account the fact that provision of a particular port installation can attract and divert both sea and land transport of goods through a particular port.

The *Anyport* model was conceived because study of successive major British ports revealed common types of installations, although arranged in varying combinations so that the total patterns of the individual ports seem very different at first sight. Moreover, it can be demonstrated that seaports develop sequentially in the same way— the same type of installations tend to be provided at any one time. This is not surprising since all the major ports of the world exist to serve the same world fleet of shipping, or similar cross-sections of it. Such a statement could be contradicted by pointing out that some ports may remain under-developed because their hinterland is under-developed and over this hinterland they exercise a port monopoly, so that both the capital and stimulus for port modernisation are lacking. This contrast in development is summed up by a ship that berths alongside a modern quay in Europe, but at the other end of her route unloads offshore to lighters at the port in a low-latitude developing country. Before summarising the model of *Anyport* (below and in Fig. 11), a *caveat* on the model, made on its first appearance, is now repeated. The purpose of using the hypothetical *Anyport* is not to display a pattern into which all ports must be forced, but to provide a base with which to compare the development of actual ports. Actual lay-outs that differ markedly from the generalised scheme will provide the greatest interest for the student of port development. *Anyport* has been designed as *Any [British] port*, and students of ports in other countries may find the concept useful, if only for the contrasts revealed between British and other ports as six eras of development unfold. It looks as though the histories of ports are going to be compared. In fact, as will be seen, each new step in the story of

Anyport involves an addition to or a change in the physical lay-out of the port, helping to build the complex pattern of a modern major port.

TABLE 6

SUMMARY OF THE GENERAL THEME OF THE DEVELOPMENT
OF A MAJOR PORT

Era	Terminated by the epoch of . . .
I *Primitive*	the overflowing of the port function from the *primitive* nucleus of the port, or the change in location of the dominant port function
II *Marginal quay extension*	the change from a simple continuous line of quays
III *Marginal quay elaboration*	the opening of a dock or the expansion of the harbour
IV *Dock elaboration*	the opening of a dock with simple lineal quayage
V *Simple lineal quayage**	the provision of oil berths in deep water
VI *Specialised quayage*	the occupation of all waterside sites between the port nucleus and the open sea

* Minimum requirements for *simple lineal quayage* have been empirically derived from a study of the development of actual ports. They are as follows: 500 m of quay in one uninterrupted line, and 9 m minimum depth alongside, with an approach channel of minimum depth of 9 m; if the quay is in an impounded dock, the entrance lock should be at least 250 m long.

Fig. 11 shows the eras of development of *Anyport*. Each era ends with an epoch-making alteration or addition to the port lay-out which can usually be dated. Note that, although an era of port development may be recognised as having ended, installations built during that time may continue to have a long working life. One of the most intriguing aspects of port study is that the vestiges of former eras of development can be seen coexisting in the modern plan. *Anyport* is taken as being first sited at an estuary head with a tidal range greater than five m. The primitive port begins at some point along *Anyport*'s estuary where an easier and therefore busier place for a harbour may be found, perhaps where a tributary enters, making an embayment, with slightly higher land giving protection on either side before the estuarine marshes begin downstream. Commerce cannot be carried on until the port is proclaimed a legal port, and the custom house is sited very close to the original port nucleus, a position it may still occupy today even though the biggest ships may berth some distance away. The port develops in a lineal fashion along the town waterfront until it is limited by some natural feature or defence work of the port. Transit sheds may line the quays, and these must not become clogged with cargo. Warehouses for longer storage are behind (see Table 7). A bridge may separate seagoing vessels from river traffic; a road transverse to the waterfront leads inland.

Eventually the lineal development of the port must outstrip the areal growth of the town; and when this can be demonstrated, the second era of *marginal quay extension* can be said to have begun. If this extension was to go on indefinitely, the port would be unduly lengthened; customs surveillance, originally based entirely on the custom house, would be made difficult. So the early port engineers strive for additional quayage without increasing the area of the port.

Marginal quay elaboration consists of short jetties or cuts in the river banks called hithes, or tidal graving docks where ships can be overhauled during the terminal turn-round. As ships grow larger, the original harbour becomes congested. Whole fleets sheer and range together in the tideway. Engineers have literally to break new ground. In the case of *Anyport*, the harbour is expanded by the excavation of a dock upon a land-encroaching site of an estuarine flood-plain. An alternative solution is to excavate mudflats between tidemarks. In both cases digging of the dock proceeds within an encircling coffer-dam, and the quaysides around the hole are built up far above high-water level by the spoil from the excavation. In the early nineteenth century sailing ships are still relatively small, and so dock engineers

TABLE 7

THE STORAGE FUNCTION AT *Anyport*

(A) *Transit storage*
     (i) balancing stock—due to imbalance in sizes of ship and land vehicle
    (ii) buffer stock—an insurance against delay
   (iii) working stocks—a reservoir of choice when making up loads in ships, containers, often in groupage depots.

(B) *Warehouse storage*
     (i) balancing warehousing—due to a difference in timing between supply (seasonal) and demand (steady), e.g. grain and timber; or between supply (one season or year) and demand (another season or year), e.g. Brazil nuts and vintage wines.
    (ii) bulk-order warehousing—to obtain economies of scale through bulk ordering
   (iii) policy warehousing—as a speculation or precaution against price movements or interruption of supplies
   (iv) marketing warehousing—whilst finding a buyer
    (v) in-process warehousing—where a process can be performed on the stock during a necessary delay perhaps while stock matures.

Source: adapted from *Ship/Shore 1980*, 51 (op. cit., *v.* p. 27).

strive for the maximum quay length possible in a given area. If the water site permits, in *Anyport*'s case if the river had been wider, peninsular jetties afford a great length of quay line within a small compass. They can be distinguished from the earlier jetties of *marginal quay elaboration* by their greater length and width. Even compact elaborate quayage in docks or jetties has to be provided progressively further away from the nucleus, and later installations of this fourth era are tied back to the central distribution area by the railway. Defects of the docks and quays with elaborate outlines become apparent as the largest ships using the port become even longer. The short runs of quays cannot easily be expanded. Engineers begin to design longer quays where the longest and shortest general cargo vessels can berth together if necessary. Such quays eliminate

---

Fig. 11 The six eras of *Anyport*

Top

    I, The *primitive* port is taken as sited where a left-bank tributary has caused an embayment, largely dry at low tide, (coarse stipple in the estuary) and upstream of estuarine marshes (fine stipple on the right of the diagram).

    II, *Marginal quay extension*, downstream of and opposite the above nucleus.

    III, *Marginal quay elaboration*, jetties and hithes (cuts in the river bank).

    W, Warehouses: quayside buildings, warehouses or transit sheds; semicircular town wall with stronghold where the wall meets the estuary downstream.

Centre:

    I–III, as Top.

    IV, *Dock elaboration* era.

    DD, Dry dock associated with later docks; Q, continuing *marginal quay extension*.

T & W, Transit sheds and warehouses.

Bottom:

    I–IV, as Centre.

    V, *Simple lineal quayage*, over 500 m in one line, with 8·5 m minimum alongside.

    VI, *Specialised quayage*, notable at T-head jetties and at large wharves in the river.

    T, Transit sheds, or in the river, jetties serving a continuous frontage of industry.

    Container berths are usually in the downstream area of ports, in reconstructed areas of docks with *simple lineal quayage*, or where deep water lies against wide areas of flat land (existing or reclaimed).

The scale has been omitted on purpose from each section of this illustration of the development of a hypothetical port.

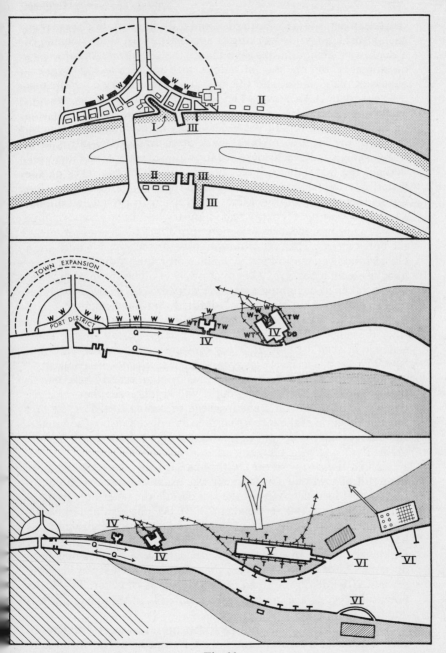

Fig. 11

short dead-end spurs for both road and rail transport, and there is no back-to-back quayside working at adjacent berths. If the opening of a dock with elaborate quayage marks the fourth era of *Anyport*'s development, the opening of a dock with *simple lineal quayage* inaugurates the fifth era, and this is a twentieth-century development.

The story of *Anyport* would end with the provision of *simple lineal quayage* if all the cargoes received were break-bulk packaged goods or goods in small lots in the holds of dry cargo liners. But side by side with the increase of break-bulk cargo trade there grows up a trade in goods specifically destined for waterside depots and factories. Perhaps the first industries to have made a distinctive mark on the waterfront are shipbuilding and ship-repairing, and fishing. But during this century *Anyport* finds it necessary to provide additional *specialised quayage* for large-scale industry and bulk cargoes. Ships have become in some instances more specialised carriers of cargoes— the bulk carriers. The first important class of such vessels were grain clippers, colliers, and oil tankers. Since oil requires distinctive port-handling techniques, provision by *Anyport* of oil berths in deep water may be taken as beginning a sixth era of *specialised quayage* provided on the grand scale. It must be admitted that conversion of quays from break-bulk cargo to specialisation on single cargo has gone on since the nineteenth century. Container cargo berths are the latest example of such a trend, and they may even call into recognition a 'special' case of *specialised quayage*—the era of *container quayage*.

Thus the growth of *Anyport* proceeds from an estuary head site to the threshold of the open sea, but it will be observed that the sixth era is fundamentally different from the preceding eras. For the first time the function of the quayage is used as a distinguishing characteristic rather than the lay-out of the berths. This has two implications: berths dating from a previous era can possibly be adapted to new specialised uses; *specialised quayage* can spread upstream, whereas the result of previous development was usually a downstream addition to port facilities. Within the last decade the innermost parts of ports, often at the estuary head site, have become hemmed in by the expanding central functions of cities; and this very expansion has boosted the real estate value of sites that make losses as ports (D. Perkins, 1970, 18). In 1969 the St Katharine Dock, which had been open merely for barge traffic on a site adjacent to the City of London, realised £1·8 million for 10 ha, including 6·5 ha of water. This is the practical effect of a more intensive form of land use ousting a less intensive form.

In Britain nearly all the major ports are of ancient foundation, sited originally, like most north-west European ports, somewhere near an estuary head and often afflicted by a high tidal range. They import mainly raw materials and export mainly manufactured goods. Two areas with very different features are East Africa and Australia, yet the *Anyport* model has been used in these areas with interesting results. B. S. Hoyle found several reasons why the *Anyport* model does not fit East African circumstances exactly. The installations have largely been provided during this century; impounded docks are unnecessary because of small tidal ranges; and the range of *specialised quayage* is not so great since the traffic flow from non-overlapping hinterlands is relatively quite small in tonnage. Hoyle found it necessary to add another era as a preliminary even to the *primitive* era of port installations—the *dhow traffic* era

extending from the earliest times to the end of the nineteenth century . . . [involving] the development of flexible hierarchies of ports at different periods; the construction of substantial port facilities was not necessary and thus flexibility of port sites was an important keynote. (1968, 166)

The end of this era and the provision of permanent port facilities appears to have coincided with the penetration of railways inland and, more particularly, the change from sail to steam—another indication that the naval architect is often the pacemaker for the port engineer.

In Australia, curiously enough, no major port was founded in a forward position, although the continent was opened up from port bridgeheads established by exogenous colonisation. This was not the result of the fears of piracy, or because of the cheapness of water transport, although this was a subsidiary factor in Queensland, but simply because the founders had to decide upon sites with a drinking water supply, and this was less likely where salt might contaminate seaboard reaches of water inlets. In some cases firm, accessible ground could only be found away from the coast, and then installations have been developed back towards the sea. The device of *Anyport* was therefore employed in Australia, although the generally small tidal range made impounded wet docks unnecessary. A counterpart to *dock elaboration* can be found in the 'solid fill' peninsulas of Sydney. This was the successor of the timber jetty of *marginal quay elaboration*, and provided an artificial peninsula with two solid fill quays and their transit sheds plus a roadway between them (J. Bird, 1968, 50–2). R. J. Solomon, 1963, put forward a scheme explaining the development of Hobart which bears close resemblance to *Anyport*. His 'four stages' and the *Anyport* counterpart are as follows: lighterage (*primitive*); marginal wharves (*marginal quay extension*); finger piers (*marginal quay and dock elaboration*); finger piers to marginal wharves (*specialised quayage* and simple *lineal quayage*).

No doubt the *Anyport* scheme could be applied to seaport study elsewhere in the world, with suitable modifications, provided it is remembered that it was designed as an aid to the understanding of the growth of really large multi-functional ports. Small ports often have only one or two specialised traffics, and thus their installation lay-out may be quite simple to understand, the complications coming perhaps within the installation itself. The whole of these small ports may perhaps be considered as one specialised component of a major port, though occasionally a series of such small ports indicate common patterns, such as once were exhibited by the coal exporting ports of South Wales, the oil exporting ports of the Middle East, and the sugar exporting ports of Queensland. Very often, such small ports depend on one major installation, and the decision to erect such a plant can mean life or death for port activities at the site. If specialisation means concentration, the through-put of cargo via a small port must either increase to justify modern port installations, or the cargo will be concentrated at one of a series of small ports to the others' disadvantage which may be mortal. But there is a role for the small port if it can be seen as one component of specialised quayage which happens to be isolated from other components for particular reasons. There are many places in the world that are proud to call themselves ports which yet export or import one basic cargo and export and receive the rest of their produce and supplies overland to and from a major break-bulk cargo port. Like their bigger colleagues, small ports must learn to adapt to the ever-increasing specialisation of port installations.

This chapter has concentrated on forms, the visible installations of a port. The casual observer might be forgiven for thinking that they are the essence of the port, but it must be stressed again that the port is basically the expression of a function—cargo transfer. When new methods of transport by sea or cargo transfer come into use, the installations of the port change and then it appears very different to the observer, although these outward changes reflect merely another way of performing the basic function. Major ports all over the world are becoming more alike as they respond to world-wide developments in sea transport. The individual component port installations in each of those major ports are becoming increasingly differentiated as they respond to the increasing specialisation of cargo carriage.

Baudelaire, J. G. (1966) *International Course in Hydraulic Engineering.* Delft.

Bertlin, D. P. (1966) Predictions for port planning, *The Dock and Harbour Authority,* **47**, 257–60.

Bird, J. (1968) *Seaport Gateways of Australia.* Oxford: University Press.

Chapon, J. (1966–7) *Travaux maritimes.* 2 vols. Paris: Eyrolles.

Cornick, H. F. (1958–62) *Dock and Harbour Engineering.* 4 vols. London: Griffin.

Culbert, F. G., and Leighton, F. C. (1963) *Application of a digital simulation model to the planning of a bulk commodity deep-sea marine terminal.* Vancouver: Canadian Transportation Research Forum.

Development of Ports: Improvement of Port Operations and Connected Facilities (1969) New York: United Nations. [Preliminary Report by UNCTAD Secretariat] TD/B/C.4/42/Rev. 1.

Eddison, R. T., and Owen, D. T. (1953) Discharging iron ore, *Operational Research Society,* **4**, 39–51.

Final Report of the Committee of Enquiry under the Rt. Hon. Lord Devlin into Certain Matters concerning the Port Transport Industry (1965). London: HMSO, Cmnd. 2734.

Fontanella, F. (1967) Impact of Containerisation on port planning, *Transportation Research Forum,* 6–9 September, Montreal, 35–7.

General Report of the Stevedoring Industry Conference (Chairman: A. E. Woodward) (1967) Canberra: Government Printer.

Greaves, F. A., and Robinson, P. R. (1955) The civil engineer's problem, *Progress in Cargo Handling,* I, 35–9.

Hoyle, B. S. (1968) East African seaports; an application of the concept of 'Anyport', *Transactions and Papers of the Institute of British Geographers,* **44**, 163–83.

Kerr, C., and Siegel, A. (1954) The interindustry propensity to strike—an international comparison, *Industrial Conflict,* A. Kornhauser, R. Dubin, A. M. Ross (Eds.). New York: McGraw-Hill.

Little, W. H. (1961) [Notes forming a basis for discussion on] *The Relative Merits of Light and Flexible Structures,* Institution of Civil Engineers, London.

New Zealand Overseas Trade: Report on Shipping, Ports, Trade and other Services (1964). London: New Zealand Trade Streamlining Committee. New Zealand: Producer Boards' Shipping Utilisation Committee.

Nicolaou, S. N. (1967) Berth planning by evaluation of congestion and cost, *Proceedings of the American Society of Civil Engineers, Journal of the Waterways and Harbors Division,* **93**, 107–31.

Oram, R. B. (1965) *Cargo Handling and the Modern Port.* London: Pergamon.

Pelcynski, Z. (1964) *The Influence of General Cargo Quay Facilities on the Costs of Transport.* Gdansk.

Perkins, D. (1970) *A Port Director's View of Planning.* Paper delivered at Semaine de Bruges, April. Bruges: College of Europe.

Plumlee, C. H. (1966) Optimum size seaport, *Proceedings of the American Society of Civil Engineers, Journal of the Waterways and Harbors Division,* **92**, 1–24.

Port Structures: An Analysis of Costs and Design of Quay Walls, Locks and Transit Sheds (1969). 2 vols. London: Report to the National Ports Council by Bertlin and Partners.

Quinn, A. D. (1961) *Design and Construction of Ports and Marine Structures.* New York: McGraw-Hill.

Reeves, S. J. (1970) Evaluation of port functioning characteristics, *The Dock and Harbour Authority,* **50**, 455–8.

Report of the Committee of Inquiry into the Major Ports of Great Britain (1962). London: HMSO, Cmnd. 1824.

Singh, D. (1970) *Port Operations and Developments: a Preliminary Analysis for Planning.* Unpublished M.Sc. (Eng.) project MS, University of Southampton.

Solomon, R. J. (1963) Four stages in port evolution: the case of Hobart, *Tijdschrift voor economische en sociale geografie*, **54**, 159–69.

Study of Port Operations, A (1967) University of Lancaster, Department of Operational Research.

Tooth, E. S. (1958) The ships' gear and quay cranes controversy, *The Dock and Harbour Authority*, **39**, 77–80.

Turn-around Time of Ships in Port, The (1967). New York: United Nations, ST/ECA/97. Mimeographed.

Working Party on the Movement of Heavy Indivisible Loads: Final Report (1970) London: National Ports Council.

3

SPECIALISED BERTHS (I):

THE TERMINAL CONCEPT

The current era of *Anyport*, that of *specialised quayage*, is a recognition of the present pervasiveness of specialisation on the waterfront, which has existed in a few respects for a very long time. The specialised functions of berths can be based on commodity type of cargo handled, ship size classification, ship sailing destination, shipping company's activities, or on shape of cargo. First, some details will be given under all these headings before considering specialised berths in two broad classes: *terminals,* where the cargo delivered is transformed within the perimeter of the installation functionally and directly connected with the berth; and, in the next chapter, *through berths* will be considered, where the cargo is taken on or delivered by specialised arrangements with land transport. Container berths are included in this second class.

The categories of specialisation

Berths specialising on one commodity type of cargo have existed for a very long time. Coal is a good example because it has always been a cargo difficult to mix with other goods, and indeed the collier generally sails one way in ballast. Coals and ores are usually unaffected by the weather, though very fine powdered materials are subject to hydration in humid climates and may have to be broken up by mechanical means. The particle size of the cargoes governs the choice of the handling equipment. Dry cargoes in powdered or granular form up to 10 mm in diameter can be handled by pneumatic equipment; for material up to 10 cm an ordinary grab is used; and for material larger than 10 cm special claw grabs or grapples may be necessary. To fit coals into this picture, it may be useful to give the classification of coals by diameter used in the Paris area (*Mechanisation of Loading*, etc., 1961, 3, 4, and 10):

80 mm/120 mm	fines, graded grains, small briquettes
80 mm/120 mm–180 mm/200 mm	screened coals
180 mm/200 mm	large screened

Thus all coals could be handled by grabs, but this is very slow compared with an installation that allows some form of tipping process, though it may not be so easy to unload the vessel as it is to load it. Obviously, coals are normally too coarse to be sucked, and thus the gravity-loading process has developed, based on different types of installation design. Methods of coal shipment have tended to vary according to the steepness of the land immediately behind the shipping point or the amount of relatively flat land transverse to the shoot (H. H. Bird, 1927–8, or older methods). An early method in north-east England was to suspend a coal wagon in a cradle, counterbalanced by a heavy weight or suspended from sheerlegs, and lower it to deck level where coal was discharged into ships' holds by bottom doors in the wagon. Where a river like the Tyne is deeply incised, elevated jetties (or staiths) could be built up over the river to deliver the coal by bottom-discharging wagons indirectly into holds by means of a hopper which feeds (perhaps by conveyor) inclined chutes or spouts. The method is economical because no hoisting is necessary since the staiths can be made self-acting by gravity. It became customary at ports in north-east England where rivers have steep banks, even being adopted at Blyth where timber staging provided the height over the flat land adjacent to the tidal basin. Hard coal of the area will tolerate rough handling. At other ports special anti-breakage appliances must be used to protect more friable coal. With shipment points on flat waterfront sites, some form of hoist up to seventy feet is necessary, with the coal then tipped through end-doors of wagons. Another method is tip the coal some distance back from the deep water and raise it to the necessary height above the berth by inclined conveyor. This last method is used to deliver coal from a stockpile to coal loaders at Newcastle (NSW) and Port Kembla, each with a rated capacity of 2,000 tons per hour. At the Conneaut coal terminal on Lake Erie, no less than four million tons of coal can be stockpiled, allowing all the year round delivery from US mines. Coal is loaded at the rate of 12,000 tons per hour. Resultant savings in transport costs allowed the Province of Ontario, where most of the coal is shipped, to continue generating power from coal, instead of switching to atomic sources within ten years. The Immingham coal terminal of the British National Coal Board effects savings on coal shipments by the rate of loading, 5,600 tons per hour; and because it can accept very large economically operated colliers, of 80,000 tons deadweight, in a location with a 24-foot tidal range. Two trains carrying 800 or 1,000 tons can be discharged simultaneously if necessary, and the system can cope with some twenty varieties of coal in its stockpiles.

Ores differ from coal in three contrasting ways: individual particles tend to be bigger, and therefore grabbing by specially designed iron ore transporter cranes is common; secondly, they have a lower value to weight ratio; thirdly, international movements of ores have increased in recent years, while for most ports coal shipments have fallen dramatically. There are thus more problems of modern port development connected with ores than with coal.

The reasons why berths become specialised because of size of ship or because of shipping route can generally be discussed under the other headings of this section. For instance, a particular type of cargo shipped in bulk may be carried in very large vessels* that can tie up only at the deepest berths in the port, which may therefore naturally specialise on that type of vessel. A ship on a constant run between two ports may dispense with ship's gear because of the facilities available at each port; then she is tied to those berths that can handle her cargo. An extreme example of this is the train ferry or roll-on vessel which must have appropriate rail tracks or berth ramps at each end of the route. Another feature of specialisation is the leasing of a berth by a shipping company. There is a tendency for shipping companies increasingly to specialise on particular classes of vessels and even on particular routes. The 'through' concept fosters this tendency to route specialisation, because if shipowners become closely involved with the landward components of routes, including inland cargo terminals, they will tend to reduce the number of land areas served in order to take advantage of organisational experience and not to spread capital too widely. The alternative is for an areally dispersed transport organisation to be run by a consortium—a group

*Some definitions may be useful. *Bulk carrier*: a single deck vessel of more than 10,000 tons deadweight, designed for the carriage of cargoes stowing between 0·45 and 1·96 cu m (16 and 70 cu ft) per ton; *ore carrier*: a single deck vessel of more than 10,000 tons deadweight, designed for the carriage of iron ore or similar ores stowing between 0·45 and 0·70 cu m (16 and 25 cu ft) per ton; *ore/oil carrier*: as above, but with a capability of loading a full cargo of either ore or oil; and *OBO* (ore–bulk–oil): as above, but with a capability of loading full cargoes of all commodities both dry and liquid.

of shipowners—the apparently logical succession to conferences of shipowners on the same route. Enough has been displayed in this paragraph to indicate that the reasons for specialisation may be multiple, and some of these reasons may appear under 'shape of cargo'.

Shape of cargo is not quite the same as commodity type of cargo. Coals and ores could be classified together as coarse-grained bulk cargoes; oils, molasses, and wine exemplify liquid cargoes; some pneumatic installations deal with several types of grain cargoes. Timber is a cargo which has in the past been normally of difficult shape, and used to demand wide storage areas adjacent to the berth for sorting or in merchants' yards for measuring and seasoning. The change to packaged timber besides enabling the cargo to be more easily handled by mechanical appliances makes carriage by sea and storage by land easier and of higher density because of standardised shapes. The ultimate in standardised shapes achieved by packaging is of course the metal container for otherwise heterogeneous break-bulk cargo. The pallet (see next chapter) piled with cargo is a unit load with a standardised shape at one end. All these different 'shapes' need specialised handling: grabs, pumps, suction equipment, straddle carriers, cranes bespoke for containers, and fork lift trucks.

Of course, some cargoes defy standardisation. They are classified as non-containerisable, and where figures appear in the following non-containerisable list they indicate the average percentage of the type that might go into standard containers or half-height containers: machinery greater than five tons in weight; unpacked cars and lorries (25); boats, hulls, aircraft; earth-moving equipment; loco-motives; chilled meat; live animals; 'long cargo', like most iron and steel pipes (25), and all rails, forgings, and ingots; structural materi-als of iron, steel, and concrete (30); and most explosives (*United Kingdom Deep Sea Trade Routes*, etc., 13). Special arrangements need to be made for fresh fruit (particularly bananas) and fresh vegetables, while steel products, petroleum chemicals, and even coal may be suitable for half-height containers.

Thus a return is made to coal with which this section opened, and the cargoes can now be reclassified according to whether the cargoes are terminating in the port area or passing through.

The terminal concept

Let it be admitted at once that very few cargoes actually terminate in port areas, but very many are vastly transformed in seaboard in-dustries. From such works oil may emerge as gasoline, ore as steel, and grain as flour. The suppliers are specialised bulk carriers which pump to tanks or dump to bins as close to deep water as possible. As far as the ship is concerned that is not only the end of the route, but also the end of her payload for the time being; she sails away in ballast for another specialist one-way cargo. If this ballast voyage is followed to the other end of the route, the ship is discovered receiving cargo in bulk at a specialised berth to which the cargo has been brought from the production hinterland. Such berths are often referred to as terminals, and this is confusing if they are merely delivery or loader berths, so perhaps these would be better names. If some form of processing is carried out adjacent to the berth so that the cargo carried is some form of beneficated or refined raw material, the word terminal is again appropriate for the installation is then the terminal of the raw material in the literal sense of that adjective. But there is no hope of this precise terminology becoming accepted. Grain 'terminals' often turn out to be nothing more than silos and pneumatic loading equipment for adjacent berths, and yet they are the exact functional counterparts of berths that are happily referred to as coal loaders.

The large-scale implantation of industries with their own sea terminals has accelerated since the Second World War, although tidewater public utilities have long been a feature of port cities far from coalfields; and in the nineteenth century industrial groups swarmed to dock areas and their associated canals. Ship-repair if not shipbuilding has always been associated with large ports. Thus port-based industries have a long history, and in order to see how circumstances have favoured the siting of large industries in port areas, several strands must be distinguished and then gathered together: temptation afforded by large volumes of cargo and relatively cheap waterfront labour, the 'Cleveland' effect, the demand-orientation hypothesis as applied to seaports, and, as might be expected, the increasing average size of specialised ships. These topics are taken one at a time, although of course they are intermixed in the present scene. Finally in this chapter, one great barrier to the present massive industrialisation of ports will have to be discussed, and this may be called the 'infrastructure-superstructure construction time differential'. This jargon is shorthand for a very important port concept, as will appear in due course.

An early version of the transformation of cargoes on the waterfront was the elementary processing of goods in warehouses. Warehouse storage is certainly necessary in a situation of un-programmed cargo flow, but some cargoes need a delay in transit for maturing or selling, if that is the way the trade is organised. Virtue was made of these necessities by carrying out simple processes on the cargoes, sorting, sampling, packaging, including bottling, or simply allowing the cargo to mature if required. For all these processes waterfront labour has been employed, because it was relatively cheap in the nineteenth century and earlier. Such labour tended to be supervised if not actually employed by organisations like port authorities and master stevedores who occupied an impartial position between seller and buyer or shipper and receiver. The past tense has been used in this paragraph not because these practices have disappeared but because they are not so widespread as formerly. Entrepot trade has declined relatively from the days when the majority of goods were dispatched on consignment and when the shipper sold his goods on an overseas market; and the growth of shipments against firm orders or indents has militated against entrepot traffic. If these processing practices persist, it is usually in those cargoes that are more valuable per unit of weight. This may seem paradoxical in that these cargoes incur high interest charges while in transit. But after processing their saleable value increases faster than interest costs, even if this means only a wait for the right buyer in highly selective trades. The point is simply illustrated by vintage wines maturing in a warehouse cellar, their value increasing each year faster than any market interest rate on their arrival value.

The 'Cleveland' effect of lowered transhipment costs at an intermediate city between producer and market has already been described (see also Fig. 1, p. 18, for Alonso's diagram).

H. H. McCarty and J. B. Lindbergh, 1966, arranged the industrial categories of the US in the order of their relative matching to the demand-orientation hypothesis.

Each category [of production, using indices of employment and income] was . . . expressed as a percentage of total production in each of the states and a coefficient of variation was computed for that type. Where those coefficients are small, as in the case of trade and certain services, the degree of association between the magnitude of the individual type and the magnitude of total production is high, and the [demand-orientation] hypothesis appears to perform rather well; but where coefficients are large, as in mining and farming, the degree of explanation is low. (109–110)

It must be stressed that the detailed figures on which this analysis is based are derived from an industrialised society that relies on a market mechanism to regulate its economy. But the scheme begins to reveal the advantages of ports for certain types of manufacturing and the relationship of ports to other economic sectors of activity.

A large port adjacent to a large city is brought into principal focus. Categories like 'wholesale and retail trade' and 'professional and related services' which closely match the demand-orientation hypothesis will find their location in such an urban complex, although the warehouses of wholesalers importing from overseas may be the only relevant premises within the port area perimeter. At the other end of the economic spectrum projected by McCarty and Lindbergh are agriculture and mining which fit the demand-orientation hypothesis least well as far as their location is concerned. These activities may be sited very far away from the port city considered as a market. Perhaps they are carried on overseas, and their products brought to the city's port in large consignments for processing immediately adjacent to tidewater because of loss of weight feature in processing and the consequent uneconomic use of land transport. For the same reason, the land haul at the other end of the route may be short to a specialised loading berth of an exporting port in the producing country, perhaps by a transport route basically at right-angles to the coast for maximum penetration of the production hinterland. The Australian continent proves an excellent example of such specialised loading ports with routes normal to the coast, and these can be generalised as radial spokes looked at continentally (J. Bird, 1968, 177–8, Fig. 4).

There remains a wide group of activities that are neither closely geared to urban markets nor manifestly out of correlation with demand location as are agriculture and mining. Perhaps the most important activities of this intermediate group are 'durable and non-durable goods manufacturing'. Such industries are broadly classed as 'footloose', but if significant economies occur with increasing size of plant, the spacious flat reclaimed land of new port developments may prove attractive for processing plants, particularly as such sites are close to the urban market of the port city and have short lines of communication to export markets by sailings from the port itself.

Seaports and industries—economic and technical links

On the demand side, ports are sources of raw materials for industry; on the supply side the primary processing industries located in ports are sources for the secondary processing and manufacturing industries (a distinction made in *The Greater Delta Region*, 1968, 33); in other words, seaport industries have backward and/or forward linkages (L. H. Klaassen and N. Vanhove, 1970, 8). Other reasons for the location of industries in seaport areas are that large amounts of low value raw materials per unit of weight are uneconomic to transport long distances overland. The optimum size of primary processing plants has become increasingly larger demanding large flat sites for basically one-storey plants. The eccentric coastal site within a nation state becomes of less transport disadvantage as the plant becomes a dominant producer in the state, able to absorb the inland transport costs on its products by reason of low unit cost of production. If the plant engages in export activities, the seaport site is a positive advantage. Finally, there are external economies in industries technically linked together or occupying the same prepared site, perhaps a reclamation area, which then functions as a marine industrial estate. (For the factors affecting the growth of the steel industry on coastal sites, see A. Capanna, 1970, 8 ff.) Developments in pipeline transport technology reduce the necessity for industries to be physically adjacent to sea terminals, and this has already happened with crude oil transport to refineries (see Table 8). However, wide reclaimed flat sites on the seaboard, with easy excavation for subterranean pipes, remain an attraction for a refinery and petrochemical complex, particularly if the site carries an in-built industrial planning permission; hence Amsterdam and Antwerp refineries lie 'inland' from Rotterdam.

A port development is often held to act as a growth pole by stimulating industrial development in the local region (L. H. Klaassen and N. Vanhove, 1970, 8 and 25). It would be simpler to demonstrate high regional outputs for regions with ports, if the following was always true:

$$\frac{P_b}{P_{nb}} > \frac{I_b}{I_{nb}}$$

where P_b is a basic* port-dependent industry

P_{nb} a 'non-basic'* (i.e. non-regional exporting) port dependent industry

I_b a non port-dependent basic industry

and I_{nb} a non port-dependent non-basic industry.

The crux of the matter is, however, not that the opportunity cost of extra investment in P_b (including the port cost) is represented by extra investment in I_b, but that by definition P_b cannot be located where I_b can flourish, and also by definition, P_{nb} cannot have backward linkages with I_b. The extent of linkages, like the magnitude of the port function as a multiplier (see p. 200), is revealed by detailed input-output information on industrial functioning, and only a very few countries compile such data.

* For discussion of the basic/non-basic concept and some difficulties of applying it in practice, and of principle, see J. H. Johnson, 1967, 61–6.

TABLE 8

LINKAGES OF SEAPORT LOCATED INDUSTRIES

Zone of enquiry: seaports from Hamburg to Le Havre; and Genoa and Trieste	
Total number of questionnaires issued (shipbuilding yards not included)	250
Replies	79
Workable replies (25 replies indicated a non-port link or installations under construction)	54
Total import tonnage (millions)	66·2
Approx. estimated increase of above in 2–5 years (an underestimate because some important enterprises reported only the next annual increase)	43·1
No. of enterprises supplied by sea	44
No. of enterprises exporting by sea	42
No. of enterprises purchasing one or more kinds of raw materials within the port area	24
No. of enterprises wholly supplied with one or several kinds of raw materials from the port area	13
No. of enterprises selling one or several products partly or entirely within the port area	27
No. of enterprises persuaded that one or several other firms settled in the port area because of their presence	10
Deductions from replies: forward and backward linkages most developed in (a) oil, petro-chemical, and chemical industries;* and (b) more maturely developed ports	

* Perhaps because of the physical ease of transporting liquid or gaseous products by pipeline. A further development of this linkage is the physical separation of port and industry via pipelines such as Rotterdam–Amsterdam, Rotterdam–Antwerp, Wilhelmshaven–Ruhr, and Marseilles–Ingoldstadt (H. Juergensen, 1970, 14–16).

Source: L. H. Klaassen and N. Vanhove (1970, 17–18, and Appendix 1).

Seaport industrial infrastructures

Industrial complexes comprising specialised deep-water terminals serving adjacent industries can be analysed from another bifocal angle. All such installations consist of infrastructure works—reclamation, dredging, quays, back-up area consolidation, and main services to sites; and also of superstructure works—the unloading and loading appliances, the factory itself, and all its ancillary plant. This division is vital because infrastructure works are usually the responsibility of the public sector such as a port authority, while individual private firms are often responsible for the factories and their terminals. Occasionally, public corporations assume this latter role, especially in the case of public utilities like generating stations and gas works. But if it is obvious that infrastructure must precede superstructure, then a time-lag is involved (see pp. 88–9 below). The two classes of development are undertaken by two different classes of executant investors. If the site is under water or so marshy that it is incapable of supporting large structures without considerable consolidation and fill, then there will be no tenants prowling around prospectively because for all industrial intents and port purposes the site does not even exist. Industrial demand often arises at remarkably short notice. Another main blocking factor is that reclamation is only economic in larger units than are required for individual plants, and thus site infrastructures are more usefully planned and constructed by public authorities for leasing as newly-won national assets. A good example is provided by the nucleus of the Ford Motor Company's activities in Britain which were shifted from Manchester in 1931 to a site on the Thames at Dagenham.

. . . an [industrial] estate [on Thameside] comprises a stretch of riverfront and adjacent land made ready for industry. This entails land reclamation and consolidation and drainage, wharf and road building, and the provision of improved sites for lease by industrial concerns. In the marshland a great deal of capital has to be recouped slowly by rental charges. Even large industrial concerns cannot afford the high double capital outlay required for first reclaiming and preparing the site, and then building the factory upon it. (J. Bird, 1952, 92)

The land on which the Ford Motor Company's factory is sited was originally reclaimed and made available by the industrial estate at Dagenham Dock, sited very near the old Dagenham Breach. The land was purchased by the industrial estate company in 1886, and by 1894 thirty acres of marsh had been built up to a height of twelve feet and level with the top of the old river wall. Most of the spoil used consisted of material excavated in the construction of London's underground railways. Even so 22,000 concrete piles were needed to support the original factory and ancillary equipment like the blast furnace, coke ovens, and generating station. Road vehicle and tractor manufacture appears to be demand-oriented to the extent that it ought to be located in a zone where there is easy access to a large market. In the US the northern part of the Middle West certainly originally filled these conditions, but final assembly plants are now necessary in every region that can absorb annually more than 100,000 cars (B. P. Birch, 1966, 373). London is in a similar zone to that of Detroit, even if the Thames site is geometrically at the south-eastern end of the central market zone often characterised as the London–Liverpool axis. Distances in Great Britain are not big enough to warrant regional final assembly plants. Significantly, the second Ford complex is at the other end of the axis close to Liverpool, although this location was a compromise after governmental persuasion, instead of expansion at the Thameside site as the company originally desired. In the inter-war years the situation of London was therefore favourable to road vehicle manufacture, and the local site qualities were recognised by Henry Ford. In 1930 he wrote:

We picked out the Dagenham site because it has water, rail and motor transport, and we can therefore put into it everything that we have learned at the River Rouge [Detroit] about economic handling of materials. (H. Ford and S. Crowther, 1930, 257)

An obvious reason for large quantities of cargo being deposited on the waterfront for some kind of processing is due in part to the specialised bulk carrier and her increasing average size. This aspect has already been discussed, making the point that the naval architect is the pacemaker for the port engineer. The chicken was separated from the egg, but H. Shinto, 1968, finds the egg elsewhere.

The trend towards larger ships has not been initiated by shipping companies nor by shipyards. It must more properly be attributed to the rapid increase of world trade and the requirements of shippers and customers. . . .
The increasing volume of production of raw materials to meet a growing market and the increasing distance to be transported have brought about the growth in unit size of carriers, which in turn has brought about the renovation and extension of shipbuilding facilities. The next evolution to be expected is the renovation and modernisation of port and harbor facilities . . . (p. 19)

The growth of world trade has certainly been a concomitant of the growth in the average size of ships and, certainly, technological innovations are usually more likely in situations of growth. But the 'increasing distance' travelled by raw materials has been a factor special to Japan rather than to every industrialised country. H. Shinto would certainly have a point if he thereupon suggested that Japan was accordingly the pacemaker in boosting up average ship sizes. Of course all this presupposes that there is a vigorous seaboard industry able to cope with vast amounts of raw imports. From 1970 Japan will have nearly thirty specialised coal and ore terminals, either newly established or enlarged to accommodate carriers of 50,000 tons deadweight or more, and five will be able to receive vessels in the 110,000–130,000-ton range.

This section has so far reiterated the advantages for many types of industries in having their own port terminals. But there remains one obstacle to discuss—that 'infrastructure-superstructure construction time differential'. Reclamation of areas annually under water is an old feature of civilisation, but modern reclamation projects in port areas may be different in three ways. First, reclamation may be of areas perennially under water, even advancing the coastline seawards (see Fig. 5). This may of course be additional to the reclamation of sandbanks, saltings, estuarine marshes, and river flood-plains. If reclamation is solely based on these features, the project is merely confirming in permanent form what is available at low tide or during periods of low land flow of rivers. Secondly, modern port projects comprise the construction of very large and heavy structures in the reclaimed area, and this entails not only massive consolidation of parts of the site, but also the provision through the site of all the necessary services to make the waterfront facilities work; and this is very different from reclamation merely for agricultural purposes. Thirdly, modern port reclamation goes hand in hand with channel excavation so that where there was once shallow water and an indeterminate land-sea boundary—the reason perhaps for considering reclamation in the first place—the result is deep-water brought close to consolidated ground. Thus the work of reclamation in ports involves very large-scale construction over a considerable time period. This provision of infrastructure has to be ready before any erection of port superstructures, such as cargo-handling facilities, including jetties, storage bins, and factories. It is ironical that the construction time period of this class of engineering work is very much shorter than for infrastructure provision, so that infrastructure projects must be embarked upon not only before the superstructure is started, so much is obvious, but before the superstructure is planned and, very frequently, *before the immediate need for the superstructure has even arisen*, because such need often arises at relatively short notice. As might be expected, this highly important point was probably first appreciated in the Netherlands.

Realisation of this time-lag, sometimes known as the 'lead time' (R. Regul, 1970, 3), gives the innermost clue to the success of Rotterdam, and clearer expression of the principle is to be found in a four-page mimeographed paper emanating from Rotterdam which appears to deal with only the administrative structure of the port, for it bears the uninspiring title of 'Position of the port management within the municipal authority', and is undated. However, the following extract sums up in a few lines one of the major principles of modern port development.

It is a heavy task for the Port Management's Directors to ensure that the essential infra-structure facilities are available on time in order that, once the decision to invest has been taken, private initiatives can be realised at the shortest possible notice. The time-lag between the decision and the realisation is much longer with infra-structure projects than with invest-ments in the supra-structure [*sic*]. This difference in time must have been bridged by the municipality[1] when private investment decisions are taken. If no short-term perspectives can be offered to private investors, the port is no longer of interest to them because, in face of international competi-tion, no positive commercial policy can be followed. The development of the infra-structure, therefore, must be a jump ahead of private enterprise decisions and experience has clearly shown that these decisions—because of the presence of actual investment possibilities—always follow quickly. This experience proves that the municipality, although it anticipates private investments, by no means anticipates the developments which lead to these investments. (op. cit.)

[1] In the formal sense, the Port Management [of Rotterdam] is a branch of the municipal services, and as such is appointed by the City Council. . . (idem)

Another reason why industrialists want their own sea terminals is that they get priority at the berths. If the berth is leased from the port authority, the rent should be equivalent to a full amortisation of the capital invested in the infrastructure. Oil refineries need import and export berths; some of the products of chemical works may be exported via break-bulk berths, perhaps in unit loads; while petro-chemical plants obtain their imports from oil refineries but may need a product export berth. At Antwerp the port authority avoids grant-ing rights to private berths if the corresponding cargo output is not equivalent to the average through-puts of comparable public berths (R. Vleugels, 1967, 10).

In 1967 the British National Ports Council engaged engineering consultants to prepare a preliminary report on maritime industrial estates where reclamation was involved. For the first time some figures were put on desirable areal and depth dimensions for MIDAS (maritime industrial development areas). Three criteria were estab-lished: nearness to water 15–18·5 m deep at mean high water neaps, without excessive dredging; the availability of at least 2,200 hectares of level land reasonably near the deep water suitable for heavy indus-trial development with or without reclamation, together with further substantial contiguous areas; and favourable broad economic geo-graphy of the location, including such factors as population, industry, inland communications, and relation to markets and other overseas ports (*Maritime Industrial Development Areas, MIDAS*, 1968; and M. H. Peston and R. Rees, 1970). Class I MIDA category embraces those sites which meet all three criteria; Class II are deficient in one or more respects, but still retain sufficient merits for MIDAS purposes; and other areas might be suitable for the establishment of a single enterprise dependent on deep-water access. The report went on to recommend that the first stage of the project should be large enough for 'take-off' at say 900 ha with each plot measuring 130–450 ha.

This section has dealt with the maritime industrial estates where the large-scale reclamation projects belong to a non-differentiated sector, characterised by a concave function (increasing returns) and marked indivisibility. This latter characteristic is met by spreading reclamation benefits over a family of superstructure users. The extreme opposite example is where one project is sited merely because of the very deep water available so that the enterprise makes use of very large vessels which tranship their cargoes into smaller vessels; and in this case the enterprise is very capital intensive with very little impact on the local area. The Gulf Oil Company's terminal at Bantry Bay is served by six 312,000 tons deadweight tankers, wholly employed in the carriage of oil from Kuwait. Smaller tankers (80,000–100,000 tons deadweight) then tranship the crude oil to refineries at Europort, Gulfhaven (Denmark), Huelva, and Milford Haven. Even with the added costs of transhipment and the £10 million expense of the Bantry Bay terminal, the transport cost from Middle East to refinery via the Cape is only half the cost of using 50,000 tons via the Suez Canal. During construction, some 1,000 men were employed in building the highly automated terminal, but only 125 local men have jobs in helping to run it. A mistake seems to have been made by the Irish Government in allowing an oil company to use the bay without paying any harbour dues, on the ground that the company provided all the installations itself. Revenue from dues might have been employed to encourage other industries to use the at present one-installation port. But if the policy was to keep further industry away from the tourist amenity of the bay, such dues could have been used further to enhance such amenity. One way of avoiding amenity interference would be to berth tankers of 250,000 tons and upwards at artificial islands with built-in tanks for oil storage which when not in use for this purpose would be filled with sea water to give stability to the structure. The Japanese call such facilities 'Central Terminal Stations', and the first began operations in Tokyo Bay in 1968. A similar island terminal is being considered for a site eleven miles from the north Welsh coast, out of sight of resorts, connected to Liverpool by seabed pipelines, and capable of berthing ships drawing 30 m. The 'Shell' system goes further and involves the discharge of the larger classes of tankers offshore into smaller tankers which have been equipped with a system of fenders, hose cradles, hoisting gear and oil transfer hose. Such a system has obvious advantages for a developing country which has not been equipped with a specialised terminal able to accept the largest class of tanker.

Bantry Bay's location is at a land's end or finisterre position with regard to a continent, and though marine terminals may be sited in such locations for depth of water, and the avoidance of shallow seas over continental shelves, it is not at present conceivable that they will give rise to vast industrial complexes of the MIDA type. These complexes have been described as depending on port terminals, but it can be seen that the word terminal is appropriate only in the sense that the ship terminates a voyage at the installation, that the vast proportion of the cargo is loaded or unloaded at the terminal, and that the cargo is transformed within the perimeter of the installation functionally and directly connected with the berth (see pp. 80–1). But that is neither the end of the story nor of the journey of the cargo, since in further-processed form it still has to reach the consumer, perhaps being even further processed or assembled several more times. The complications of all these zig-zag joggings to the ultimate consumer are not found adjacent to the Bantry Bays of this world, but are becoming established on the threshold of already large ports with reclaimable areas towards the sea.

Birch, B. P. (1966) Locational trends in the American car industry, *Geography*, **51**, 372–5.

Bird, H. H. (1927–8) The shipment of coal with reference to the lay-out of approach roads and sidings, *The Dock and Harbour Authority*, **8**, 3–10.

Bird, J. (1952) The industrial development of Lower Thameside, *Geography*, **37**, 89–96.

——(1968) *Seaport Gateways of Australia*. Oxford: University Press.

Capanna, A. (1970) *Aspects et problèmes de la sidérurgie côtière dans le monde et dans la CEE*. Paper delivered at Semaine de Bruges, April. Bruges: College of Europe.

Ford, H., and Crowther, S. (1930) *Moving Forward*. New York: Doubleday.

Hallett, G., and Randall, P. (1970) *Maritime Industry and Port Development in South Wales*. Cardiff: University College, Dept. of Economics.

Johnson, J. H. (1967) *Urban Geography: an Introductory Analysis*. London: Pergamon.

Juergensen, H. (1970) *The Investment Policy of European Maritime Ports with Regard to Regional Implications*. Paper delivered at Semaine de Bruges, April. Bruges: College of Europe.

Klaassen, L. H., and Vanhove, N. (1970) *Macro-economic Evaluation of Port Investments*. Paper delivered at Semaine de Bruges, April. Bruges: College of Europe.

McCarty, H. H., and Lindbergh, J. B. (1966) *A Preface to Economic Geography*.

Maritime Industrial Areas (MIDAS): Report to the [British] National Ports Council (1968).

Mechanization of Loading and Unloading Operations in River Ports (1961). Economic Commission for Europe.

Oberman, L. S. (1965) Functional planning of bulk material ports, *Proceedings of the American Society of Civil Engineers, Journal of the Waterways and Harbors Division,* **91,** 17–25.

Peston, M. H., and Rees, R. (1970) *Maritime Industrial Areas: a Preliminary Report.* London: National Ports Council.

Position of the Port Management within the [Rotterdam] Municipal Authority. Mimeographed, undated.

Regul, R. (1970) *Future Development of Maritime Transports and Its Implications on Harbour Facilities in Western Europe.* Paper delivered at Semaine de Bruges, April. Bruges: College of Europe.

Shinto, H. (1968) Ships, *Canadian Transportation Research Forum,* Vancouver, 1–3 May 1968.

United Kingdom Deep Sea Trade Routes: the Potential for Containers based on Physical Cargo Characteristics. University of Lancaster Department of Operational Research. London: Report to the National Ports Council.

Vleugels, R. (c. 1967) *The Industrialisation of Port Areas with Special Reference to the Port of Antwerp.* Antwerp. Mimeographed.

4

SPECIALISED BERTHS (II):

THE THROUGH CONCEPT

On a wide view, and in economic terms, the port is an interface between two modes of transport linking producer and consumer. As such it is an economic barrier, but economies of scale in one of the modes of transport or in the manufacturing process may make the jumping of the barrier a relatively minor cost. This happens when bulk cargoes are brought to large waterfront factories; but not all cargoes are susceptible of bulk consignment. Goods that need little further processing before they reach the ultimate individual consumer, and are consequently bound for many destinations, are very different from the bulk cargoes that are to be processed once or many times before they become individual consumer commodities. Grain for a tidewater mill is here being compared with a cargo of eating apples; just as raw goods may be compared with manufactured goods. Break-bulk cargo has always encountered both a physical and an economic barrier at seaports. Except in the very few cases where ship side-ports are used, imports have to be lifted up and out of the ship and then across and down. In rare cases the cargo descends direct on to the feeder vehicle. More generally, the load is placed on the quay to await the land carrier, in which case double handling is involved. As has been shown, increasing the size of the conventional break-bulk ship to gain increasing economies of operation only increases the time of turn-round in port. Unit transport avoids this difficulty.

R. B. Oram, 1968, succinctly summed up the factors that led to the progressive mechanisation of through cargo. He dates major mechanical intervention into port work from the inter-war years in the shape of the electric truck, later the fork lift truck. From this his first principle of mechanisation is derived, and this gave rise to two further principles which are extracted from his article and telescoped together below.

First Law . . . If you improve a stage in the process of cargo handling you will immediately have to improve the stage before and after that one [because productivity improvement in one stage induces a bottleneck at the join with the next stage] . . . Second Law . . . The unit of cargo should be the largest that is practicable; it must remain as a unit for the longest possible time in its journey from producer to consumer. . . . Third Law . . . The process of mechanisation must be commenced at the earliest possible stage in the journey from producer to consumer and it must be maintained for the longest practical portion of the journey.

There arises a problem of terminology. Everyday words like 'unit' and 'container' are used in specialised senses and seem to fit into a hierarchy of meanings as suggested in Fig. 12. There are everyday counterparts of these forms of cargo: a bundle of letters is a unit load, and a number of such bundles in a mail bag is a packed unit load; a household tray performs the same functions as a pallet, with the two hands of a maid the counterpart of the prongs of a fork lift truck; and a shopping bag is a container, non ISO standard of course! The old-fashioned tea chest and jute sack could be classed as unit loads; often small parcels were bound together and again could be regarded as embryonic unit loads. But it must be remembered that the weight of each individual item was light, necessitating much repeated handling on the waterfront. The bundle, the mail-bag, the tray, and the shopping bag have been cited to show that there is nothing very new about the idea of unitising cargo. The revolution lies in the fuller application of the through concept that the mechanised implementation of the idea permits.

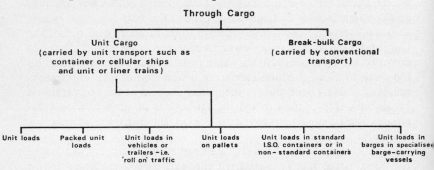

Fig. 12 Suggested hierarchy of terms for through cargo.

Roll-on traffic

A long-established method of avoiding the difficulty of the smallness of unit was the roll-on method, first for trains in train ferries and then for road vehicles and trailers in converted tank-landing ships and later in specially designed vessels with bow or stern loading. For train ferries a perfect match is needed for loading and unloading, but for other vessels connection between shore and ship is generally by means of three ramps: the shore ramp from the quay to the bridge ramp, a suspended roadway, usually hinged at the shore end and supported near the outer end. This is the main link and it may have a telescopic or hinged outer extension before connecting with the ship ramp, which is the door at the bow or stern of the vessel. The length of the bridge ramp depends on the range of water level but should not exceed a gradient of 1:20. A working party of the British National Committee of the Permanent International Association of Navigation Congresses recommended some optimum dimensions for the maximum interchange of roll-on vessels between terminals (*The Standardisation of Ferry Terminals*, 1966, 18): depth to cater for vessels of up to 6·1 m draught with a beam of up to 24·4 m. The recommended draught indicates that few terminals are expected to accommodate deep-sea roll-on vessels. Variations in plan design of roll-on terminals have been classified by T. Rogge, 1965, and summarised in Fig. 13.

In roll-on traffic, railway carriages, trucks (with their drivers) and trailers are the unit loads. Speed of cargo-handling is faster by roll-on method than by any other, and is obviously the universally preferred method for tourist-accompanied cars. Roll-on traffic has the additional advantage of ease of assembly of cargo from many destinations—it assembles and disperses itself. But since speed of cargo-handling is the only advantage over pallets and containers roll-on is used where cargo-handling forms high proportions of total line-haul and terminal costs, i.e. on the shorter ferry routes. There are several reasons why roll-on methods are costly. It has been estimated (*Containerisation*, etc., 1967, 52; and *1970 Outlook*, etc., 1967, 17) that roll-on vessels cost twice as much as container vessels of the same exterior size but have only half the payload capacity. The reasons are that roll-on vessels must be more strongly constructed and have spare internal capacity for manœuvring. Road vehicles and even trailers cannot be as tightly stowed (or stacked) as palletised loads and containers. It is reckoned that a trailer must be provided with twice its capacity of cargo space. Stabilisers may also be necessary, and there has to be rest room provision for drivers, for truck drivers as well as tourists. The tween-deck structure of the ship has to be built with additional strength to support high bearing loads.

Trucks and trailers are the most expensive form of cargo packing on board ship; they are of course inert during the voyage, and the truck driver is not earning his keep. Trailers and railroad wagons effect some economies of weight (absence of motive unit) and of wages (absence of drivers), without losing the speed of cargo-handling. Such services need a high degree of shore organisation and can be operated only by large concerns with the assurance of a very regular traffic in two directions. For all these varied reasons, roll-on traffic is most suitable for shorter ferry routes where the extra costs incurred in carrying out the voyage can be traded off against the savings achieved by fast turn-round. The critical distance beyond which roll-on services become uneconomic compared with other forms of unit cargo is not simple to determine. If the cargo is homogeneous, or can easily be made homogeneous, and if it is easy to assemble, the decision will swing away from roll-on methods. On the other hand, if the cargo demands door-to-door transit or is high value per unit of weight, or is perishable, then roll-on traffic may be preferred, but in these cases air freight becomes a competitor. Each mode of transport has its sector of most economic traffic; if this was not so, they would not co-exist, for one would take over another. One last odd feature of roll-on traffic may be mentioned. In most countries drivers are restricted to certain maximum periods on the road before taking a compulsory rest period which can be organised to coincide with the voyage, just as many tourists 'save a day' by using overnight ferry services. B. Janryd and G. Alexandersson, 1968, have concluded that the increase in roll-on services during the 1960s was due to the expansion of tourism and motor traffic generally allied to the increase of international trade, particularly across the North Sea and English Channel.

Fig. 13 Six types of roll-on ferry terminal

(1) side-loading, rather rare, examples at Kiel and Oslo;
(2) for bow- or stern-loading, quite common;
(3) for larger type of vessel needing shelter and guidance, examples at Antwerp and Oslo;
(4) for greater precision of guidance, especially for train ferries, examples at Bremerhaven and Ostend;
(5) for even greater guidance, for large modern vessels. Solid auxiliary walls as at Grossenbrode and Puttgarden; dolphins at the car ferry terminal, Dover;
(6) impounded dock, the only example being the train ferry dock at Dover, the vessel raised or lowered by varying the water level to make a perfect rail match.

Source: T. Rogge, 1965, 358.

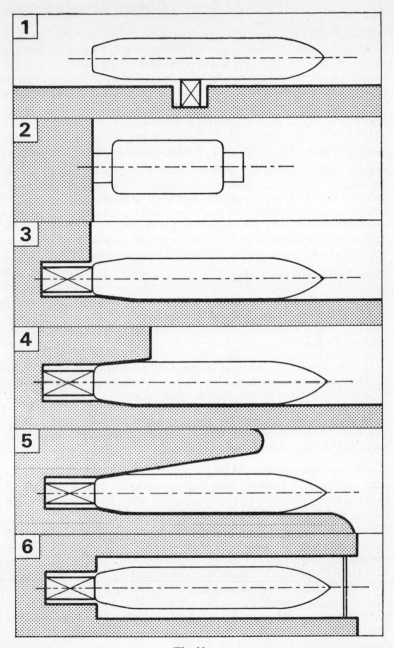

Fig. 13

Palletised cargo

A significant change came over cargo-handling when unit loads were placed on pallets and when containers came into general use. These two devices permitted the mechanisation of cargo-handling on a large scale using flow-line methods first developed in manufacturing industry. 'Pallet' and 'container' must have many legal definitions all over the world if port authorities wish to refer to them in their statutory regulations and catalogue of charges. Adopted here are the admirably clear definitions of two international organisations:

A pallet is a device on the deck of which a quantity of goods can be assembled to form a unit load for the purpose of transporting it, or of handling and stacking it with the assistance of mechanical appliances. This device is made up of two decks separated by bearers, or of a single deck supported by feet; its overall height is reduced to the minimum compatible with handling by fork lift trucks and pallet trucks; it may or may not have a superstructure. (*European Convention*, etc., 1960, Art.1)

Sea-going pallets may also have eyes welded at each corner for hoisting.

A freight container is an article of transport equipment
(a) of a permanent character and accordingly strong enough to be suitable for repeated use;
(b) specially designed to facilitate the carriage of goods, by one or more modes of transport, without intermediate reloading;
(c) fitted with devices permitting its ready handling, particularly its transfer from one mode of transport to another;
(d) so designed as to be easy to fill and empty;
(e) having an internal volume of 1 m^3 (35·3 ft^3) or more.
The term freight container includes neither vehicles nor conventional packing. (*ISO Recommendation R–668*, 1968)

Pallets and containers could be presented as key components of two rival systems, and then the question would arise as to which would beat the other in a fight to the death. The issues involved are not so simple, and the matter will be discussed at the end of this chapter.

Pallets are made of wood, steel, aluminium, or plastic. They are designed for use with a fork lift truck, and the combination has been around for a long time on the factory floor. After the Second World War the fork lift truck became a familiar tool on the waterfronts of the world, but it was basically a quay runabout for moving cargo from the place where it was deposited and lifted by quayside cranes, and for stacking and unstacking cargo in the shed. The next step was to employ fork lift trucks in the ship, but then the bottleneck was the quayside crane operation with the long traverse of the crane hook to and fro with one unit at a time . . . many time losses occurring in the coordination of crane hook movement with the work of gangs on board and ashore. (*The Philosophy of the Unit Load*, 1966, 5)

So the next development was the 'truck to truck deck to deck' operation with fork lift trucks loading through side-ports some five metres wide, provided in specially designed ships.

The impact on the quayside lay-out is first to discover that quay-side cranes, quayside rail tracks, and any road vehicle access to the quayside are an embarrassment since they provide obstacles to the free access to the ship's side-ports by fork lift trucks. Nor must the quay apron be too wide, perhaps between 10 m and 20 m is best; otherwise the quay fork lift truck has too long a transit to and from the stack in the transit shed to the side-port of the ship. For this system of cargo-handling, the quay lay-out demands a covered transit shed with at least four metres of headroom to take two man-high units. Land transport must be separated from fork lift truck movement, and import and export movements also separated. Side-port operation cannot cope with some 30 to 40% of cargo, which has to be slung by crane hook; but mobile cranes serving ship's gear are preferred to quayside cranes because of less interference with access to side-ports required by the palletised goods. Some specially de-signed ships are equipped with conveyors from the side-ports, and internal lifts distribute the cargo to various decks. Such are the *Black Watch* and the *Jupiter* of Fred Olsen Lines, Oslo, for the London–Canary Isles run, with a cargo-handling rate of 300 tons an hour. Scandinavian shipping lines have been the great proponents of palletised methods of cargo-handling, and great improvements over conventional methods are apparent. But some critics have pointed out the difficulties of palletising vast quantities of goods back from the waterfront at the production end of the route and have said that palletisation is essentially a quay-to-quay operation. The mechanisation of pallet stowage within the ship is not so simple as with containers; unit loads should overlap the pallets so that the pallet runners do not rub against cargo; and pallets need lateral support if they do not get it from each other (*New Zealand Overseas Trade*, etc., 1967, para 354). However, E. Heirung, vice-president of Fred Olsen Lines, has vigorously advocated palletisation instead of a full containerised system:

We are viewing a fight between a capital intensive system requiring little labour and a system requiring somewhat more labour but little capital. But it is also a fight in which the USA is desperately trying to regain its position as a shipping nation.

From an owner's point of view this fight is fatal. Every liner operator has to take risks. To stay out is impossible and to compromise is extremely difficult. If he makes a wrong choice he will at least lose huge amounts of money, most probably he will be out of business in a very short time. We believe that the unit load/sideport technique offers the best solution to the benefit of shippers and shipowners. (E. Heirung, 1967)

This is dramatically put. The reason why some Scandinavian operators have become identified with the pallet system is that they do not command the financial resources of the newly-arisen shipping consortia which can face the high capital cost of containerisation. Scandinavian shipowners are often placed in the role of common carrier between two non-Scandinavian countries, perhaps with a minority share of the trade. They are thus less able to contemplate complete through systems of containerised transport door-to-door, or at least to and from inland depots. Significantly, in 1969, Fred Olsen Lines announced that they had ordered eight multi-purpose vessels, all able to carry appreciable numbers of containers, and due in service by the end of 1971—six designed for North Sea routes, and two others will serve Portugal and Morocco. These vessels look like each-way bets on both containers and pallets. Another complication must be introduced into what is not exactly a straight fight between two systems. Very often they are combined when palletised loads are put into containers. At present several standardised pallet dimensions exist, but certain sizes waste more space inside an 8-ft container module than others.

The European UIC Rail Pallet Pool uses a size 1,200 mm × 800 mm, incidentally an ISO standard size; but this wastes over 30% of the width inside an 8 ft-wide container. Many European factories have been designed with the 'European' pallet in mind, however, and Western Germany alone holds twelve million of them. Britain, USA and certain central American countries have advocated a pallet 1,200 mm × 1,000 mm (48 in × 40 in) which uses up to 89% of the stowage width of the eight-foot wide container. The larger pallet can be loaded 'T' fashion to produce a combined width of 2,200 mm. It is certainly more stable and stronger than the European pallet, and is accordingly more suitable to go to sea, whereas the European pallet is really a land animal designed to fit the standard European rail wagon, and also conditioned the non-ISO dimensions of the Federal German Railways inland containers.

The container ship

The most important design feature of the bespoke container ship is that for the first time in the history of naval architecture the compon-

ent dimensions of the cargo for a break-bulk vessel were precisely known in advance. The designers start with a remit of the number of containers the ship is to carry. But there is a snag in that each unit of this homogeneously shaped cargo may have a different stowage factor ranging from the weight when empty to full container weight capacity. When Overseas Containers Limited was formed as a ship-owners' consortium in 1965, there were no design precedents; previous container carrying vessels were adaptations of conventional ships. From the estimated optimum ship container capacity for the Europe–Australia route, all else followed (see below).

Given   container capacity requirement: 1,300 ISO containers (20-ft length equivalents)

=blocks 18 containers long by 9 wide by 9 high (6 below and 3 above deck)

=*length* 745′ 9″ (227·30 m), from 18 × 20 ft, plus loading distance between cells, plus cooling equipment requirements, plus machinery space fore and aft

=*beam* 100 ft (30·48 m), from 9 × 8 ft, plus sufficient to allow for structure, port and starboard (maximum dimension permitted by the Panama Canal; increases in beam must be in multiples of 2·8 m, 9 ft)

=*depth* 6 × 8 ft, plus addition to cope with 8 ft 6 in containers, plus depth of the double bottom, minus the coaming height

=*profile* high flared forecastle to prevent solid water meeting deck-stowed containers and often bridge structures right forward for the same reason

=*draught* 30 ft (9·14 m)

The average size of container ship in the world fleet of converted and specially-built vessels will always be very much less than the largest vessels, since the fleet is composed of some old vessels and includes many short-sea and coastal ships. But the enormous disparity at the beginning of the 1970s and the fourfold increase of the maximum size in the decade 1960–71 indicate that many ports are going to have to expand their container parks if the berths were bespoke to the first generation of specially-designed deep-sea container ships.

Such vessels are not likely to be as deep draughted as bulk vessels of similar dimensions, because container cargo is less heavy per unit of

TABLE 9

SIZE OF CONTAINER VESSELS

	Maximum number of 20-ft container equivalents in fully converted or specially built vessels	Average number of 20-ft container equivalents in vessels of world fleet
1960	500	
1962–3	830	
1966		385
1969		449
1971	1974	

Source: E. Hunter and T. B. Wilson, 1969, 201, and calculated from Table 12

volume than bulk cargo. Deadweight tonnage of the vessel will vary with the cargo; for example when exporting wool from Australia there are only 12 tons in each container, whereas during the fruit export season there may be as much as 20 tons per container (M. Meek, 1969).

The first generation of Atlantic Line container ships was different in that there is dual capacity of container space to trailer space in the proportions 75–80:25–20, because these appeared to be the proportions of containerisable:non-containerisable cargo on the north Atlantic route. It is interesting to observe that in the second generation vessels after 1970 the roll-on capacity is the same, but container capacity has been increased by half.

The barge carrier method of unitising transport has excited great interest particularly with the entry into service of the *Acadia Forest* in 1969, a vessel which uses one of four proposed methods of barge carrying (K. Moen and T. Adland, 1970). This LASH system (lighter aboard ship) is based on the concept of a cellular ship for floating containers in the form of lighters which can be taken aboard the mother ship or discharged by means of a shipboard travelling gantry crane of 500-ton capacity. The first ships were designed to carry about fifty lighters, 18·76 m × 9·50 m × 3·96 m (61 ft 2 in × 31 ft 2 in × 13 ft), and some 200–350 standard 20-ft containers (*Report of the Conference*, etc., 1970). J. L. Goldman, 1970, the inventor of LASH, has described how the dimensions of the barges were arrived at. The upper limit of deadweight tonnage was 500, the capacity of the largest shipboard crane of highest possible reliability. Obviously, barges cannot be used for consignments of less than five tons, though a minimum of 50 tons was taken as a working base. Within the range

50–500 tons it must be remembered that the smaller the size of barge, the less the volume and weight of cargo that can be carried in a vessel of given size. The larger the size of component barges the cheaper is the capital cost per unit of volume and per ton of dead-weight. Lighters also need large hatchways since they are in fact the cargo holds of the ship. They must therefore be strong and also able to cope with being loaded and unloaded and towed; and they should last twenty years. All these factors pushed the tonnage of barges up within the 50–500 range, until the 9·50 m beam limitation was reached in the case of European canal navigation. The solution was a barge of 375 deadweight tons, giving the length and depth dimensions, and the dimensions of the mother ship. It is claimed that the barge carriers can bring the container concept to ports that would be too shallow to receive the 'conventional container ship', to coin a confusing phrase; barge draught is only 2·64 m (8 ft 8 in). Receiving ports must have quite sophisticated towage facilities and a 3-ton lift if the barge hatch covers have been rendered watertight. The most suitable cargoes are those not requiring ventilation such as forest products. There is a danger that the shipboard crane may break down where it cannot be repaired. K. Moen and T. Adland, 1970, 22–3, made some cost comparisons between conventional ship, barge carrier, container ship, and pallet carrier, but this was before experience had been gained of barge carriers in service. In such circumstances they came to the conclusion that barge carriers would be the cheapest type of vessel where other ships suffer delays in ports or where dispatch is slow. Another factor seems to be the presence of suitable cargo close to an inland waterway shipping point. The barge carrier waiting at the estuary mouth then avoids the double handling of other inland waterway/ship systems.

Perhaps a pointer to the future of seaborne container carriage is the Trisec design of Litton Industries Marine Division (*Containerisation International*, 5, no 1, 1970, 40). This abandons three aspects of cellular container ships by means of a twin-hulled catamaran design. First, the payload part of the ship, completely clear of the water, is no longer of the displacement type, faster speeds are possible, and storage can be box shaped for optimum cargo capacity. Secondly, all sizes of containers can be accepted, involving a third new aspect— horizontal movement for loading and within the vessel. The impact of such vessels on ports would be to stimulate even quicker methods of turn-round by mobile container movers rather than by fixed gantry lifting cranes. If container cargoes of many different shapes and sizes become common, then really sophisticated methods of storage and retrieval of containers at ports will become necessary.

The development of container berths

This section concentrates on the container itself, then the container berth, which like the ship is designed around it, and finally the focus widens to view the operation of a container service. There is a great flood of literature on containers for all forms of transport, and as a general guide to this literature the reader should consult the latest edition of the HATRICS bibliography of 760 entries (2nd ed., with all material published before 1960 omitted, *Containerisation: a Bibliography*, 1968).

A container seems such a simple device that the question arises as to why it took so long to make an impact on transport generally and on sea transport in particular. Of course, large containers with small consignments inside had been used by inland transport for several decades before strategic thinking in the US began to attack the problem of the accelerated turn-round of vehicles and the maximum dispersion of stores to avoid vulnerable amassing of supplies at ports. At the US National Defence Transportation Association Meeting in 1959, the military needs for a container were stressed. Subsequently, many orders by the US military stimulated container manufacturers who in turn promoted their wares among possible commercial users, including shipowners (R. T. Crake, 1963). It seems generally agreed that it was in 1966 that commitments to containers by shipowners and port authorities passed the point of no return (*New York Journal of Commerce*, 1967; and *1970 Outlook*, etc., 1967, 2). There had been no technical barrier delaying introduction of containers until such a late date, and this could be recognised when the general introduction of seagoing containers was still a talking point (J. Bird, 1963, 420). But with the benefit of hindsight, it can be seen that the reasons for delay and the causes of the rather sudden container revolution are multiple. Of all the links in the international transport chain, the sea passage is the most open to international competition. In the mid 1960s operators of deep-sea break-bulk cargo services came to realise that if they did not go over to container ships a rival might sail over the horizon. Decisions to containerise were therefore not so much a gallant gamble on a shining future but rather a fear of *force majeure*, particularly a *force americaine*. This seems to have been the most powerful factor, and shipping companies have been the innovators of international container movements. Without the fear of competition, they might merely have continued to pass on the rising costs of cargo-handling to their customers, as had always happened in the past, thereby avoiding the massive injections of capital necessary to set up through services.

A source of rising costs in conventional cargo-handling was port labour, not only because of its direct cost, but also because of the indirect costs of delays in ship turn-round due to low productivity, labour disputes, and restrictive practices. But to be fair to the men, the low productivity also resulted from the absence of a standardised cargo to handle. The McKinsey Report to the British Transport Docks Board in 1967 (*Containerization; the Key*, etc., 1967, 3–10) placed standardisation of the cargo as the key contribution of containers to higher productivity. F. C. Margetts, 1968, showed that there were multiple reasons, no less than eleven, why British Rail container traffic grew so slowly in the inter-war years, though containers had been introduced in the 1920s. A chief factor seems to have been the regarding of the container as something that had to be fitted into an existing transport network, without having that network integrated and even designed around a standardised module.

Since the drawing up of international container standards by the ISO in 1965, the standardised unit for sea and land carriage has not only welded different parts of the route together, but has encouraged mechanisation and flow-line methods on the waterfront, and horizontal amalgamation of shipowners, with vertical integration of transport functions as shipowners grab their cargoes further back from the quaysides and carry them closer to the ultimate destination. Table 10 gives the ISO standard variations of the 8-ft (2·438 m) container module, a dimension based on the first American standardisation in 1959 (G. van den Burg, 1969, 38 ff.). A proposed ISO standard is developed and agreed by an ISO technical committee and circulated to some fifty or more countries for acceptance, comment, or disapproval. When accepted by more than 60% of those voting, the ISO Council may issue the standard as a recommendation which is voluntary for all members. Such is the status of the 8-ft container module. This module was a development of the container dimensions used for military purposes in supplying American forces in Europe—ammunition boxes fitted in exactly.

Special purpose containers within the standard module are designed for the carriage of liquids; with retractable basal hoppers they can carry granular cargoes; and with side openings they are suitable for rail yard work. As far as mechanical handling gear is concerned, the standardisation consists of regulation corner fittings for lifting gear and standard size channels or pockets for the forks or prongs of fork lift trucks. Within the standardised frame all kinds of specialised containers are possible. Insulated and refrigerated containers are available. Gondola open-topped containers are used for heavy machinery that has to be lifted from above, and are also used for the stowage of automobiles. Half-size (four feet high) containers

TABLE 10

CONTAINER DIMENSIONS

Designation	Height		Width		Length		Gross weight		Approx. interior cubic capacity	
	ft	m	ft	m	ft	m	tons	metric tons	cu ft	cu m
ISO series 1										
IA*	8	2·438	8	2·438	40	12·192	30	30·4814	2189	62
IB	8	2·438	8	2·438	29–11¼″	9·125	25	25·4012	1624	46
IC	8	2·438	8	2·438	19–10½″	6·055	20	20·3209	1077	30·5
ID	8	2·438	8	2·438	9–9¾″	2·990	10	10·1605	530	25
IE	8	2·438	8	2·438	6–5½″	1·969	7	7·1123	318†	9†
IF	8	2·438	8	2·438	4–9½″	1·460	5	5·2080	†	†
Non standard										
Sea-Land	8′ 6″	2·591	8	2·438	35	10·668	22·5000	23·0438	2088	59
Matson	8′ 6″	2·604	8	2·438	24	7·315	22·3214	22·8614	1415	40

* In October 1969 ISO also approved a draft proposal for a 40′ × 8′6″ [2·587 m] container as a Series 1 type, originally recommended in February 1968 (ISO, R–668) (E. S. Tooth, 1970, 125).
† Not in common use. Interiors vary greatly.

are for heavy items like steel, ores, and other heavy minerals and liquids. These heavy dense cargoes reach the weight capacity of the container well before they occupy the cubic capacity. The ideal cargo in this respect appears to be Scotch whisky, an eighteen-ton consignment almost exactly filling a twenty-foot container and also close to the maximum tare weight.

This volume–weight ratio needs more precise discussion to bring out the point. Assume a 20-ft container has an available volume of 1,000 cu ft [30·5 cubic metres] and a tare capacity of 18½ tons. Then any cargo with a volume to weight ratio of greater than 2·7 cu ft per cwt—1,000 ÷ (18·5 × 20)—will be put into containers to fill the available space. If the volume–weight ratio is less, the inside of the container will not be filled before the weight limitation is reached. If the volume to weight ratio is less than 1·35 cu ft per cwt the cargo ought to be placed in half-height containers. In practice up to 25% of the internal capacity of the container is not used because of stowage problems, rising to a peak with uncrated machinery. This is separate from the problem of so organising the traffic that each container has a maximum load either by volume or weight. Where the cargo is heavy, leaving a large portion of the container unfilled, careful stowage is necessary, but there is always a great saving in packaging costs compared with conventional break-bulk cargo. Inflatable dunnage is one ingenious method of securing cargo inside containers.

It seems hard that two container pioneers, both American, should find their containers classified as non-standard in 1965. Malcolm McLean, founder of Sea-Land Service Inc., a subsidiary of McLean Industries Inc., was originally a long-haul trucker in the US and en-

visaged the container as a unit to be detached from his trucks ready
for other modes of transport by rail and sea. Sea-Land's container
dimensions derive from McLean's highway trailer bodies. On 20
April 1956 saw the real beginning of through containerisation with
the carriage by the then Pan-Atlantic Steamship Corporation, a
McLean subsidiary, of sixty trailer bodies on a special deck structure
aboard a T–2 tanker, the SS *Maxton*. In 1958 six converted vessels
(C–2s) carried containers, with regular services from New York coastwise and to Puerto Rico; in 1962 a service connected New York and
California via the Panama Canal, using jumbo-ised T–2 tankers;
Alaska was served by 1964; and on 23 April 1966 Sea-Land began a
weekly service from Elizabeth (New York) and Boston to Rotterdam,
Bremen, and Grangemouth, starting off the great container race
(*A History of Sea-Land Service Inc.*, 1966). The 1966 international
developments were made when Sea-Land realised that there was nothing in the Hague Rules to prevent a shipowner accepting a wider
areal responsibility for goods if he so wishes and if conference
arrangements permit (see p. 115 below).

Matson Navigation Company has operated a Pacific service since
1882. A container service was begun in August 1958 to carry truck
bodies as deck loads only on conventional vessels. This first phase
was selected because it was the lowest level of operations that would
test the service. All developmental capital had to come from cost
reductions within the company since profit margins were insufficient
to attract capital from outside. Cargo-handling costs were half the
total costs of operating the service, and ships spent half of their
time in port. The system of six 'deck-only' vessels was the largest
scale that could be contemplated considering that failure was possible
if labour refused to cooperate. This involved the company with
labour problems and helped to usher in the famous longshore agreement (see p. 60), so that by the autumn of 1959 an all-container
ship, the *Hawaiian Citizen*, a completely modified 'C–3' vessel, could
be contemplated. These details are from F. L. Weldon, 1963 and
1964, the designer of this system, and it is of interest to quote him,
the second extract being a rather sad reply to why Matson containers
are non-ISO standard:

The first phase of the improvement programme—outfitting the six 'deck-
only' container ships—was selected because it represented the lowest case
test of the service and at the same time it was the highest level we could
afford considering the financial risk involved if the longshore union
refused to cooperate with work-saving innovations. (1964, 28)

The fact that our containers are non-standard is part of the price paid
by a pioneer. (1963, 35)

The Matson size of container was chosen to obtain maximum pay-loads when operating in tandem on roads of Hawaii and the western US.

From 1958 Matson pioneered the use of the A-frame gantry quay-side cranes which are now becoming familiar at container berths all over the world. For these first portainers, research specified the crane cycle that would make operations economical. At that stage the engineers took over to ensure that the equipment met these operational requirements (F. L. Weldon, 1964, 39). The specification for such cranes would be a lift of 25 tons for 30-ft containers, though ports are now having to face 40-ft containers requiring a 30-ton lift. Spreaders distribute the lift to the four corner posts of the container; and latest spreaders permit a twin lift of two 20-ft containers. 'Portainer' cranes operate a ship-quay motion, with ancillary equipment to move the containers to and from the storage area. 'Transtainer' or 'Goliath' cranes are overhead travelling cranes with a ship-quayside storage motion. Obviously, transtainers have a lower output than portainers, but they eliminate other quayside equipment and capital investment is thereby reduced for berths of less intensive through-put (G. van den Burg, 1969, 132).

In spite of the early developments by the two American pioneers, ISO appears to have selected an eight-foot module because this had been chosen as an internal American standard in 1961 and seemed to be the size most likely to be more widely used, bearing in mind the restrictions imposed by inland transport. However, in some countries, it is possible to take the greater height of 8 ft 6 in. For example, although British Rail converted their Freightliner fleet to the 8-ft module, it is now found that they can accept the larger container, On board ship a tolerance of 6 in can sometimes be accommodated. and of course this is certainly possible if the containers are carried on deck. On the question of length, American operators have complained that 20 ft is too short for efficient stuffing and stripping, to use the picturesque verbs in vogue; and the different lengths between standard and non-standard containers while posing few difficulties on land may be impossible to mix on board ship.

Another American container pioneer, Grace Line, has operated a service from the US to central and south America with shipboard container cranes, since most of the non-US ports do not have lifting facilities. But such cranes displace a great deal of weight, and their cost and maintenance are high. They are unlikely to be employed on regular container routes but may be useful for feeder services and in particular to help under-capitalised ports in developing countries (J. C. Koster and N. H. Tilsey, 1968, 14 ff.).

On shore the container is moved to and from the container park by various devices: tractors and container trailers; straddle carriers that can stack containers two high, as can heavy duty fork lift trucks; and the above plus a 'Goliath' crane, which is able to move on a gantry spanning the whole of a container park, piling three high; and various automated systems. The latter are not yet in use though an American system has been described embracing an automated tower storage facility for 2,000 standard 20-ft containers in an area only 98 m by 34 m (R. D. Fielder, 1967, 312), or about one-third of a hectare, compared with the normal requirement of 2·5–5·0 hectares. A British system, the automatic container warehouse, is designed to give a random fast access system for a large number of containers. The warehouse is a steel skeleton with the necessary number of container stowages to match the desired through-put and storage capacity of the berth. Containers enter the warehouse to be moved vertically by gantries and horizontally by a 'motive beam'. This is a self-powered rail truck with arms that can deliver or extract containers to or from the stowages, and one such motive beam runs along the length of the building on each 'floor'. Such a system is particularly useful where area is limited. This type of system, with variations, will presumably be necessary when container handling becomes more automated, and is particularly useful when containers do not arrive in a planned sequence, the likelihood of this being progressively less as total numbers grow. The proponents of the system have estimated that it would break even on cost at through-puts servicing two 750-capacity container ships per week (K. C. Weaver and J. C. Hebbes, 1969; see also the 'containerport' vertical storage scheme, *Containerisation International*, **4**, no. 5, 1970, 26–9).

A container berth simulation study has been carried out by W. S. Atkins and Partners in conjunction with staff of the British National Ports Council, and the results have been published (*Research and Technical Bulletins*, 1967–9). The four systems studied were:

(1) crane, tractor, and semi-trailer system;
(2) crane and straddle carrier system;
(3) transporter crane system (able to stack containers up to five high;
(4) quay crane, tractor/trailer, and 'Goliath' container park crane.

Naturally, several operating and cost assumptions had to be made but kept constant for all four simulations. For low volumes of traffic the transporter crane system had the lowest costs, but as through-put increases the differences decrease and are even reversed.

As might be expected, perhaps the most important point . . . is that variations in traffic volume make large differences to the unit cost of the system [i.e. cost per container falls with rising through-puts]. Hence, if any system has particular characteristics which can attract business, this could have a greater effect on profitability than its relative cost. (*Research and Technical Bulletin*, 1969, 238)

It could be added that the 'attractive characteristics' might be connected with one of the other aspects of a port's function once it had been equipped with a container berth, however operated, such as the port's relative location to a container-load generating hinterland.

At a container berth the mean duty cycle of a portainer is the time required to move a container from the quayside vehicle to the ship and vice versa, and return for the next. The datum point in the ship is the geometric centre vertically and horizontally, any deviations in one direction during one cycle being compensated in the other direction during other cycles. The capacity of the cranes may be as high as 40 cycles per hour, but in practice 30 may be a maximum due to delays on the quay and in the ship, and 20 cycles per hour may be a reasonable working average (*1970 Outlook*, etc., 1967, 49–51). This is because not all cycles of the crane are double working cycles. Obviously when a ship arrives at a container berth, the crane, without carrying a load, moves to the first container cell in the vessel where containers are stacked six high. Once the first container cell has been removed, a container can then be loaded into the bottom of the empty cell. Three minutes are needed for the double cycle. When a complete row of cells has been discharged, the last cell must be loaded in a single-cycle operation. So the proportion of double cycles depends on the beam of the ship, and it may be assumed that 80 % of the containers can be worked on double-cycle operations, since the quayside crane does not move to the next row of cells until one row has been completely discharged and loaded. Thus one crane manufacturer estimates performance as the equivalent of eighteen double cycles per hour, or handling thirty-six containers. This estimate assumes that the container is placed on the quay and removed by stackers. If the container has to be placed on a vehicle standing on the quay, the locking elements have to be precisely aligned, and this might reduce the handling rate to the equivalent of twelve double cycles or twenty-four containers handled.

Suppose thirty-six containers contain 900 tons of cargo and if this was accomplished in an equivalent of one-ton lifts by conventional handling, this would take 900×5 minutes, the average time for conventional loading, or 75 working hours. And this is the cargo that might be loaded and unloaded in one hour by container cranes. That is the measure of the speed of cargo-handling at a container berth.

The operation of a through container berth

This section will naturally concentrate on the advantages of container services, but there are some obstacles to the implementation of through services, and these fall into four categories of diminishing importance: organisational, by far the most important; composition of the seaborne trade; physical limitations on land; and the requirements of regional planning. Organisational difficulties include the attitude of port labour and redundancy problems. There are also the difficult decisions facing shipping companies in deciding how to reduce the number of ports serviced. Some ports provide insufficient aggregate cargo on their own to act as a container port. On the other hand, there is the cost and organisational problem of assembling sufficient cargo at one port and the question of equalisation of transport rates from outlying regions or ports with feeder services. The composition of seaborne trade may be unbalanced between imports and exports at one end of the route; cargo flows may be unbalanced in direction; or the trade may be seasonal in volume; or the cargo one way may be difficult to containerise, such as carcass meat. Inland transport may not be able to cope with containers either because of route limitations, such as the dimensions of bridges and tunnels, or because of axle limitations of rail wagons and road trucks, and sharp corners and narrow widths of roads; or, at best, container lengths may be limited to twenty feet. Regional planning policies may be upset at the withdrawal of direct liner sailings from ports not equipped with direct container ship sailings. If land transport equalisation rates are not implemented, industries and consumers away from ports where container services are concentrated could find themselves at a freight disadvantage for all kinds of break-bulk cargo. The withdrawal of cargo services implies insufficient total volumes of cargo coming forward which in turn implies an outlying region; and the freight disadvantages that may result would only increase the relative disadvantages of location compared with more developed regions that scoop the container services.

A berth with specialised container-handling and container-parking facilities is essential to a port for more economic cargo-handling; but one of the problems for port authorities is to decide whether or not this is to be used exclusively by one operator or be a common-user facility. Operators of through container services will naturally prefer to have exclusive rights where there is sufficient traffic, the more easily to control the container flows and programme the service. Port authorities, as owners of the berths, wish to see a high return on the investment and maximum use of the berth. Berthing and cargo-handling charges could be so arranged that they could compensate for any short-fall from a desired berth occupancy factor. Container service operators would no doubt like to have exclusive control of their own depots, but customs authorities may be reluctant to give clearance at a depot where there is no free access to all in the trade.

Table 11 is a summary of information furnished by the general manager of the Port of Gothenburg and provides an interesting comparison of the operation of conventional, roll-on, palletised, and container berths. The costs quoted are from 1966, but it will be remembered that this is an interesting date, because it was then that commitments to deep-sea containers by ports and shipowners were set irrevocably in motion (p. 104). It may be surprising that the capital cost of conventional and container berths should have been the same. This is because there are several balancing contributory costs. The $27\frac{1}{2}$-ton container crane cost more than the five conventional quay cranes, but the conventional berth is equipped with a

TABLE 11

COMPARATIVE COSTS OF OPERATION OF SIX BERTH TYPES
IN THE PORT OF GOTHENBURG

Type of berth	Length (m)	Area (sq m)	Total capital cost (million dollars 1966)	Annual tonnage of goods handled	Capital cost per ton handled (dollars)
North Sea trade					
Conventional	2 × 90	8,000	1·6	110,000	1·45
Roll-on	—	30,000	{ 1·3	100,000	1·30
			{ could rise to	150,000	0·87
Palletised	5 × 90	20,000	2·7	205,000	1·31
Container (Roll-on)	—	47,000	2·2	200,000	1·10
Deep-sea trade					
Conventional	200	20,000	2·8	120,000	2·34
Container	200	40,000	2·8	260,000	1·08

Source: S. Axelson, 1967.

three-storey shed occupying 4,000 sq m. The conventional berth has to have rail tracks on the quay apron, but the container berth needs hard standing over twice the area. The savings manifestly come from the higher through-put of cargo resulting in a saving per ton of cargo handled of almost 60%. This views the data from the angle of the port authority, since if charges are made on tons of cargo handled, the end column is then a return on capital originally invested, exclusive of annual costs.

The operation of a through container service

Another example of comparative costs of operation, this time from the point of view of the container service operator, is provided by Arthur D. Little Ltd. (*Containerization on the North Atlantic*, 1967), comparing a fleet of conventional break-bulk ships with a container fleet. The detailed results of such a comparison depend heavily on: how the trade is organised; the number of ships in each fleet and their bale capacity; number of containers carried; ship speed; length of route; type of berth; and quayside unloading methods are also important (one- or two-crane container berth for example). It is doubtful if any valid contemporary cost comparisons will become available simply because once a container service is established, a completely parallel conventional service ceases. Later it should be possible to compare before and after costs on routes that have become containerised. From the Little model investigation it is apparent that the chief savings are the 80% reduction of the cargo-handling costs, and this is the item that may account for over half the cost of operating a conventional fleet. Container methods have thus attacked the most costly item involved in cargo transport by sea, though other savings accrue to shippers on other legs of the route (*Containerization: Full Steam Ahead*, 1970, 14). The only brake on the cumulative decline of conventional cargo services is put where governments are unwilling to allow capital invested in existing facilities to be written off (e.g. South Africa) or where large-scale labour redundancies pose political problems (E. Argiroffo, 1967).

Concerning the flows of containers within any given container route, there are five variables to be considered: the number of ships in service; the length of the voyage; the number of complete container loads in the pipeline (the number of sets); the load factor; and the pattern of the return of containers to the service. The pattern of return of containers from being stuffed and stripped to actual movement on the route may be linear against time, or it may be convex, a happy situation for the container operator, since it may mean an early return of containers, or concave, meaning a late return. E. C.

Emerson, 1968, operated a statistical model to show how the load factor would vary if the number of sets of containers were constant but the number of ships allowed to vary:

TABLE 12

Container service operator	Ships	Sailing period	Sets	Load factor		
				Concave	Linear	Convex
A	2	2	3	46	62	88
B	1	4	3	44	54	74
Combined	3	1·3	3	44	64	92

Secondly, if the load factor is kept constant, the number of sets is least with a combined fleet, assuming a fourteen-day linear return of containers:

TABLE 13

Container service operator	Ships	Sailing period	Sets	Load factor
A	2	2	3	46
B	1	4	2·6	46
Combined	3	1·3	2·2	46

The Gothenburg example quoted an annual through-put for a one-crane container berth of 260,000 tons, whereas a two-crane berth might conceivably achieve a through-put of one million tons. But, as was shown in the last chapter, the high berth occupancy factors that such a high through-put implies result in queuing delays for ships. No berth is yet operated at through-puts approaching one million tons, and when through-puts have risen, operators have opted for second berths. At the moment the total economies of a through route seem to be best achieved by operating the container berth well below its capacity, since after all it is only one stage in the through route. In other words, container berths have allowed improvements in cargo-handling far outstripping what sea and land transport can cope with. In eliminating the bottleneck of cargo transfer that is characteristic of conventional berths, they have thrown the role of bottleneck on to the line haul sections of the route. It seems to be the case that where there are different vehicles moving an object in a through-route situation (counting container berth straddle carriers and cranes as vehicles), or where the cargo pauses en route, it will be very difficult to devise a system in which some kind of delay does not occur because of a traffic bottleneck, a term which may be dignified by the expressions 'warehousing' or 'container park' but which will nevertheless connote a delay.

The paperwork of a through service in containers should theoretically be much less than with conventional break-bulk cargo transit, with downgrading of the importance of the bill of lading issued for the maritime leg of the route (see Sir Osborne Mance, 1945, 29–30; and H. D. Tabak, 1970, 28 ff.). Until Sea-Land's initiative in 1966, the accepted interpretation in shipowners' bills of lading was to assume and disclaim responsibility at the ship's rail, but Article VII of the Hague Rules as long ago as 1924 permitted the possibility of through transport (a point first suggested by S. Johnson, 1969).

Nothing herein contained shall prevent a carrier or a shipper from entering into any agreement, stipulation, condition, reservation or exemption as to the responsibility and liability of the carrier or the ship for the loss or damage to or in connection with the custody and care and handling of goods *prior to the loading* on and *subsequent to the discharge* from the ship on which the goods are carried by sea. [Italics added] (see E. R. H. Ivamy, 1968)

In the Atlantic Container Line bill of lading the carrier accepts reponsibility for the goods from the time when they are received by him either at the seaport or at any inland point in Europe or the US. Legal responsibility for the goods follows the system normally operating for each leg of the route, and this is known as the 'network' system. There is the problem of ascertaining where damage to goods occurred, and a special clause in the bill of lading takes care of this :

When the goods have been damaged or lost during the through-transportation and it cannot be established in whose custody the goods were when the damage or loss occurred the damage or loss shall be deemed to have occurred during the sea voyage and the Hague Rules shall apply. (see K. S. Schalling, 1967, 4)

While this network system is a practical solution, the original Hague Rules are the least favourable to the shipper of any international convention. They limit the liability per container to £100, whereas the international road convention (CMR) allows up to £3,500 per ton. The Hague-Visby amendment of February 1968, when ratified, would allow £276 per package (10,000 Francs Poincaré*) or £842 per ton (30 Francs Poincaré per kilo), whichever is the higher, unless the

* A unit consisting of 65·5 mgs of gold of millesimal fineness 900.

nature of and value of the goods have been declared by the shipper
before shipment and inserted in the bill of lading. The development
of container berths and 'through' container routes plainly outran the
legal rules for the international carriage of goods. But by 1970 the
work of several international bodies had culminated in agreed standard conditions of a combined transport negotiable document of
title of goods known as the FIATA Combined Transport Bill of
Lading. A convenient survey of international trade documentation
is contained in the SITPRO *Report*, 1970; while T. F. Poole, 1967,
surveys the insurance implications.

Since a through container service is highly capital intensive, it is
important that it be closely matched to the real-life flows of cargo, or
diseconomies will soon be apparent. This is not to deny that container services may cause diversion of trade when established. But as
at present constituted, some routes of world trade are more suited to
containers than others, and the clearest categorisation of world trade
routes in this respect has been provided by H. J. Molenaar, 1967.
He argues that as a result of conventional deep-sea cargo-handling,
port time/sea time ratios vary from 40:60 to 60:40. High port time
duration results from numerous ports of call or port cargo-handling
performance, or a combination of both. Molenaar classifies trade
routes of the world into four categories, warning that these are not
definitive judgements, but rather the result of a model technique
designed to contrast the various factors involved, assuming that
cargo is available and suitable for containerisation.

(1) High stevedoring expenses and relatively slow dispatch (more
than 50 days' port time for every 50 days' sea time). Such routes are
eminently suitable for containerisation; e.g. UK and Europe to
Australia and New Zealand; and US to developing countries, because slow dispatch at one end of the route is combined with high
American stevedoring costs, the savings on which might even offset
the possible necessity to stuff and strip containers on the quayside at
the developing country end of the route.

(2) High stevedoring expenses and good dispatch. The savings on
stevedoring must be very high to provide operating economies. An
example is the north Atlantic route, where it is estimated that half
the traffic will be groupage traffic, which may reduce somewhat the
savings over conventional handling.

(3) Low stevedoring expenses and slow dispatch. The conditions
here seem less favourable to containerisation. Examples are many
of the routes between two developing countries, though it might be
worth while if significantly large amounts of cargo were available

at one port; the savings would then arise from the increase in ship turn-round speed.

(4) Low stevedoring costs and good dispatch. The conditions here seem least favourable to containerisation. An example of the European continent to Far East trade.

The above comments are made in the light of the two variables noted above. One important factor to be taken into account is a bandwagon effect which might be called 'container emulation'. Molenaar refer to this in discussing his fourth category.

. . . the trade between the European Continent and the Far East would not for some time yet qualify for such radical moves as are involved in fully containerised services. However, the large volumes of manufactures moving both ways, commercial pressures brought to bear upon the shipping industry and developments in the United Kingdom/Far East trade (in which longer port times justify an earlier shift to containerisation) can easily make the industry decide to move ahead. (op. cit., 15)

The decision to start in 1971 came in October 1969, only two years after the above was written.

Problems in the wake of containers

Faced particularly with the capital demands in establishing a through container route, and also the other attendant problems, it is little wonder that many shipping companies, British, European, and Japanese, have associated themselves in various container consortia. Apart from the problems at the port and inland, cellular vessels are more costly than conventional vessels of similar size and power. Moreover, the drastic reduction of ship numbers which follows upon the introduction of bespoke designed container services would have in any case caused the shipping lines to associate and rationalise their services, and this was another contributory factor to the setting up of consortia. These large bodies may have monopolistic tendencies upon some routes, and certain countries have looked askance on this, Australia keeping a wary eye on the situation since 1968 (*Report from the Senate Select Committee*, etc., 1968, para 278). The first container operator conference, across the north Atlantic, was registered with the US Federal Maritime Commission in 1969 (for conferences see S. G. Sturmey, 1962, 322–58).

Sir Donald Anderson, chairman of P & O shipping group, a partner in the consortium Overseas Containers Ltd, said in 1969 that he envisaged a new breed of container ships of 50,000 tons, when existing flows of cargo had been altered and merged. These larger container ships would reap the economies of scale which larger tankers achieved in the 1950s and 1960s. More transhipments would then be necessary to assemble and disperse the great instalments of cargo that these vessels would carry (see also *Transhipments in the Seventies*, etc., 1970).

The following model of the possible rise of transhipment with increasing volumes of a commodity has been based on P. M. H. Kendall, 1970, 7, although the presentation in 'stages' is not his.

TABLE 14

CONCERNING THE CARRIAGE OF A COMMODITY (INCL. A CONTAINER)
INCREASING STEADILY IN TRADE VOLUMES

Initial stage
Entry of commodity into international trade; annual volumes small; many ports of origin and destination; carried in ships with other cargoes.

Emergence of specialised routes
Demand for product increases; increasing annual volumes; emergence of specialist ships geared to the volumes and the distance between ports.

Concentration of routes
Growth of volume on particular routes from a single source justifies the use of larger ship which tranships at a pivot port to smaller ships serving feeder ports.

Growth of transhipment
Once the above critical point has been reached, where costs of transhipment are overcome by the economies of a larger ship on the long route, transhipment grows rapidly.

Pivot-feeder port relationship spiral
The trade at the pivot port increases even faster since it now also deals with the trade of the commodity in question for all its feeder ports, and this increased trade supports even larger ships. Feeder ports are serviced by smaller ships geared to the relatively short distance from the pivot port.

Necessary associated circumstances
(1) Where pivot port and feeder port are in different countries, the government
  ·   of the country in which the feeder port is located must be willing to contemplate such international transhipment taking place. This may be less of a problem with the emergence of larger economic groupings.
(2) The delay to the big ship while transhipment is in progress must be minimised. This is an organisational problem and is probably the biggest stumbling block to the model progress outlined above.

Transhipment might reduce the frequency of delivery of cargoes, and here arises a problem for shippers and receivers. They may have to accept slightly less frequency of service in the interest of lower freight rates. Perhaps the equilibrium will be reached when reductions in freight rates no longer offset the interest charges of increased goods in the stockpile awaiting fast shipment or having just been massively delivered (R. B. Oram, 1969).

Containers raise another set of problems for developing countries which produce relatively light amounts of containerisable cargo (more to the raw material end of the cargo spectrum than that of consumer durables). There is less volume of cargo coming forward from such countries making economic shiploads less regularly available; there is the low cost of stevedoring, allowing less saving when mechanical handling is introduced; and many of the inland transport arteries of such countries are not suitable for the passage of containers. Already on some short-sea unit load services, carriers base tariffs on the cubic capacity or length of the container, without reference to the cargo inside. This is contrary to the general freight rate practice of charging what the traffic will bear. Under this circumstance high value per unit of weight goods are charged relatively more per ton/mile than low value per unit of weight commodities. Rate equalisation among cargoes coming into force would discriminate against developing countries with their predominantly raw material exports, without corresponding freight decreases on manufactured goods imported, since these are normally so much lighter.

Port authorities have their problems too. Container berths and the associated facilities are of course expensive to construct and equip, yet the result may be fewer total number of ships visiting the port giving rise to 'expansion in reduction'—an expansion of trade in a reduction of area. It is doubtful if the port charges on the relatively few cellular ships will compensate for the loss of the fleets of conventional ships made redundant. Quay rates on goods will not diminish, but there is the problem of the conventional berths made redundant by unit cargo berths. Ports may also lose some of their ancillary services. Perhaps port authorities face greater problems than shipowners because the results of their investment cannot be switched in location to follow the trade. R. P. Holubowicz, 1967, goes so far as to foresee the era of the no-port. Sorting, storing, inspecting, marketing, packaging, and general administrative services may certainly take place where the loaded container first enters and leaves the through service. This will happen at depots where there is the largest amount of cargo coming forward. Port authorities need not blench too much at this. The ships themselves will need a host of services, and many major seaports are indeed themselves the places where much cargo is generated, so that there may be many depots closely associated with container berths, though not necessarily physically adjacent, and, admittedly, not necessarily under the control of the port authority. Two main classes of container ports are pivot container ports and feeder container ports. The terms are almost self-explanatory, and the two can be distinguished by defining a pivot port where delivered containers (or lighters) may yet have a water leg before reaching their final destination, and that conversely containers loaded at the port may have arrived by water.

The most convenient way for a cargo to enter a through system is for a manufacturer to provide a full container load, and the most economic location for him to do this as far as economies of overseas freight are concerned is as close to the container berth as possible, or as close to the receiving depot inland, if freight equalisation arrangements are practised. The Association of British Chambers of Commerce has already expressed alarm over the possible regrouping of industry close to a relative handful of deep-sea container berths.

A final return is made to the problems of the growth of containers vis-à-vis other unit cargo systems. Enough has been displayed to show that each system has considerable advantages over conventional methods of break-bulk cargo-handling. Unit loads on pallets cost much less to initiate than a full container service. But for both systems the organisation of the trade is probably a bigger obstacle than technical difficulties, which have long since been overcome. If this deduction is correct, then the implementation of unit cargo services is the result of decision making by entrepreneurs in a spirit of competition or emulation. From this it may be further deduced that containers are here to stay and grow in numbers. There is the paradox that shipowners faced with two solutions; a system that requires moderate capitalisation for substantial economies (pallets) and a system that requires massive capitalisation for massive economies (containers) have in general opted for the second solution, leap-frogging the first, since most of them feel they dare not be left behind. They have huddled together in giant consortia for mutual protection. This is not to say that other unit load methods do not have their place, perhaps as a feeder service, and particularly for services to underdeveloped ports. These are the two classes of route where the through routing of massive numbers of containers are less likely to apply. On short-sea routes pallets and roll-on methods have a vital role, since it is not possible to operate the most economical size of container ship where the port time/sea time ratio is unsuitable. In any case, short ferry routes require frequency of service rather than less frequent massive consignments of cargo, and since their approach dimensions are modest, there is a future unit load role apparent for the well-located specialist small port.

For the foreseeable future the various systems of unit load carriage will be in evidence, but the destiny of most long distance break-bulk cargo is surely to be stuffed into containers and carried in the fast-sailing, fast-turn-round cellular ship of ever-increasing size until the frequency of the service matches the requirements of the trade.

Argiroffo, E. (1967) *Social Repercussions of the Introduction of Unit Load Systems.* Paper submitted to the Interregional Seminar on Containerization, etc. organised by the United Nations in co-operation with the U.K. Government, London 1–12 May.

Axelson, S. (1967) The Seaport, *The Dock and Harbour Authority*, **48**, 13–15.

Bird, J. (1963) *The Major Seaports of the United Kingdom.* London: Hutchinson.

Containerisation: a Bibliography (1968) Hampshire Technical Research Industrial Commercial Service (HATRICS). Southampton: Central Library (2nd ed.).

Containerization International (1967) Annual volumes and year books to date.

Containerization: Its Trends, Significance and Implications (1966) Report by McKinsey and Co. Inc. to the British Transport Docks Board.

Containerization on the North Atlantic: a Port-to-Port Analysis (1967) Report to the British National Ports Council by Arthur D. Little Ltd.

Containerization: the Key to Low-cost Transportation (1967) Report by McKinsey and Co. Inc. to the British Transport Docks Board.

Container Shipping: Full Ahead: a Forecast of how Containerization of Oceanborne Foreign Trade will Develop by 1975 (1967). Port of New York Authority.

Crake, R. T. (1963) Long distance container economics, *ICHCA Journal*, **1**, 29–36.

Emerson, E. C. (1968) Aspects of container flows, *Proceedings of International Container Symposium.* London: Chamber of Commerce.

European Convention on Customs Treatment of Pallets used in International Transport (1960). Geneva, 9 December.

Fielder, R. D. (1967) Vertical container storage, *The Dock and Harbour Authority*, **48**, 312.

Goldman, J. L. (1970) How LASH was born, *ICHCA Journal*, **4**, 29–36.

Heirung, E. (1967) *Shipowner [and] Unit Load Ships.* Paper read at Eighth Technical Conference of ICHCA, Antwerp, 22–6 May.

History of Sea-Land Service, Inc., A (1966) Elizabeth: Sea-Land Service Inc. Mimeographed.

Holubowicz, R. P. (1967) *Port Arrangements between the Ship and Road Transport and the Ship and Rail Transport.* Paper submitted to the Interregional Seminar on Containerization etc., organised by the United Nations in conjunction with the UK Government, London 1–12 May.

Hunter, E., and Wilson, T. B. (1969) The increasing size of tankers, bulk carriers, and containerships with some implications for port authorities, *Research and Technical Bulletin*, **5**, 180–224.

Immer, J. R. (1970) *Container Services of the Atlantic.* Washington: Work Saving International.

Ivamy, E. R. H. (1968) *Payne's Carriage of Goods by Sea.* London: Butterworths.

Janryd, B., and Alexandersson, G. (1968) Seaborne tourists and cargo in North-western Europe: roll-on traffic capacity in the North Sea and across the English Channel, *Ad Novas*, **8**, 86–95.

Johnson, K. M., and Gurnett, H. C. (1970) *The Economics of Containerisation.* London: Allen and Unwin.

Johnson, S. (1969) The seaports of the future, *Ports and Harbours*, **14**, 7–8.
Kendall, P. M. H. (1970) *Transhipment and the Importance of Ship Size*. Paper delivered at Semaine de Bruges, April. Bruges: College of Europe.
Koster, J. C., and Tilsey, N. H. (1968) *Container Guide*. London: National Magazine Co.
Latham-Koenig, A. L. (1970) *The Development of Container Transport*. Paper delivered at Semaine de Bruges, April. Bruges: College of Europe.
Mance, Sir Osborne (1945) *International Sea Transport*. Oxford: University Press.
Margetts, P. C. (1968) Why should we use containers? *Proceedings of International Container Symposium*. London: Chamber of Commerce.
Meek, M. (1968) *The first OCL Container Ships*. Paper read at the Royal Institution of Naval Architects, 28 March.
Moen, K., and Adland, T. (1970) The barge carriers, *ICHCA Journal*, **3**, 18–23.
Molenaar, H. J. (1967) *Basic Economics of Containerization and Unitization in Ocean Shipping*. Paper submitted to Interregional Seminar on Containerization, etc. organised by United Nations in co-operation with UK Government, London, 1–12 May.
New York Journal of Commerce Container Supplement (1967) May.
New Zealand Overseas Trade: Report by the Container Cargo Handling Committee (1967) [Molyneux Report].
1970 Outlook for Deep Sea Container Services: Report to [British] National Ports Council by Arthur D. Little Limited (1967).
Oram, R. B. (1968) The three principles of mechanisation, *The Dock and Harbour Authority*, **48**, 311–12.
——(1969) Is the 75,000 ton container ship feasible? *The Dock and Harbour Authority*, **50**, 194–5.
Philosophy of the Unit Load, The (1966) Oslo: Fred Olsen Lines, Stevedoring Department.
Poole, T. F. (1967) The insurance of containers and unit loads, *The Dock and Harbour Authority*, **48**, 16–18.
Report from the Senate Select Committee on the Container Method of Handling Cargoes. Commonwealth of Australia, 1968.
Report of the Conference on the LASH SYSTEM organised by ICHCA (Netherlands Section) (1970) Amsterdam: ICHCA, 27 February.
Research and Technical Bulletins. London: National Ports Council.
Rogge, T. (1965) Ferry berthing installations: six basic types of structure, *The Dock and Harbour Authority*, **45**, 358–61 [an abbreviated translation of the original article in Hansa (1965) 3].
Schalling, K. S. (1967) *The Carrier's Liability on Combined Transportation and Insurance Problems*. Paper read at First International Conference on Containerisation, Genoa, 19–21 October.
SITPRO *Report* (1970) Prepared by the UK Committee for the Simplification of International Trade Procedures. London: NEDC.
Standardisation of Ferry Terminals, The (1966) Report by a Working Party of the British National Committee of the Permanent International Association of Navigation Congresses, reprinted in *The Dock and Harbour Authority*, **48**, 13–18.
Sturmey, S. G. (1962) *British Shipping and World Competition*. London: Athlone.
Tabak, H. D. (1970) *Cargo Containers: their Storage, Handling, and Movement*. Cambridge, Maryland: Cornell.
Tooth, E. S. (1970) Standardisation of freight containers, *The PLA Monthly*, **45**, 125–7.

Transhipment in the Seventies—a Study of Container Transport (1970) Report to the [British] National Ports Council by Arthur D. Little Ltd. Summarised in *Research and Technical Bulletin*, **6**, 259–75. London: National Ports Council.

van den Burg, A. (1969) *Containerisation: a Modern Transport System*. London: Hutchinson.

Weaver, K. C., and Hebbes, J. C. (1969) *The Container Port Random Access Problem*. Barrow: Vickers [Paper read to Port of London Marine Officers' Association, 23 January].

Weldon, F. L. [Director of Research, Matson Navigation Co.] (1963) Research in Steamship Operations, *Fairplay Cargo Handling* Supplement 3 October, vii–ix; and [in answers to discussion on above] *Fairplay*, 10 October, 35; and (1964) *Progress in Cargo Handling*, **4**, 23–44.

5

HINTERLANDS AND FORELANDS

Pedantic or not, this chapter must start by discussing definitions. A confusing variety of meanings is ascribed to both hinterland and foreland, which basically and respectively refer to the area served by a port at home and overseas. Here arises the major topic of connectivity, of transport links to the places inland, and the destination ports of the ships. A contrast is apparent: the hinterland is usually thought of as continuous, literally the area behind the port; whereas the foreland may well be discontinuous, indeed split into several components in five continents if the port has world-wide trading connections. But this general discussion is running ahead of what the two terms have meant to various writers in the past, and what may be now put forward as useful working meanings.

Hinterland is a naturalised German word and began life in English as meaning the 'back country', the district behind that lying along the coast or along the shore of a river (see the *Oxford English Dictionary*). Later this meaning was extended to the region from which ports received and dispatched passengers and cargo. Urban geographers have also used the expression 'urban hinterland', though in this sense the word seems to be losing ground to 'umland' (German: lit., 'around land'; see E. Van Cleef, 1941; entries in L. D. Stamp, 1962; and R. L. Singh, 1955, 116–17). Where a port is also a large city, the two terms primary hinterland and umland seem interchangeable. A. J. Sargent, 1938, found the hinterland idea rather vague and wished to confine the meaning to:

an area of which the greater part or a substantial part of the trade passes through a single port . . . (15)

This avoids the fiction of a continuous isotropic area served by a port. Indeed, G. C. Weigend, 1956, is in agreement with F. W. Morgan, 1958, that one port may have a great number of hinterlands dependent on the cargo criteria adopted: imports or exports, bulk or break-bulk cargoes, or even hinterlands of groups of commodities and single commodities. Hinterlands might also be defined by method of inland transport used. The following definitions are suggested based on the reasoning of F. W. Morgan, 1958, 118, and expanded in the light of the demands of practical application by N. M. Shaffer, 1965, 142 ff. and J. Bird, 1968, 222.

TABLE 15

SOME HINTERLAND DEFINITIONS

Immediate hinterland—port area itself and the port city (N. R. Elliott, 1969, 167)

Primary hinterland or *umland*—includes the above and the area where port and city assume a commanding role in the life of the area

Secondary hinterland or *competitive hinterland*—difficult to distinguish from above but for working purposes is taken as where less than 70% of an area's traffic is forwarded by or received from the port in question

Advantage hinterland—an area which may fall within the sphere of traffic influence of one port due to the non-linearity of inland tariffs from ports in competition

Commodity hinterland—based on indicated direction of shipments of particular commodities or groups of commodities

Hinterland functional overlap—occurs when the hinterland of a large port overruns that of a smaller port for certain cargoes because of the greater range of port functions, perhaps due to the greater number of sailings from a large port

Hinterland areal overlap—occurs where there is competition between ports of comparable size for cargo of the same type to and from the same area

In an American context the immediate hinterland is the port city's metropolitan area, the primary hinterland the 'outer low rate area' and the 'overnight truck zone'. The secondary hinterland of the ports of the north-eastern US and New Orleans would appear to be the shared area of the Eastern Midwest, with the Gulf port pushing an advantage hinterland northwards because of the 'traditionally depressed rail rates of the Mississippi, Ohio, and Missouri Valleys ...' (J. Kenyon, 1970, Figs. 1, 2, and 3; and p. 19).

Table 15 implies a flexible approach and acknowledges that hinterlands include a punctiform pattern of origins and destinations of the cargo in question—the texture of the hinterland (D. J. Patton, 1960). Presumably, hinterland boundaries could be drawn around a stated density of points, but even if some universally agreed critical density could be agreed to define hinterlands, the flow volumes of cargo are as significant as areal distributions. There are even further difficulties of principle. While goods statistics are available for most railroads, the ever-increasing road traffic is usually counted, if at all, by means of vehicle transits, although flows of goods would be more meaningful. As to imports there is the problem of how to treat goods that undergo physical change. For example, grain for food may be milled on the dockside with the result that flour distribution might be a better hinterland determinant. For exports, the place of manufacture is required rather than the intermediate depot, such as a wholesaler's warehouse or railroad station of consignment (J. Bird, 1969, 284, citing K. F. Glover, 1966, and D. J. Patton, 1958, 455). Often the 'origins and destinations' available to the port student are not the first origins and ultimate destinations.

The meaning of foreland was not crystallised* until G. C. Weigend, 1956, discussed it and later provided a formal definition (1958, 195):

Forelands are the land areas which lie on the seaward side of a port, beyond maritime space, and with which the port is connected by ocean carriers.

He also rightly pointed out (1956, 3) that while maritime space has been organised by ocean carriers, they have done so as servants of the land areas with which ports are connected. In economic terms, ports and their associated hinterlands and forelands are the pacemakers for ocean carrier developments—an interesting reversal of the relationship between ports and ships when technical developments are in question. J. N. H. Britton, 1965, 109, concluded that there have been many studies of port hinterlands because of the close links with urban umlands where many concepts and techniques have been developed to delimit urban spheres of influence. Before reviewing some of this work to distill what is most useful for port geography, it might be prudent first to consider the general conditions under which cargo flows are generated, and the major contrasts in the type and quantity of flow.

Cargo generation

Cargo moves from its origin to a port, moves across the sea, and moves from another port to its destination. These movements form

* J. Mikolajski, 1964, 228, contends that the concept of the foreland was first introduced by S. Berezowski, 1949, in Zaplecze i region [Hinterland and region], *Gosp. Morska*, 2, 378–84. The concept of foreland is often held to originate with M. Amphoux, 1949, 1950, 1951.

three 'sets', to use the language of the Venn diagram*; and these sets join or even overlap at ports. Thus there is a port-to-port set, traversed by the ship. Traditionally, shipowners have scarcely concerned themselves with the transport organisation of the hinterland, though if they become operators of a through service then they have to do so. This section is concerned with the 'set' or group of movements on land. In general terms, it is possible to postulate the conditions under which contrasting types of flow will occur. Table 16 is based on the deductions of A. Pred, 1964, with one important amendment. The assumption here is that a large seaport is in question and that this seaport is in itself a large market and source of skilled labour for industry. Thus the headings of high, intermediate, and low accessibility refer to accessibility to the port itself, and that locations with these characteristics are therefore in the port's near, middle, and far hinterland, the adjectives referring to relative accessibility. Pred himself suggests that his typology may be used at different scales, including 'metropolis and hinterland' (loc. cit., 72). The typology consists of four sets of three variables:

(1) manufacturing industry, divided into three types according to the dominant way it is oriented;
(2) relative accessibility of the industry's location to the market, in this context taken to be the port, even if the product is export cargo destined to pass through the port;
(3) relative length of the predominant cargo flows; and
(4) relative size (in weight) of the predominant cargo flows.

Turning to section (A) of Table 16 it can be seen that the heaviest weight of cargo flows is associated with raw material- or power-oriented industry, and the relative length is dependent on the relative distance of the industry's location from the port. If the port is the largest manufacturing centre and market in its hinterland, then the generation of flows of market-oriented industrial goods will decline with distance away from the port. The labour- and agglomeration economy-oriented industries will also generate flows that decrease in the same manner, but since these industries are likely to produce goods of the highest value per unit of weight, the total weight of the flows is relatively very much lighter than the products of market-oriented industry.

In section (B) of Table 16, there is by contrast assumed to be a large inland manufacturing centre exporting goods via a port. By

---

* Based on a suggestion of P. H. Sinclare, Research Director of the British National Ports Council.

TABLE 16

RELATIVE CARGO GENERATION

Note: below the relative length of the haul is indicated by the
relevant adjective: short, medium, or long; and the relative weight
of flow by the relevant type: LONG, Long, *Long*, in decreasing order
of weight.

(A) *Hauls to a port which is itself the largest urban market in its hinterland*

| | Accessibility | | |
Type of manufacturing industry	Near hinterland	Middle hinterland	Far hinterland
Raw material- and power-oriented industry	SHORT	MEDIUM	LONG
Market-oriented industry	SHORT	Medium	*Long*
Labour- and agglomeration economy-oriented industry	Short	—	—

(B) *Cargo generation from a large manufacturing centre in the port's middle hinterland*

Type of manufacturing industry	Exports	Imports
Raw material- and power-oriented industry	—	*Medium*
Market-oriented industry	MEDIUM	—
Labour- and agglomeration economy-oriented industry	Medium	—

(C) *Cargo generation from an inland exploited raw material source*

Accessibility	Flows
Near hinterland	SHORT
Middle hinterland	Medium or MEDIUM
Far hinterland	Long or LONG

definition this centre will send manufactured goods rather than raw
materials, and the relative weight of manufactured goods issuing
from its market-oriented industries may well be heavy because its
factories will have taken advantage of the economies of scale. The
products of the labour and agglomeration economy-oriented industries, though probably just as valuable, will be much lighter because
of much higher value per unit of weight. The only imports to such a
centre which do not compete with the centre's own industries will be
the products of raw material- and power-oriented industries but these
cargoes are not likely to flow in massive quantities, because in that
circumstance the industries using them would be more economically

located at the port. (This last sentence ignores the fact that in the most advanced economies sophisticated manufactured goods are exchanged by industrial nations each taking advantage of the economies of scale to specialise on particular goods, or even on goods of the same functional use, but different in size and style.)

Finally, in section (C) of Table 16, the export cargo generated from an inland exploited raw material source is considered. Weights of flow are likely to be relatively heavy, except where some inland processing centre in the middle or far hinterland transforms the raw material so that it loses some of its bulk. This may happen even with short hauls, but then such benefication is likely to be undertaken at the port itself.

Hinterland penetration and selective port success

The simplest penetration of a hinterland is by a link at right-angles to the coast, *Anyport*'s transverse track (see p. 69), and perhaps this consists of a river in the first instance, later the first railroad.

Dead end main lines [one of eight categories in W. H. Wallace's (1958) classification of world railroad patterns] are a much more important part of rudimentary railnets than of complex rail systems . . . and are the dominant element of the rail pattern in all scantily railed areas. Many of the world's dead-end main lines form links between ports and their hinterlands in areas where traffic is relatively little developed but external or foreign trade is of great importance . . . (373)

Gradually, the routes will increase in number if the hinterland develops, radiating fan-wise from the port, and the ultimate in this direction will be routes parallel to the coast from a successful port encroaching on the hinterland of port sites on either side, perhaps by road and rail links along the coastlands, or by coastwise shipping services. The modern counterpart of this development is the route by which containers are brought from a groupage depot actually in the urban area of an overrun port city by road or unit trains or coastwise feeder service. To demonstrate the manner in which certain ports grow relative to their neighbours, which are sometimes robbed of trade absolutely, P. J. Rimmer, 1967, adapted a transport model first put forward by E. J. Taafe, R. L. Morrill, and P. R. Gould, 1963, which demonstrated route development of a hinterland to show the corresponding concentration of trade on successful ports. The text below and Fig. 14 are conflations of these two models, with slight adaptation where necessary to make them fit together. The 1963 model was erected as a part-explanation of patterns in west Africa (particularly Ghana and Nigeria), and was used by Rimmer

E

in a general discussion of the evolution of the spatial pattern of Australian ports. Thus the model seems particularly appropriate to developing countries where the sequence or inter-regional develop-ment may be telescoped into one or two centuries.

The first phase represents a series of tiny ports along a coast each with its own hinterland, served by a route transverse to the coast, and serviced by the occasional ship, represented by a route line at right-angles to the coast, and with coastwise links (represented by pecked lines on Fig. 14a). In the second phase, certain lines of interior communication appear to serve growing interior centres (I_1-I_4), and therefore ports P_1, P_2, P_3, and P_4 grow at the expense of their neighbours. In the third phase, port concentration is accentu-ated because P_2 and P_4 develop for the faster growing inland centres I_2 and I_4, and the important routes between these ports and their hinterlands may develop the first nodal centres N_1 and N_2, each with their own embryonic umlands. There are also the beginnings of hinter-land interconnection. Coastwise links may show a hierarchy of three routes of different levels of importance.

The fourth phase finds P_2 able to overcome all rivals except P_4 which is late in being joined up to the rest of the network focussing on P_2; and by the time it is eventually linked up, there is sufficient momentum of development to enable P_4 to coexist with P_2 as the major ports of the coast, having extinguished their rivals, aided per-haps by the decline of the coastal trade with improved landward communications. Finally the hinterland may see the emergence of high priority through routes, such as improved waterways, motor-ways, unit train routes, and confirming the supremacy of the success-ful ports, the most successful of which may become so busy that special annexes must be constructed, container berths (P_{2a}), a maritime industrial estate (P_{2b}), and an oil port (P_{2c}). Taafe, Morrill, and Gould linked the phases of their model to the model of stages of economic development put forward by W. W. Rostow, 1960:

The scattered, weakly connected ports might be considered evidences of the isolation of Rostow's traditional society; the development of a pene-tration line might be viewed as a kind of spatial 'takeoff'; the lateral-interconnection phase might be a spatial symptom of the internal diffusion of technology; and the impact of the auto on the latter phases of the

Fig. 14 Hinterland penetration and selective port success

For explanation of development through five phases see text.

Sources: E. J. Taafe, R. L. Morrill, and P. R. Gould, 1963, 504; and P. J. Rimmer, 1967, 43.

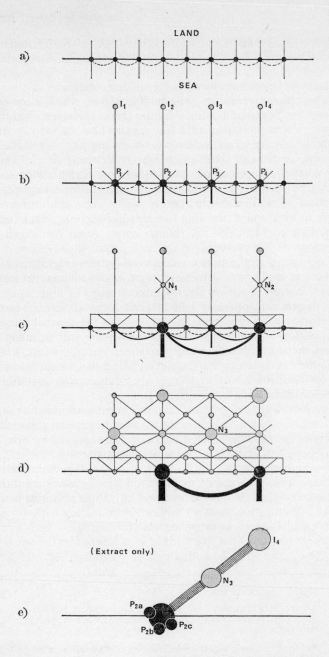

a) LAND / SEA

b) I_1 I_2 I_3 I_4 — P_1 P_2 P_3 P_4

c) N_1 N_2

d) N_3

e) (Extract only) I_4 / N_3 / P_{2a} P_{2b} P_{2c}

Fig. 14

sequence [the emergence of the high priority through routes] might be an expression of certain aspects of higher mass consumption . . . (loc. cit., 505)

The model does not allow for the sudden emergence of a new port nor the resurgence of an old-established one, which may happen because of the attraction for shipping serving tidewater industry or assisting the exploitation of a raw material source made economic by the developments of technology. In an old-established hierarchy of ports, such as in the eastern US, J. Kenyon, 1970, 23 ff., has stressed the importance of 'great inertia (or perhaps momentum)'. In this he includes the commercial, financial, and organisational structure of well-established ports which may lead their traffic-graph upward via a nothing-succeeds-like-success spiral (see also D. J. Patton, 1958, 454–5), though ample room for 'downstream development' is a prerequisite for such persistent *Anyports*.

Following a model that concentrated on the development of the network of land communications, another dynamic model may now be put forward based on the developing shape of hinterlands. This very theoretical approach will at least focus thoughts upon how hinterland space is organised and suggest the normal shape and organisation of a hinterland from which there will be many diver-gences in reality due to many particular circumstances. But once again the discussion enters the clean clinical theoretical world where the complication of 'other things' are conveniently forced into the limbo of 'being equal'.

The model spatial pattern that has stimulated most thought in human geography is based on the shape of hexagonal areas tributary to central places. This is the basis of central place theory originating with W. Christaller, 1933, and which has given rise to a vast litera-ture—almost a central place industry in itself (B. J. L. Berry and A. Pred, 1961). The use of the hexagon shape derives from the fact that such polygons will pack together; only three polygons with sides of equal length pack together without overlap, and without residual intervening spaces: squares, equilateral triangles, and hexagons. Hexagons are now firmly embedded in central place theory, and it is hard to quarrel with the contention of W. Bunge, 1966, 152, that in

Fig. 15 Hinterland shapes

Above: The hexagonal net distorted by transport arteries and a disuniform population distribution. Adapted from W. Isard, 1956, 272.

Below: Brisbane's hinterland diverging northward to capture the back country of other Queensland ports, rendered diagrammatically.

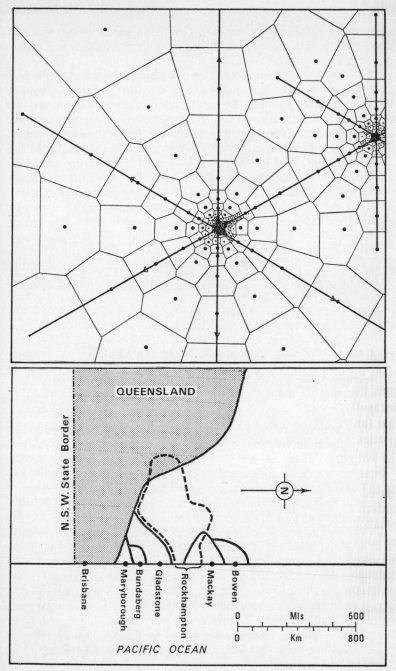

Fig. 15

areas which are served by central places, hexagonal service areas will appear if the distortions caused by a disuniform surface and transport are allowed for.

The complications introduced into central place theory by transport become severe when ports are in question, because they are usually eccentric places as far as the land is concerned. A way of approaching this problem is to consider the famous attempt to show an hexagonal grid distorted by transport arteries in an area of disuniform population distribution. In this diagram (part of which is reproduced here as Fig. 15 top), W. Isard, 1956, 272, attempted to cope with the disuniform population decreasing in density from the urban centres, but not decreasing so fast along routeways. The instructions given to his cartographer are interesting and presented in edited form below.

(1) retain the Löschian deduction [refers to A. Lösch, 1954] that each producer of any given commodity operates at approximately the same cost so that the boundary separating the markets of any pair of neighbouring producers is a perpendicular bisector of the line connecting the two;

(2) adhere to the hexagonal market areas in so far as possible . . .;

(3) depict hexagonal market areas which increase in size with distance from the core in any direction; and

(4) construct the hexagonal market areas so that, along any circle drawn with the core as centre, the size of the market areas in general tends to decrease as we approach the transport axis of a city-rich sector and increase as we approach the transport axis of a city-poor sector. (274, *n*. 17)

It will be seen that following these constraints built into the diagram —the instructions to the cartographer as outlined above—the hexagons become distorted, but in every case the end of the distorted hexagon nearer the major centre is narrower than the distal ends and that this is particularly so for hexagons aligned along the transport arteries. This apparatus of deduction is now borrowed in considering the evolution of port hinterland shape.

First, there is postulated a series of five ports of equal size, evenly spaced along a coastline (Fig. 16a). One certainly cannot suggest a pattern of hexagonally-shaped hinterlands, because a honeycomb of hexagons does not consist of edges which make up a straight line to be laid along the coastline (Fig. 16b). Simpler geometric forms packing exactly together might have been chosen—the square or the rectangle, but then all the ports would be similarly equipped with hinterlands, and any development would be due to extra-hinterland factors (a shipping development, or an entrepreneurial initiative, at

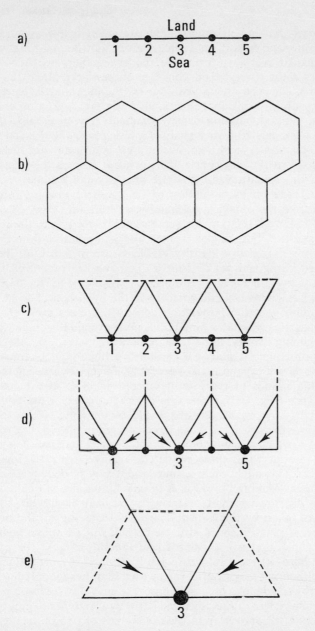

Fig. 16 Theoretical port hinterlands on a straight coast
For explanation see text.

some ports but not at others). The argument below assumes that extra-hinterland factors are equal. A group of triangular hinterlands is postulated over a uniform area. To fit together, two sides of the triangles must diverge and converge successively along the coast (Fig. 16c). The ports are now equipped with hinterlands of equal area, but they are not of equal functional importance. At this point C. Clark's, 1951, population density gradient may be employed. The gradient was derived from a study of a wide range of cities and shows that population density decreases at a constant rate with increasing distance from the city centre. This concept ignores the absence of residential population in the centre of a city and assumes a central density based on extrapolation of the gradient inwards (and up-wards) from the outskirts of the city. J. Johnson (1967, 53 ff.; see also P. T. Kivell, 1969) makes some useful correctives to the concept of the gradient, but the general idea works in practice, for a number of reasons. Population density gradients are in fact built into the distorted hexagonal net of Isard's diagram. The tapering of these hexagons towards the city centre is very significant for the triangular hinterlands successively disposed upon the hypothetical coast.

Assuming that the population density decreases away from the port cities, then go-ahead hinterlands must expand to compensate for this declining density, like the hinterlands of ports 1, 3, and 5 (Fig. 16c). Consequently, and still considering hinterland factors alone, these ports will expand their spheres of influence by sharing the captured hinterlands of the even-numbered ports to give rectangular hinterlands (Fig. 16d), if the rate of development of the odd-numbered ports was equal, but this would be unlikely. Notice that the hinterlands of ports 2 and 4 can be considered in Fig. 16c as focussing on port 3, which might come to serve the whole area between ports 1 and 5, considered as three equilateral triangles or a semi-hexagon (Fig. 16e). This might seem a roundabout way of deducing that the whole area would fall into the economic hinterland of one port, but the fan-like arrangement of triangles is probably revealed in the direction taken by the transport arteries focussing on the port. In Fig. 16e, if ports 2 and 4 still exist, they will be subservient to 3 whose hinterland will overlap theirs functionally. At the extreme coastal edges of the semi-hexagonal hinterland of port 3 there may be neighbouring major ports, each with a semi-hexagonal hinterland. The arrowed triangles focussing on port 3 may also focus on ports at the extreme edges of the diagram. These two triangles then represent examples of areal overlap of the hinterlands of two ports.

An example of the diverging hinterland of a large port compared with the converging hinterlands of small ports is included as Fig. 15,

based on Queensland. The southern boundary of Brisbane's hinterland is not included because of complications induced by the state
border, but the northern boundary diverges to capture the back
country of several smaller ports. R. Dugrand (1964, Map 37) gives
an example of five French Mediterranean centres extending their
influence back from the coast of Languedoc. Only Narbonne has an
area of immediate urban influence that tapers inland, and its various
secondary zones of urban influence are the smallest of the five towns
in question.

The search for a datum—hinterland measurement

Some of the ideas of the preceding two sections may be combined in
the concept of a cargo generation gradient—that cargo destined for
a particular port decreases as the distance between the port and
location of generation increases; and that for a given location larger
ports attract a proportionally greater share of cargo generated than
smaller ports at any given distance. A method of testing these two
hypotheses is by radial analysis. Rings of fixed incremental radius are
drawn centred on the port and calculations are made of the proportion of cargo handled in the port which originates in the zones boun-
ded by the various rings; secondly, there is the proportion of the
cargo generated in each zone which is handled by a particular port.
If the rings are centred on the cargo-generating location, there can
be found the proportion of cargo passing through ports in the various
zones. A worked out example of radial analysis can be found for
British ports (*Portbury*, etc., 1966, 45–6), and such an analysis presupposes a comprehensive set of origin and destination data on cargo
flows. The discussion of the method has introduced the basic notion
that size of port and distance of cargo generation areas from it
influences the amount of cargo it receives, and this double idea ushers
in yet another model applicable to hinterland study.

The gravity model has long been recognised as a possible datum
for predicting flows between settlements. Credit for early use of the
model in the nineteenth century is given to H. C. Carey, 1858–9, and
A. Schäffle, 1875–8, by F. Lukermann and P. W. Porter, 1960, and
A. Pred (loc. cit.). Sometimes the concept is known as Reilly's Law
of Retail Gravitation from a monograph of that name (1931), but
first put forward by him in 1929; other names are interaction or
interactance theories (E. L. Ullman, 1956; and S. C. Dodd, 1950,
245). The gravity model relies on an analogy from physics: 'the
gravitational energy between two masses divided by the first power
of the intervening distance' (F. W. Lukermann and P. W. Porter,
1960, citing J. Q. Stewart). In fact, experience has shown that differ-

ent exponents may well be necessary for different forms of flow. The
model can be stated as follows:

$$I_y = k\frac{P_i P_j}{D_{ij}^h}$$

where I_y = interaction between places i and j
$P_i P_j$ = size of places
D_{ij} = distance between i and j
k and b = empirically derived constants

This is the basis of the gravity model used in *Portbury*, etc. (op.
cit.) as an 'explanation' of actual flows to and from British ports and
helped to prove correct two hypotheses:

⚹ (i) The further away the port, the less proportionately of the region's
    exports it attracts. This supports the distance hypothesis;
⚹ (ii) The larger ports also attracted, proportionately, goods from further
    afield than smaller ports, which supports the second hypothesis (op.
    cit., 46) . . . that, for a given exporting region larger ports attract a
    larger share of exports than smaller ports at any given distance (ibid.,
    45).

The working of the model is set out in Annex 4 of the Portbury
paper, but quoted below is the basic equation which represents the
flows of exports from an inland hinterland characterised by 'zone i'
to a port j.

$$T^*_{ij} = A_i B_j O_i X_j^a f\,(d_{ij},\, b)$$

where T^*_{ij} = exports from zone i through port j, as produced in the
             model
A_i = set of constants associated with the zone i
B_j = set of constants associated with the port j
O_i = the total amount of exports originating in zone i
X_j = the total amount of exports handled by port j
a, b = the parameters of the model
f = a function of the distance and parameter b
d_{ij} = distance between zone i and port j

A_i is really a term representing port competition; it decreases for
the port in question if there are several other ports sharing the
hinterland. The parameter b represents the amount of decline of the
port's pull with increasing distance from regions. The model flows
fitted the actual flows well (with variance exceeding 0·9 for imports
and exports), and was then used to predict future flows. It is essential

to realise that such a model merely redistributes forecast future increased total trade in the same proportions as the attempted best fit to current flows. If this model seems unduly theoretical, two important points should be remembered. Given the total size of the port, the total amount of cargo generated in an area and its distance from the port, actual flows could be produced mathematically (cf. columns 2 and 3 of Table 6, Annex 4, *Portbury*, etc., op. cit., 46). The flows predicted using the model were part of the evidence causing a minister not to authorise the construction of a major port expansion. Thus was theory translated into practice.

Recently, gravity and interactance models have come under fire because their margins of predictive error may be wide. I. G. Heggie, 1969, reports that the weighted average error (weighted by actual traffic volumes in the base year) of the Portbury model was 14%. He suggests two simple methods of traffic forecasting: (1) expanding an existing origin-destination table to give future movements, with stated assumptions about growth rates; (2) a prediction equation for traffic as a function of relevant growth parameters. He prefers these simple methods to the gravity model approach, though was immediately faced by a 'rejoinder' on this question by A. G. Wilson, 1969, and the debate no doubt continues.

This section on hinterlands may have left the impression that as a port's trade develops its hinterland must become larger in area by piracy of other ports' hinterlands. This is not necessarily the case. If the population of an area increases, if the economy of an area demands more maritime exchanges, or if a new market or a newly-exploited resource increases overseas trade, then the port will expand without any concomitant increase in hinterland area. Under one or more of the foregoing conditions, the port's trade could actually increase with hinterland shrinkage. Hinterland shrinkage might well occur for a port that abandoned break-bulk cargo for bulk cargo imports to waterfront industries. As far as break-bulk cargo is concerned, it appears that the rise of unit cargo will tend to concentrate on fewer ports with larger hinterlands. Any vertical integration of transport between sea and land carriers on through routes will tend towards the aggrandisement of hinterlands of ports employed, as shipowners obtain the cargo further back on the through route and take it closer to its ultimate destination. Symbols of this hinterland enlargement are the equalisation of through rates when cargo is handed in at various places at unequal distance from the container berth, and a second symbol is the reception depot.

These inland depots have three main functions: they enable the through route to start and end further back in the hinterland, perhaps carried from the port by unit train for dispersal by road transport; they are customs clearance areas; and they act as a consolidation centre both to make up unit train loads and for groupage traffic of less than container loads. Cargo consolidation is necessary because on some routes up to 70% of break-bulk cargo consignments are five tons or less. A. Scherrer, 1967, suggests basic reasons for three different locations for cargo grouping and distributing centres: (1) alongside cargo berths (for part-load traffic not grouped by the forwarding agent); (2) in port upland (operated by individual or grouped forwarding agents); (3) inland (where there is a compact area of export break-bulk cargo generation, often at a transport node). Rivalta Scrivia began life as an inland satellite for the Port of Genoa, 67 motorway kilometres to the north. This port is notorious for its lack of upland area or back-up area for the quays and also suffers from obstructive labour practices. The depot was opened in 1966, but the build-up of traffic was slow. However, the centre covers some thirty hectares, with two-thirds of the accommodation covered. It has inland customs clearance facilities for TIR and bonded rail traffic. Italian and international container trains now serve the centre, so it appears to have a developing future. The abiding problem remains for the hinterland delimiter. Old-fashioned warehouse, wayside railroad station, or modern inland container depot are hardly sufficient for 'origin' and 'destination' of cargo which is manufactured or consumed somewhere else. And if inland depots are successful in grouping traffic for a wide area, someone may have to start investigating the hinterlands of container depots.

Finally, N. R. Elliott, 1966, 115–16; and 1969, 167, has referred to the 'symbiotic existence' of the hinterland and foreland. And R. Robinson, 1967, has argued that the extent and intensity of hinterlands may also depend on the orientation of hinterland space through the ports towards its internal origins or markets overseas. For imports through Vancouver he found that a critical variable in 'structuring the spatial pattern' was foreland orientation (46).

The search for a datum—foreland measurement

The measurement of a port's foreland, in total and according to cargo commodity mix, and comparison with forelands of other ports, like the work on hinterlands, depends heavily on data availability—this time the destinations and origins of cargo overseas. This information is readily available at the level of nation states; indeed it forms basic items in the national balance of payments. But it is often very difficult to obtain the same information broken down by port of entry and departure. This is frustrating, because the information is collected for customs purposes; even if the trade is coastwise, or intra-state, the figures are known for port revenue purposes. A comparison of port trade is constantly needed for port planning purposes. But there is an inherent data blockage. The assembly of the information has usually involved an enormous amount of special book-keeping and collation of statistics, whereas the value of the work has been in the sphere of port and regional planning rather than in the realm of national accountancy. Only when port and regional planning are held to be vitally important activities will such material be readily available; and computerised book-keeping should make the availability much easier than it has been in the past.

The basic objective attack on foreland measurement and comparison has been via the statistical benchmark, borrowed from work on industrial location by P. Sargant Florence, 1943. The principle behind his location quotient is to make a relative comparison between the performance of an individual with the average total performance of all the individuals in the universe, the latter forming the benchmark for the comparison. An example of the application of this principle to the directions of world trade at the nation state level are to be found in G. Alexandersson and G. Norstrom, 1963, 17–29, with illustrative maps. In simple terms their trade distribution index works on the principle that if country A has seaborne trading connections with other nations such that the trade mix perfectly matches the composition of world trade, the foreland indices of country A would work out at 100 for every other country, each of which would constitute a foreland at this level of the aggregation of statistics. But if the trade between country 1 and country 2 is twice the hypothetical situation (where the share of country 1's trade going to country 2 is twice that of 2's share of the world trade), then the index is 200 and so on pro rata. The index is stated mathematically as follows:

$$I = \frac{\dfrac{T_{1-2}}{T_1}}{\dfrac{T_2}{T_w}} \times 100 = \frac{T_{1-2} \times T_w}{T_1 \times T_2} \times 100$$

where I =trade distribution index
    T_{1-2}=total trade between country 1 and country 2
    T_1 =the total foreign trade of country 1
    T_2 =the total foreign trade of country 2
    T_w =the sum of all imports and exports in the world

J. N. H. Britton, 1965, used the Sargant Florence benchmark idea at the level of the individual port when he considered Melbourne's trade. A similar method was employed by J. Bird, 1969, for an analysis of the flows via individual ports in a nation state, this time not to other nation states but to thirteen 'world trading areas' arbitrarily defined from British customs weight analyses and published in the annual British *Digest of Port Statistics.* 'Location of trade quotients' were worked out for each of fifteen major British ports for each of the thirteen world trading areas (quoted as Table 17). The highest quotient was found to be representative of Southampton's trade with South Africa, but it must be remembered that this represents only a comparison of the relative proportions of Southampton's trade with South Africa compared with the proportion of the total British trade with that country. (Actual tonnages in 1966 were, in thousand tons: Liverpool, 512; London, 395; Southampton, 353.) The closer the series of location of trade quotients is to 100, the closer is the port to matching the national trade mix to the forelands. So the coefficient of variation was worked out upon the thirteen location quotients for each port (actually on the logarithm of each quotient, for whereas 200 represents twice the national average, half the average is represented by 50). As might be expected, the largest ports had the lowest coefficient of variations (last column of Table 17), and were therefore the closest to being regarded as truly national ports. But the comparison against port trade and variation cannot be examined mathematically because of the arbitrary nature of the thirteen world trading areas which differ remarkably in size. Nevertheless, where a port with a relatively low tonnage had a relatively low coefficient of variation, it was a pointer to look further into the absolute statistics to see why this was so. The Clyde was only Britain's fifth ranking port in 1966 as far as total cargo tonnage (excluding fuels) was concerned, yet the port has wide trading connections to many forelands overseas, emphasising Glasgow's role as a port for all Scotland, with a wide range of liner services that start at this port, attracted by good bottom cargo (metals and manufactures) and valuable export cargo (whisky); and there are a number of ship repair facilities available. But the date of the statistics is 1966, before the rise of deep-sea container services in specially designed cellular ships. The Clyde has not so far attracted a regular deep-sea through container service; indeed container operators to Australia offer the same through rates to shippers if the cargo is delivered to a Glasgow depot as if it was delivered to the depot close to the London container berth. This indicates that the sailings of break-bulk cargo liners to forelands overseas from Glasgow will not be so far-flung in the 1970s. In statistical terms the coefficient of variation of Glasgow's foreland location quotients is expected to rise.

TABLE 17

LOCATION OF TRADE QUOTIENTS FOR THE TOTAL TRAFFIC (EXCLUDING FUELS) OF FIFTEEN BRITISH PORTS IN THIRTEEN OVERSEAS TRADING AREAS, 1966

Port	Near and short sea trades				Deep sea trades									V* log Port's location of trade quotient
	Irish Republic	European Economic Community	Scandinavia and Baltic	Iberia and Mediterranean	West Africa	South Africa	East Africa	India and Persian Gulf	Far East	Australasia	North America	South America	Central America and West Indies	
London	31	95	79	108	71	96	166	137	169	180	97	76	162	10
Southampton	—	148	34	65	54	1336	152	31	90	82	69	38	210	38
Bristol	106	41	34	48	65	143	97	202	15	204	234	50	182	19
Newport	87	28	85	146	320	5	4	12	25	16	112	258	10	41
Cardiff	10	24	69	127	233	103	3	81	—	72	139	112	323	45
Swansea	38	58	66	135	29	386	74	117	189	148	130	178	8	22
Liverpool	200	27	21	78	132	160	253	194	264	196	117	250	148	17
Manchester	104	54	131	72	20	81	68	70	28	15	187	54	65	17
Clyde	30	25	89	59	112	126	109	96	56	110	148	145	142	13
Grangemouth	—	158	173	62	45	22	14	39	137	—	83	8	10	55
Leith	—	129	102	63	18	47	84	—	—	117	170	15	240	62
Tyne	3	88	152	19	159	55	39	2	2	53	121	163	3	54
Tees	6	90	125	102	262	96	48	202	153	19	54	35	46	25
Hull	2	129	133	75	56	87	80	72	42	92	107	47	68	26
Grimsby and Immingham	18	115	136	194	102	81	17	14	80	109	41	20	111	23

Based on data in *Digest of Port Statistics 1967*, London: National Ports Council, 1967.

* V = 'coefficient of variation of . . .'

J. N. H. Britton was a pioneer in the use of the location quotient in respect of a single port (1965). The method of calculation is the same as for the trade distribution index. He went on to employ another device of Sargant Florence, the 'coefficient of specialisation':

The coefficient is calculated as follows; percentage shares by commodity for the imports (or exports) of an area are compared with the percentage commodity composition of all imports (or exports) for all areas totalled and the sum of the positive (or negative) differences of an area from the total pattern for the port produces the coefficient. (112, *n.* 15)

As the commodity composition of the port relative to a particular foreland approaches the total pattern for all the port's forelands, the coefficient becomes smaller, approaching zero. The measure does not work very well if the imports or exports are concentrated on a few commodities. In that case Britton borrows a technique devised by A. O. Hirschmann, 1945—an index of traffic concentration.

The index is calculated as follows: if P_1 represents the percentage share of the first commodity in an area's imports (or exports) from Melbourne, and a total of 'n' commodities accounts for all imports (or exports), then $I = \sqrt{P_1{}^2 + P_2{}^2 + \ldots P_n{}^2}$ (loc. cit., 56, *n.* 18)

One port's hinterland is another port's foreland, but it is clear that to be of any use these concepts must somehow be described statistically. There is ever present the danger of dividing up a country into hinterlands or the world into trading areas, and then 'proving' that one area is more important than another, not avowing that part of this importance is due to the way the area was divided up. Port students rarely have the opportunity of following the optimum statistical approach; the required data are not available. This is a lacuna also to be faced by regional planners, for ports do generate a great deal of land transport in their hinterlands. If a large port is also a large city, and this is the normal case, it is essential that traffic to and from the port by road and rail should not be confounded with traffic serving the city as a regional centre, to their mutual diseconomy. This does not necessarily mean duplication of long-distance arteries, but certainly does mean separate links to the port and city taking off on the boundary of the city region.

To most people a port is rather a hidden function of a city. The quays are down river, the docks may be far out in a delta or at the entrance to a bay, but there is steady demand on the access routes by land, with cargo traffic far in excess of that generated by inland cities of comparable population. R. Lutz, 1967, 4, once made a dramatic comparison between an inland city with 360 degrees of umland and a port of roughly similar population size with a hinterland direction of only 180 degrees. Yet Hanover generated cargo traffic of 7,527,000 tons based on the full 360 degree circle while Bremen had 30 million tons of cargo movement, 12,185,000 via the Weser and 18,062,000 on the half circle of land movement to and from the port. Converting the land figures to tonnage per degree of hinterland, the inland city generated 20,908 tons while the port generated 100,344 tons, nearly five times as much. The problem of transport provision to move so much tonnage is where the subjects of hinterland development and regional planning are closely intertwined.

Alexandersson, G., and Norstrom, G. (1963) *World Shipping: an Economic Geography of Ports and Seaborne Trade*. London: Wiley.

Amphoux, M. (1949) Les fonctions portuaires, *Revue de la Porte Oceane*, 5 (54), 19–22.

——(1950) Des horizons terrestres aux horizons maritimes de l'activité portuaire, *Revue de la Porte Oceane*, 6 (57), 15–18.

——(1951) Géographie portuaire et économie portuaire, *Revue de la Porte Oceane*, 7 (70), 5–8.

Berry, B. J. L., and A. Pred (1961) *Central Place Studies: A Bibliography of Theory and Applications*. Philadelphia: Regional Science Research Institute Bibliography Series.

Bird, J. (1968) *Seaport Gateways of Australia*. London: Oxford University Press.

——(1969) Traffic flows to and from British seaports, *Geography*, 54, 284–302.

Britton, J. N. H. (1965) The external relations of seaports: some new considerations, *Tijdschrift voor economische en sociale geografie*, 56, 109–12.

Bunge, W. (1966) *Theoretical Geography*. Lund: Gleerup.

Carey, H. C. (1858–9) *Principles of Social Science*. 3 vols. Philadelphia: Lippincott.

Christaller, W. (1933) *Die zentralen Orte in Süddeutschland: Eine ökonomisch-geographische Untersuchung über die Gesetzmassigkeit der Verbreitung und Entwicklung der Siedlungen mit stadtischen Funktionen*. Jena: Fischer. Trans. C. W. Baskin (1966) *Central Places in Southern Germany*. Englewood Cliffs, NJ: Prentice-Hall.

Clark, C. (1951) Urban population densities, *Journal of the Royal Statistical Society, Series A*, 114, 490–6.

Dodd, S. C. (1950) The interactance hypothesis—a gravity model fitting physical masses and human groups, *American Sociological Review*, 15, 245–56.

Dugrand, R. (1964) *Villes et campagnes en Bas Languedoc*. Paris: Presse Universitaire.

Elliott, N. R. (1966) The functional approach in port studies, *Northern Geographical Essays*, Ed. J. W. House, Newcastle-upon-Tyne: Oriel Press for University Dept. of Geography.

——(1969) Hinterland and foreland as illustrated by the Port of the Tyne, *Transactions of the Institute of British Geographers*, 47, 153–70.

Florence, P. Sargant (1943) The technique of industrial location, *The Architectural Review*, 93, 59–60.

Glover, K. F. (1966) Traffic flows to and from ports, *The Dock and Harbour Authority*, 46, 286–7.

Heggie, I. G. (1969) Are gravity and interactance models a valid technique for planning regional transport facilities? *Operational Research Quarterly*, **20**, 93–110.

Hirschman, A. O. (1945) *National Power and the Structure of Foreign Trade*. University of California Press.

Isard, W. (1956) *Location and Space Economy: a General Theory Relating to Industrial Location, Market Areas, Land Use, Trade, and Urban Structure*. MIT.

Johnson, J. (1967) *Urban Geography: an Introductory Analysis*. Oxford: Pergamon.

Kenyon, J. (1970) Elements in inter-port competition in the United States, *Economic Geography*, **46**, 1–24.

Kivell, P. T. (1969) Gradients of urban influence, *Process and Patterns of Urbanization*, Institute of British Geographers, Study Group in Urban Geography, Keele, September Conference.

Lösch, A. (1954) (1st edition) *The Economics of Location*. New Haven: Yale University Press.

Lukermann, F., and Porter, P. W. (1960) Gravity and potential models in economic geography, *Annals of the Association of American Geographers*, **50**, 493–504.

Lutz, R. (1967) *Modern Development of Seaports and their Landward Traffic Approaches*. Bremen.

Mikolajski, J. (1964) Polish sea-ports, their hinterlands and forelands, *Geographia Polonica*, **2**, 221–9.

Morgan, F. W. (1948) The pre-war hinterlands of the German North Sea ports, *Transactions of the Institute of British Geographers*, **14**, 47–55.

——(1958) *Ports and Harbours*. London: Hutchinson. 2nd ed.

Patton, D. J. (1958) General cargo hinterlands of New York, Philadelphia, Baltimore and New Orleans, *Annals of the Association of American Geographers*, **48**, 436–55.

——(1960) *Port Hinterlands: the Case of New Orleans*. University of Maryland. Mimeographed.

Portbury: Reasons for the Minister's Decision not to Authorise the Construction of a New Dock at Portbury, Bristol (1966). London: HMSO.

Pred, A. (1964) Toward a typology of manufacturing flows, *Geographical Review*, **54**, 64–84.

Reilly, W. J. (1929) *Methods for the Study of Retail Relationships*, University of Texas, Monograph 2944.

——(1931) *The Law of Retail Gravitation*. New York: Reilly.

Rimmer, P. J. (1967) The search for spatial regularities in the development of Australian seaports 1861–1961/2, *Geografiska Annaler*, **49b**, 42–54.

Robinson, R. (1967) *Spatial Patterns of Port-linked flows: General Cargo Imports through the Port of Vancouver*. University of British Columbia, Department of Geography. Mimeographed.

Rostow, W. W. (1960) *The Stages of Economic Growth*. Cambridge: University Press.

Sargent, A. J. (1938) *Seaports and Hinterlands*. London: Black.

Schäffle, A. (1875–8) *Bau und Leben des socialen Korpers*. 4 parts. Tubingen.

Scherrer, A. (1967) *Grouping and Distribution Centres*. Paper read at the Eighth Technical Conference, ICHCA, Antwerp, 22–6 May.

Shaffer, N. M. (1965) *The Competitive Position of the Port of Durban*. Evansto, Illinois: Northwestern Studies in Geography No. 8.

Singh, R. L. (1955) *Banaras: a Study in Urban Geography*. Banaras: Kishore.

Stamp, L. D. (Ed.) (1962) *A Glossary of Geographical Terms*. Longmans.
Taafe, E. J., Morrill, R. L., and Gould, P. R. (1963) Transport expansion in underdeveloped countries, *Geographical Review*, 53, 502–29.
Ullman, E. L. (1956) The role of transportation and the bases for interaction, *Man's Role in Changing the Face of the Earth*, Ed. W. L. Thomas. Chicago: University Press, 862–80.
Van Cleef, E. (1941) Hinterland and umland, *Geographical Review*, 31, 308–11.
Wallace, W. H. (1958) Railroad traffic densities and patterns, *Annals of the Association of American Geographers*, 48, 352–74.
Weigend, G. C. (1956) The problem of hinterland and foreland as illustrated by the Port of Hamburg, *Economic Geography*, 32, 1–16.
——(1958) Some elements in the study of port geography, *Geographical Review*, 48, 185–200.
Wilson, A. G. (1969) Heggie on gravity and interactance models: a rejoinder, *Operational Research Quarterly*, 20, 489–96 [includes a 'reply' by I. G. Heggie and a 'further rejoinder'].

6

SEAPORTS EXEMPLIFYING GENERALISATIONS (I):
EUROPE AND NORTH AMERICA

This chapter and the next are rather grandly labelled as the 'exemplification of generalisations', with a two-fold world division based on Europe and North America on the one hand, and the rest of the world on the other. In the preceding chapters, theories or principles have been emphasised rather than descriptions of actual ports. Real places have been introduced only to give illustration of the generalisation in question. This approach is also followed in the final two chapters on ports and planning. Meanwhile, in this chapter and the next, the approach is in the reverse direction; but the intention is still to keep a close link between the data about actual ports and the way that data may support theory, or at least illustrate a generalisation valid over more than one port. There is a massive information bank about all the ports of the world,* and it is obvious that in the few pages that follow, only a very selective scoop into the treasure chest of fact is possible. However, if the objective is to provide information that supports generalisations, some guide-lines are at least laid down for the selection and presentation of material. Where a particular illustration of a general point is made elsewhere in another chapter, an italicised page number in square brackets gives the appropriate reference. This cross-referencing also enables the reader to refer forwards to the two chapters on ports and planning, which are placed at the end of the book because this topic seems best considered against the maximum amount of information on ports. Sometimes the connection between examples and theory may strike the reader as oblique rather than direct, but such cross-reference is nevertheless

* See 'A Note of References', pp. 26–7.

made in the hope of setting up a resonance in the reader's mind that may prove of value.

The preceding paragraph has discussed the guide-lines which set out the way in which material has been rather ruthlessly selected. The subjects will change rapidly and the scene shift swiftly across the world. But if it is remembered that exemplification of theory is the prime aim that animates this chapter and the next, then they may appear to be more than a mere dilettante dip into the world port bibliography and documentation.

European seaports

Europe exhibits a fascinating series of contrasting countries as far as relationship of area to length of seaboard is concerned. On the one hand, there are countries with a very long coastline, either because they are insular or peninsular, such as Great Britain, France and Spain; these countries have many ports. Italy and Scandinavia do not have the large numbers of ports often found in this peninsular category for different reasons; one coast of Sweden has much longer sea approaches than the other, and moreover this coast is seasonally icebound; Italy's peninsula is not the country's most important hinterland, so that three of her four largest ports are located to serve the Po Plain, almost a southern annexe of central European mountains and basins (L. Gatti, 1967). However, 'Project 80' envisages four port systems: Alto Tirreno (Savona to Leghorn); Alto Adriatico (Venice–Trieste); Basso Tirreno (Naples–Salerno); and Basso Adriatico (Bari, Brindisi, and Taranto) 'in order to prevent the Italian peninsula assuming the character of a hinterland for better equipped foreign ports' (G. Dagnino, 1970, 7). In Poland, Western Germany, Denmark, the Netherlands, and Belgium there are only one or two major ports, so that national planning is easier. Port functions are concentrated in Poland, Western Germany, and the Low Countries because of short runs of coast, with estuary or delta distributary foci. There is then a broad contrast between centripetal coastlines with few ports, and centrifugal coastlines with many ports [23–4], such that Britain, France, and Spain have faced problems of national planning of ports in the last few years—discussed below.

The main recommendation of the 1962 Rochdale Committee on British ports (*Report of the Committee of Inquiry*, etc., 1962) was the proposal for a National Ports Authority (paras 140–53):

We have devoted a good deal of thought to this matter and we are firmly of the opinion that there is a need for some central machinery which, while still seeking to take the fullest possible advantage of local initiative and responsibility, will make it possible for a national policy for ports to be formulated on the basis of the recommendations made in this Report, and for the execution of this policy to be kept under continuous supervision (para 140).

This report attempted to combine the advantages of a national authority with those accruing to a system of port trusts [*199*], autonomous except in the field of national policy-making. As a result, the British National Ports Council was set up in 1964 as an advisory body. The idea of central policy making was strengthened in a 1969 Government White Paper, going further than the Rochdale Committee, which had advocated a National Ports Authority with specific non-operational functions.

The authority must have power to determine the nature, and shape of the British ports industry, whose efficiency is of fundamental importance to the economy and life of the community. Such power can only be entrusted to a body which has the discipline of knowing that it is fully responsible for the success or failure of its policies: this must mean national ownership.

The National Ports Authority will have an immense task to fulfil if it is to plan the future development and rationalisation of physical facilities whilst at the same time adapting the organisation of work in the ports to modern needs. The first necessity is to enable the proposed new Authority to concentrate resources and management on essentials. (*The Reorganisation of Ports*, 1969, paras 2–3)

However, it must be remembered that port nationalisation is not the policy of the Government elected in 1970.

Perhaps one of the hardest tasks facing national port planning in Britain is that the ports with the greatest potential for development are not located in those regions of the country which the government desires to help on national planning grounds in order to spread economic growth more evenly. A perhaps over-simplified cliché of British geography is contained in the two-fold division of the country into Highland Britain and Lowland England, separated by a line joining the Tees to the Exe. However coarse this division, there is a certain rough justice as far as coastal sites are concerned. The Tees and estuaries to the south offer reclaimable fringing flats and sands; and the tidal range permits the contemplation of berths without access through lock gates. Moreover, the south and east coasts face continental Europe, enabling ports on these coasts to share in the buoyant ferry traffic across the North Sea. None of these advantages appertains to ports on England's west coast, afflicted by high tidal ranges. In Scotland the position is reversed, for the Clyde has become the country's national port, an example of the 'proclaimed impulse' [*24–5*] of a bishopric and market calling forth a port on a shallow estuary, later canalised and deepened, with the port moving downstream (J. Bird, 1963, 76–97).

The chief disadvantage faced by ports on England's east coast is the depth limitation in the Pas de Calais area [36], and this has led to the idea of a transhipment roadstead, partially based on the Goodwin Sands (A. H. Beckett, 1969). Since this site might be held to be outside British territorial waters, an international transhipment port has been proposed, where transfer is made from vessels too big to enter the North Sea, a development from the 'land's end' or 'finisterre' location typified by Bantry Bay [90–1].

During the period of the Third French Plan (1958–61), it was first realised that the ports of that country were lagging behind in their development (L. Poirier, 1963, 65). Three reasons seem to have been responsible. First, fierce competition had come from state-subsidised Rhine delta ports, particularly from Antwerp which had emerged as the leading port for French exports to North America. Secondly, there was the antiquated method of financing French ports, in which the government, as central authority over the ports, charged *droits de quai* (on ships and cargo); and *taxes de péage* were levied by local Chambers of Commerce where they had been allowed to provide certain superstructural facilities under laws dating back to the turn of the century. Only Bordeaux, Le Havre, and Strasbourg were free of this dual control. Thirdly, the numerous French ports on the long isthmus coastline had been protected from international competition in the nineteenth century and first half of the twentieth by the very protectionism of French trade policies, particularly through exclusive sea links with French colonies. The process of decolonisation together with the progressive weakening of the internal boundaries of the European Economic Community had exposed French ports to the full force of European international transit trade. As a result, an Act was passed on 29 June 1965 establishing a new administrative structure for French ports. Six *ports autonomes* were set up (Bordeaux, Dunkirk, Le Havre, Marseilles, Nantes–St Nazaire, Rouen). This was a French version of 'autonomy', since there is no question of decentralising decisions of capital expenditure. The 'autonomous' port's Administrative Council has half its twenty-four members nominated by the state, as is the port's director who assists the Council. An important distinction is made in the matter of financing. Expenditure occurring at very infrequent and moderately infrequent intervals, or infrastructure provision is held as dependent on the natural features of the site and provides benefits for many generations. This is financed under the national budget. Superstructure facilities, like cargo-handling appliances, must be financed by the port in such a manner that the projects pay their way (J. P. Chapon, 1966). Here is the French solution to the problem of indivisibility of major port infrastructure projects [205], and also to the division of responsibility for long-term planning (the state), and intermediate- and short-term planning (the local authority) [217].

A. Cordesse (1968, 89) recommended that development ought to be concentrated on Dunkirk, Marseilles-Fos, and the ports of the lower Seine, and this was confirmed by the Social and Economic Council at Paris (A. Cordesse [Avis], 7). These three ports are close to the growth axis of the Community, from the Rhine through southwest Germany to north Italy. Here is a good example of port developmental strategy being conditioned strongly by land situation in an asymmetrical direction [23]. In particular, the development of Marseilles is an interesting variant on 'downstream development' [72].

From the ancient Vieux Port, Marseilles was forced to expand along the coast—a water encroaching site—protected by a mole parallel to the shore. The limit of this type of development was reached in 1960. Meanwhile, separate port development on the Etang de Berre was formally linked within the port in 1919, with a physical canal link in 1929. By these means Marseilles had expanded on to the deltaic area of the Rhône, making use of one of the lakes that deltaic distributaries frequently cut off from the gulfs they invade. No doubt the Gulf of Fos would have become a further étang, if the distributary that had formed the Port St Louis peninsula had been given time to close off that water area. Instead, two docks, 4,000 and 4,500 m long, are laid out with an industrial estate of 3,000 ha, a typical maritime industrial area (MIDA) [89]. The state is bearing 80% of the dredging costs (23·5 m depth for 130,000-ton deadweight vessels) and 60% of the costs of dock construction (B. S. Hoyle, 1960; H. D. Clout, 1968; and I. B. Thompson, 1970).

The main objectives of a national port plan for Spain in 1964 (*Plan de puertos 1964–7*) were to favour the concentration of external trade and to develop the specialisations of a reduced number of commercial ports, constructing quays for international traffic with at least ten metres alongside for break-bulk cargo, and twelve to thirteen metres for bulk loading. The policy of concentration [139] led to the ban on all new superstructure works at ports which dealt with less than 100,000 tons annually. The Spanish solution to the problem of the balance between the necessity for national strategic port planning and local autonomy veers towards centralisation. Three authorities are involved: the Ministerio de Obras Publicas in Madrid approves development projects and all matters relating to port installations; the Junta de Obras at each port receives its authority from the Madrid ministry, undertakes day-to-day decisions, and is responsible for maintenance dredging and general maintenance; finally, the Dirección de Puerto is the executive body in each port. There is thus some attempt to separate long- and short-term planning on the one hand [217]; and also to distinguish between infrastructure and superstructure decisions on the other [87 ff].

Following the above discussion, it might be assumed that European countries with few major ports, like the Netherlands, Belgium, and Portugal, would face fewer port planning problems compared with Britain, France, and Spain. Where there are only one or two ports in a country, problems of concentration and specialisation do not arise, but other problems may be present. The Rhine delta ports have had a spectacular tonnage increase in the decades following the Second World War, with Rotterdam at its apogee of success as the 1970s progress (J. Bird, 1967). But this port's great increase in tonnage since the inter-war years has been achieved by a great reliance on oil traffic, accounting for some 80% of all tonnage handled. The Dutch have seen great petrochemical complexes arise in the Botlek and Europort areas (H. Kuipers, 1962). These large-scale industries, financed by international share capital, are by no means labour intensive. It may appear by the end of the century that there is a broad division between seaboard capital-intensive industries and labour-intensive high value added industries which will be market-oriented [83] close to the inland conurbations of Europe, particularly in West Germany. The Netherlands may fall behind relatively in the establishment of such industries, with the country having to cope with the progressively rising cost of dealing with air and water pollution from the capital-intensive industries. Secondly, North Sea ports will not be able to receive tankers larger than about 275,000 tons deadweight fully laden. Should the next generation of tankers of supposedly minimum economic size for the transport of crude oil rise significantly above 275,000 tons, oil terminals at 'finisterre' locations will thrive [91] or more 'central terminal stations' will come into existence [90]. Finally, European ports like Marseilles, Lisbon, and Bordeaux have more forward positions for European trade with low latitude countries, and might profit if the cost of the land leg of international deep-sea transport were to fall because of rapidity of service.

In the case of Belgium, there is an interesting long-term investment dilemma for port planners. The alternatives are investment at Antwerp, or at Zeebrugge on the coast. Antwerp suffers from a twisting approach channel, and there are projects to replace the silt-prone sixty kilometres from the sea by a canal. Antwerp also plans to expand on to the left bank of the Scheldt. Both these plans depend on agreement with extra-Antwerp authorities. The lower Scheldt is in Dutch territory. In addition, the left bank of the Scheldt is in the province of East Vlaanderen, administered from the city of Ghent (K. W. Flitcroft, 1968, 214). Such is the penalty paid by a port which is administered by a municipality whose boundaries are not disposed over the whole of the potential port area [*199*]. The Zeestad project (M. Anselin, 1970, 26–9) would involve developing Zeebrugge for ships of 225,000 tons deadweight, with a canal accepting 125,000-ton ships to Antwerp's left bank, giving 26,600 ha of industrial sites. The project has been put forward accompanied by a cost-benefit analysis (*Le Projet Zeestad*, 1969) [*209*]. The decision as to which port gets the major developmental funds rests with the Brussels government, where the lobbying power of Antwerp must be formidable.

At Lisbon the cost of waterfront labour is very low, and this hardly stimulates mechanised cargo-handling development. There are insufficient demurrage charges, so that there is little incentive to clear transit sheds [*69*], and the port is hemmed in by urban development which makes spacious redevelopment difficult [*72*] (*General Cargo Handling in Three Efta Ports*, 1968, 38–44).

Fig. 17 shows the great contrast in the port scene in Poland before and after the Second World War and the triangle and the trapezium symbolise the different shapes of the national hinterland. The pre-war position is an extreme example of a centripetal type of coast [*23*], exacerbated not only by political factors but also by the fact that the chief Polish area for the generation of overseas cargo has always been some 300–500 kilometres from the coast. In the inter-war years Szczecin (Stettin) was cut off from Poland by a political and economic border, and within Germany its overseas trade was curtailed in favour of Hamburg; Szczecin later became very important to the Nazi war effort (B. Kasprowicz, 1963).

Fig. 17 A changed national hinterland: Poland

Above: Pre-1939. Gdansk (Danzig) was the only Polish outlet to the sea until 1928, when the 'free' city, directed from Berlin, indicated that no links with Poland were desired. Poland constructed the new port of Gdynia 15 kms from Gdansk. The chief area generating overseas trade is shown by a stippled polygon.

Below: Modern Poland. The chief area for generating overseas trade has expanded but is still distant from the ports; and the country no longer focusses centripetally on the exclusive Gdynia outlet.

Source: B. Kasprowicz, 1963, 5.

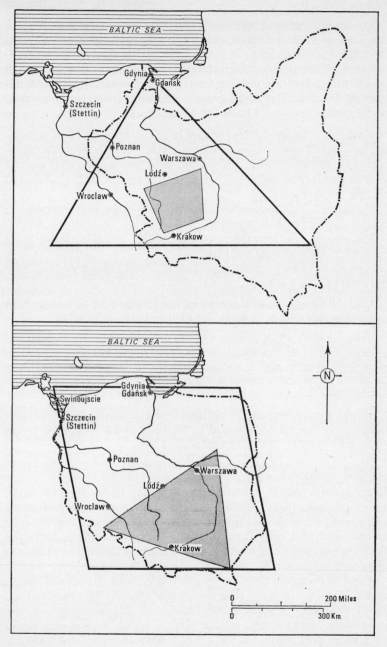

Fig. 17

The Polish national port plan (*The Economic Tasks of* [Polish] *Commercial Seaports,* 1960) adopts the principle that the total plans for traffic-handling in the ports should be higher than the mathematical sum of the economic projections. Presumably, this is to take account of unforeseen developments. In this connection four variations of the division of seven groups of cargo between the two sets of ports were adopted as a basis for planning.

Variation 1. This provides for a more or less equal division between the two sets of ports—Gdansk-Gdynia (GG) and Szczecin-Swinoujscie (SS). The proportion under this variation between GG and SS is respectively coal and coke, 1:1; ores, 2:3; grain, 3:2; timber, 1:2 to 1:3; break-bulk cargo, 2:0·9; and fuel, 1:2.

Variation 2. This puts more stress on SS in order to strengthen the transit position of Polish ports.

Variation 3. This puts the emphasis on GG, assuming a dominant increase in Poland's national trade.

Variation 4. This is a maximum plan assuming high growth in both national and transit trade.

Under Poland's planned economy, the existence of two major port areas does not permit of free competition between them.

... the stream of cargo is directed to a port in accordance with the national economy as a whole, due attention being paid to the economic advantages offered by the geographical situation. In this case there is competition only for transit goods, and even this can happen only on the borderline of states with a different socio-economic system. (E. Dobrzycki, 1963, 9)

It would appear that in the realm of port planning few important decisions in Poland are allowed to be made at an areal scale below national level [*227–8*] (T. Szczepaniak, 1968).

North American seaports

In these pages 'North America' is confined to the briefest survey of US ports, with three examples of major port problems, from the east and west coasts with one 'inland' port. In Canada there will be room to include a brief glance at east–west routes—the St Lawrence Seaway, and the idea of a land bridge, a concept that has applications elsewhere in the world.

The US possesses three long coastlines, with little tidal range, and plenty of places to construct ports cheaply (F. W. Herring, 1955). American ports have been developed extensively rather than intensively. Note the reasons given for the typical lay-out of a break-bulk cargo port before the advent of container berths and parks.

Piers were scattered from hither to yon and built, more often than not to serve one industry or one steamship company. Exclusive occupancy and exclusive use of piers in convenient locations seem to be the most important factors in our port growth. As a result, our piers had to be built on a more economical basis than those in Europe, for instance, where a high utilisation is possible. Finger piers, rather than marginal wharves [70–2] were built to consume as little of the relatively high-value water frontage as possible. (loc. cit., 92)

The author went on to explain that housefalls and burtoning [56] were developed to obviate expensive cranes, which would not have been possible on piers economically built with low load properties. Piers had narrow aprons and two decks to increase transit room. There were so many cheap installations that none could support costly cargo-handling appliances, and in any case a crane cannot compare with a housefall if the berth occupancy factor [62 ff] is as low as 25%.

As might be expected, the tonnage of almost all US coastal ports is dominated by petroleum, except for three ports: Tacoma, where wood products predominate; Mobile, alumina; and Galveston, sulphur. The Great Lake ports are differentiated because their trade is dominated by iron ore, coal, or crushed limestone, servants as they are of the US steel industry (R. E. Carter, 1962).

New York as leading break-bulk cargo port has been forced to expand on one of the annexes of the Hudson River in the State of New Jersey. Fortunately, the Port of New York Authority was established as a self-supporting corporate agency of both the States of New York and New Jersey by means of a 1921 treaty between them. Thus the port could expand away from the Hudson where there is no large area of flat land readily reclaimable as there was adjacent to Newark Bay (Fig. 18), in the State of New Jersey—a clear example of how port limits must not be shackled by local government boundaries [199]. The site of 371 hectares consisted of glacio-lacustrine deposits with subsequent organic sedimentation. Compressible organic silt and peat lie over silty sand and clay until the shale bedrock is reached at depths varying from 12 m to 30 m. There was no difficulty in hydraulic dredging, but the various types of wharf construction [53] had to be reviewed very carefully, and in view of the site conditions, the method chosen was a concrete relieving platform supported on timber piles. Where buildings or other heavy structures had to be placed on the compressible site behind the wharves, a preloading technique was used. This is simply a method which involves placing a surcharge fill on the area of substantially heavier weight

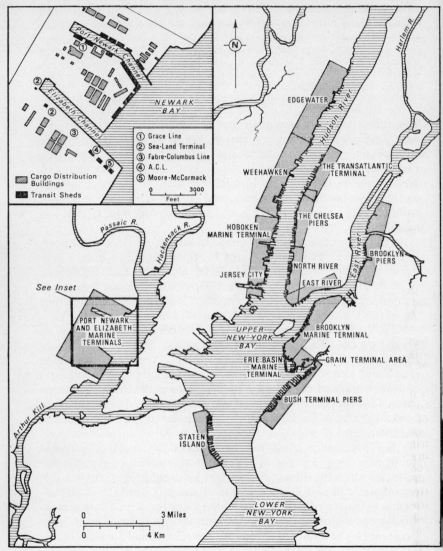

Fig. 18 Location of Port Newark and Elizabeth marine terminals within the Port of New York

than the eventual desired loading. There is room for twenty-five container berths by 1975.

New York has had a special problem as premier American passenger port. In 1965, 902,000 passengers used the port, 515,000 crossing the Atlantic, and there were 387,000 cruise passengers (*A Plan for a New Consolidated Terminal*, etc., 1967). The 1967 plan forecast that these numbers would rise to 850,000 in 1985, only 310,000 transatlantic, and 540,000 cruise passengers. Since passenger-handling in the port had been notoriously slow and uncomfortable, partly owing to the unsuitable pier sheds, but also to a US law requiring every piece of baggage to be examined, the Port of New York Authority had to plan a complex of nine berths, allowing four passenger ships to be dealt with simultaneously if necessary. It must be emphasised that 1985 passenger through-puts were not arrived at by straight line extrapolations of trends; and it may be of interest to list below the very varied factors that were allowed to modify the forecasts up or down:

(1) price comparability on transatlantic route sea/air;
(2) price comparability of cruises versus air travel to Miami and a stay in a de luxe hotel;
(3) rise in disposable income of the inhabitants of the north-eastern US;
(4) ships being built and likely to be in service in 1985.

This last factor proved to be the most powerful in reducing the cruise passenger total from the straight line forecast of 740,000 to 540,000 per annum, and for increasing the transatlantic forecast from 290,000 to 310,000. This is a special and vivid example of how port planning follows developmental planning of a sector of the world's fleet [*195*], and the port engineer comes last in line since he has to design the structure required by the port plan.

At San Francisco, consultants recommended a major locational shift in port activities from outmoded finger piers in the northern waterfront area (equivalent to the dock elaboration era [*70*]) to the India Basin at the southern end of the port (*Port of San Francisco: an in-depth Study*, 1968). An interesting feature is that when the northern Embarcadero loses its cargo liners, commercial and recreational development will supervene and help finance new port construction. This exemplifies how a more intensive type of land and water use is able to oust a less intensive use [*72*]. In physical planning terms the port function no longer requires a central urban position, and its removal from the centre reduces congestion for other functions.

The inland port of Houston has risen to third port of the US in terms of tonnage of cargo. The extent of Houston's development is at first sight astonishing considering its original site at the ultimate head of navigation, for vessels drawing not more than three or four feet of water, on a shallow stream (or bayou) fifty miles inland from the Gulf of Mexico. Houston's growth could be presented as a narrative of the success achieved by a series of men with initiative, and the actors themselves believed this to be the reason.

There was a time when it was thought that San Felipe, Velasco, and San Luis [Texan river or Gulf settlements] would become large towns, and why did they not? They were well situated—their owners lacked enterprise. Compare the two towns of Columbus and Houston;—the one situated at the head of tidewater on the largest river in the State, in the centre of the richest planting section in the world—the other on a shallow Bayou, naturally incapable of navigation to any extent, surrounded by post oak and pine barrens and boggy prairies—one has all the advantages of situation [and site] [29] the other of an energetic people. (*Tri-Weekly Telegraph*, 13 April, 1857, quoted by M. M. Sibley, 1968, 76)

But a port or a city cannot lift itself by its own bootstraps without a consensus of views that it will be successful, and these factors have been grouped under the term 'proclaimed impulse' [24]. In Houston's case, two of the factors were self-proclaimed. The very name attracted attention, riding on the hero-worship of the victor of San Jacinto. Secondly, the original promoters understood the value of self-proclamation; Houston was the only new town so advertised in the Telegraph and Texas Register during the critical final months of 1836 and so won the battle to become the first capital of Texas.

In the railway era Houston benefited at the expense of the gulf port of Galveston because the adoption of the Corporate Railway Plan, another form of the proclaimed impulse, made Houston a node of the trans-continental system, whereas the unsuccessful State Plan would have focussed state railroads on Galveston. By 1918 the Petroleum Refining Company had a refinery on the north side of the Ship Channel dredged to the bay. After the Second World War came the establishment of the petrochemical industry, with the final industrial accolade awarded by the National Aeronautics and Space Administration, and how that bayou had been transformed!

Chief among these [advantages] was the fact that Houston's Ship Channel and port facilities provided an excellent means of transporting bulky space vehicles to other NASA locations, especially to Cape Canaveral [now Cape Kennedy]. (S. B. Oates, quoted by M. M. Sibley, 1968, 206)

Montreal exhibits problems of comprehensive city planning of the central downtown waterfront area, and the future of the port resides in sites eight to twenty-four kilometres downstream. The inland route of the St Lawrence Seaway has two features of particular interest affecting Montreal: an approach to the labour problem and the competition from other modes of transport. This second feature involves consideration of a wider topic—the idea of land bridges.

In 1966 the Shipping Federation of Canada and the Canadian International Longshoremen's Association agreed in advance to accept the findings of an inquiry commission on operational problems such as productivity and guarantees of employment. As a result dockers at Montreal secured a guaranteed standard work week's employment for thirty-seven weeks, since the port is inactive during the winter freeze-up. The extent of the guarantee was made dependent on the maintenance of productivity. The standard work week is fixed at forty hours if productivity is equal to that of 1964. If productivity falls below that level, the hourly guarantee falls by a sliding scale to thirty-five hours, corresponding to a productivity only 88 % of that of 1964. The guarantees are covered by a Job Security Fund fed by payments from employers. Corresponding guarantees have been worked out for Quebec and Trois Rivières. The basic idea is that guarantees about employment and income are exchanged for the abandonment of certain work practices leading to flexibility in the use of waterfront labour [60] (*Report of the Inquiry Commission*, etc., 1967).

The Seaway is basically an east–west route extended by the Great Lakes, and as such it faces competition from the railway over part or most of its length. A container service operating through Halifax can serve hinterlands such as Montreal, Toronto, and Hamilton by means of Canadian National Railways' 200-container capacity unit trains, an example of the unit train versus the container ship [*163*]. The international Association of Great Lakes Ports has complained that the CNR has filed a tariff on export-import containers of 1·14 cents per ton-mile between Montreal and Toronto–Hamilton, and this compares with 1·89 cents for traffic originating domestically. The container rate looks like a loss-leader to undercut Seaway shipping, which also faces a rise in toll costs, since the Seaway is required to liquidate its capital cost within fifty years—a 'pay your way' requirement.

And yet they don't apply the same logic to other areas. Dredging is carried out in many parts of Canada without charge to the direct users. It's considered a national benefit and absorbed by the economy as a whole. Why

F

stop when you get to the Seaway and Ontario? (J. H. Jones, President of the International Association of Great Lakes Ports, 1969)

This is part of a recurring debate on port economics: either ports are completely self-financing or subsidised in some way because they create external economies and are in this respect at least to be regarded as national assets, especially as regards their dredged approaches [204].

A container service using a rail haul via Halifax–Montreal could be said to be using a half-span land bridge, and the same applies to Far East and African imports to Toronto and Montreal via Vancouver (R. Robinson, 1967, Fig.3.5). The land bridge concept involves a through transport movement using a land haul to connect two sea legs of the complete route. Three major land bridge sites have emerged: Far East to Europe, via the trans-Siberian railway; in Israel, Ashdod on the Mediterranean coast to Elath on the Gulf of 'Aqaba, the only land bridge using road transport, on a nine-hour trip via Beersheba; and, most notably, across the North American continent for Far East–Europe traffic, avoiding the Panama Canal. The land bridge full span within inter-continental routes depends on a number of factors: the proportion of higher rated cargo carried on the route; the differential freight rates between unit trains and container ships; the savings in time translated into cost savings because of less goods in the pipeline and revealed by inventory costs savings; organisational problems involved in transhipment, matching train and ship schedules, and documentation simplification; and the willingness of shipowners to service the land bridge. Some of the savings were revealed by trial shipments via the Euro-Asian land bridge commencing in 1967, travelling 12,000 kilometres across eight countries from Japan, using the Russian port of Nakhodka. This saves some 20 days on the 50–60-day Yokohama–Europe door-to-door route by sea.

A forerunner of the half-span land bridge in the nineteenth century was effected by the so-called 'silk trains'. The high value of Japanese silk, its fluctuating market, and its liability to deterioration in transit made it necessary to have it delivered as soon as possible on the New York market. Canadian Pacific Railroad ordered fast ships for the Pacific run, and the silk was transferred to express transcontinental trains, being delivered to New York thirteen days after leaving Japan (H. A. Mann, 1969a, 13–14). This idea of the half-span land bridge may well become more important in North America whereby goods from the Far East are landed on the Pacific Coasts for forwarding by unit train perhaps right across the continent; and in the reverse direction European traffic landed on the Atlantic Coast would be onward delivered west. This emphasises the importance of route orientation for hinterland definition [140]. Reverse directions would of course be taken by exports (H. A. Mann, 1969b, 13). For the half-span land bridge, only one port transhipment is necessary, and it should be easier to organise since the span and destination are within the same country, or continent. The consultants McKinsey and Company Inc. estimated in 1967 that a 1,200-container capacity vessel was only cheaper than unit trains when the route was longer than 3,300 miles (*Containerization*, etc., 1967, 30). Although the US West Coast to the East Coast is 6,000 miles via Panama, it is only 3,000 miles by train, saving about six days, even if 25-knot ships are used on the all-water route.

Turning to the concept of the full land bridge across North America, the first consideration is the savings of distance which are matters of fact; then comes the deduced savings of time and cost which are matters of estimate.

TABLE 18

DISTANCE COMPARISON: HAMBURG TO YOKOHAMA
(sea, via Suez, 24,430; Panama, 23,694)

	all distances in km via					
	Halifax–Vancouver	*St John–Vancouver*	*Quebec–Vancouver*	*Montreal–Vancouver*	*New York–Seattle*	*New York–San Francisco, Oakland*
Atlantic	5,416	5,885	5,664	5,992	6,719	6,719
North American Continent	5,873	5,384	4,888	4,631	4,670	5,149
Pacific	7,897	7,897	7,897	7,897	8,162	8,405
TOTAL	19,186	19,166	18,449	18,520	19,551	20,273

N.B. 1 nautical mile = 1·853 km
      1 land mile   = 1·609 km
Source: H. A. Mann, 1969b.

Estimates of the time saving on the Japan–Europe route via the land bridge compared with the all-sea route vary from seven days

(H. P. Schneider, 1968) to five days (H. A. Mann, 1969b, 12); but both agree that the real saving is in the interest charges of goods not in the transport pipeline. A. E. Gibson, 1969, calculates that the savings in time disappear when 26-knot ships are used on the all-sea route.

TABLE 19

US FULL-SPAN LAND BRIDGE *v*. ALL-SEA ROUTE

	Time in days				
	20-knot ship (900 containers)		26-knot ship (1200 containers)		Dollars per 20 ft container
	All water	Land bridge	All water	Land bridge	
Yokohama to Rotterdam	28·8	—	21·3	—	1,100
Yokohama to W. coast US	—	10·9	—	8·1	721
Ship/railroad transfer time	—	2·0	—	2·2	—
W. coast to E. coast US	—	3·2	—	3·2	186
Railroad/ship transfer time	—	2·0	—	2·2	—
E. coast US to Rotterdam	—	7·7	—	5·7	553
TOTAL	28·8	25·8	21·3	21·4	1,460
RATE DIFFERENCE					360

Source: A. E. Gibson, 1969.

If US railroads reduced rates to make the land bridge competitive with the all-water route Japan–Europe, then they would face a potential loss in domestic revenues, and this would be a factor against the quotation of lower rail rates. The *New York Journal of Commerce* (13 May 1968) sounded two further notes of caution. If non-Japanese vessels are used exclusively on the Atlantic leg of the Japan–Europe route, Japanese shipping would lose much ton-mileage, and because shipping carriage is an important contributor to the Japanese balance of payments, the Tokyo Transport and Finance Ministries might consider the land bridge concept a threat to their country. It has also been estimated that there will be an imbalance of trade, twice as much cargo moving east-about as westbound. Finally jumbo jets may well cream off more of the higher value per unit of weight cargo, the very merchandise that would give the greatest saving by reduction of time in the transport pipeline.

Containers have made their impact on every major north American port, with no coordinated provision on the US coasts, as has been the traditional free-for-all manner of US port development. Competition between ports is perhaps fiercest in the US compared with any other developed country. As break-bulk cargo becomes concentrated on the most successful container berths, over-provision of break-bulk cargo installations elsewhere will become ever more apparent. On the other hand, the industrial role of US seaports will increase—well exemplifying the dual approach of this study and its title.

Anselin, M. (1970) *Les fonctions des ports belgiques et les projets d'investissement.* Paper read at Semaine de Bruges, April. Bruges: College of Europe.
Beckett, A. H. (1969) An international transhipment roadstead, *The Dock and Harbour Authority*, **50**, 157–8.
Bird, J. (1963) *The Major Seaports of the United Kingdom.* London: Hutchinson.
——(1967) Seaports and the European Economic Community, *Geographical Journal*, **133**, 302–27.
Carter, R. E. (1962) A comparative analysis of United States ports and their traffic characteristics, *Economic Geography*, **38**, 162–80.
Chapon, J. P. (1966) The recent changes in French port administration, *The Dock and Harbour Authority*, **46**, 345–8.
Clout, H. D. (1968) Expansion projects for French seaports, *Tijdschrift voor economische en sociale geografie*, **59**, 271–7.
Containerization: the Key to Low-cost Transportation (1967). British Transport Docks Board: Report by McKinsey and Company Inc.
Cordesse, A. (1968) *Rapport sur l'adaptation des ports français aux nouvelles exigences du trafic et à la concurrence du Marché Commun.* Paris: Conseil Economique et Social, 26 March, and *Avis* [on the above, same date].
Dagnino, G. (1970) *Notes schématiques pour un rapport d'orientation sur certains problèmes de la situation portuaire italienne.* Paper delivered at Semaine de Bruges, April. Bruges: College of Europe.
Dobrzycki, E. (1963) *The Role of the Port of Szczecin in the Economic Organisms of Germany and Poland.* Poznan.
Economic Tasks of [Polish] Commercial Seaports up to 1980, The (1960) Draft directives of the Commission appointed by the Polish Ministry of Shipping. Warsaw-Gdansk.
Evans, A. A. (1969) *Technical and Social Changes in the World's Ports.* Geneva: ILO.
Flitcroft, K. W. (1968) Antwerp's left bank development scheme, *The Dock and Harbour Authority*, **49**, 213–14.
Gatti, L. (1967) *Italian Ports vis-à-vis the Development of Containerisation.* Paper read at First International Conference on Containerisation, Genoa, 19–21 October.
General Cargo Handling in Three Efta Ports (1968). Geneva: European Free Trade Association.
Gibson, A. E. (1969) Land bridge—fact or fiction, *ICHCA Journal*, **3**, 14–23.

Herring, F. W. (1955) US port organization and its effect on cargo handling, *Progress in Cargo Handling*, **1**, 35–9.

Hoyle, B. S. (1960) The Etang de Berre—recent port expansion and associated industrial development at Marseilles, *Tijdschrift voor economische en sociale geografie*, **51**, 57–65.

Kasprowicz, B. (1963) *The Polish Seaports*. Poznan.

Kuipers, H. (1962) The changing landscape of the Island of Rozenburg (Rotterdam Port Area), *Geographical Review*, **52**, 362–78.

Mann, H. A. (1969a) The land-bridge concept, *Shipping Register and Shipbuilder*, **52**, 11–14.

——(1969b) The Canadian land-bridge, *Ports and Harbours*, **14**, 7–14.

Miller, I. S. (1968) *The British General Cargo Ports*. Unpublished Ph.D. thesis. University of Lancaster.

Plan de puertos 1964–67—Memoria—Plan de desarallo economico y social. Madrid: Dirección General de Puertos y Señales Maritimas.

Plan for a New Consolidated Terminal for the Port of New York, A (1967) Port of New York Authority.

Plowman, E. G. (1967) *The situation in North America*. Paper submitted to Interregional Seminar on Containerisation, etc., organised by United Nations in co-operation with UK Government, 1–12 May.

Poirier, L. (1963) Situation et problèmes des ports de commerce de l'Europe occidentale, *Journal de la Marine Marchande*, **14**, 38–91.

Port of San Francisco—an in-depth Study (1968) Report by Arthur D. Little Inc.

Ports of the Americas: History and Development (1961) American Association of Port Authorities Inc.

Projet Zeestad, Le: analyse de ses possibilités techniques de réalisation et de son interêt économique (1969). Brussels: Banque de Paris et des Pays Bas.

Reorganisation of the Ports, The (1969) London: HMSO [Government White Paper], Cmnd. 3903.

Report of the Committee of Inquiry into the Major Ports of Great Britain [Rochdale Report] (1962) London: HMSO, Cmnd. 1824.

Report of the Inquiry Commission on the St Lawrence Ports (1967) Ottawa: mimeographed.

Robinson, R. (1967) *Spatial Patterns of Port-linked Flows: General Cargo Imports through the Port of Vancouver, 1965*. University of British Columbia: Department of Geography. Mimeographed.

Sibley, M. M. (1968) *The Port of Houston: a History*. Austin: University of Texas Press.

Sobisch, H. (1970) *Facilities and Development Programme of the Port of Hamburg*. Paper delivered at Semaine de Bruges, April. Bruges: College of Europe.

Szczepaniak, T. (1968) The Polish model of port administration and organisation of the port services, *Fifth International Harbour Congress*, 2–8 June. Antwerp. Paper 8.1.

Thompson, I. B. (1970) *Modern France: a Social and Economic Geography*. London: Butterworth.

7

SEAPORTS EXEMPLIFYING GENERALISATIONS (II):

AFRICA, MIDDLE EAST, ASIA, AND

THE SOUTHERN CONTINENTS*

Some problems of developing countries with prominent reference to African seaports

The first ports discussed in this chapter are in developing countries, and the major question is the extent to which containerisation will penetrate their seaborne trade. From the established trans-ocean container services between developed countries, it can be deduced that the shipping operator is the innovator of a through service which involves inland transport. A. O. Hirschman has called such a developmental spread a 'trickling-down' effect (1958, 193–4), and this is especially apt for major seaports in developing countries for they are all linked directly with the highly developed world. But it would be unwise to extend seaport theory to developing countries without some preliminary comment.

Manufacturers 'tropicalise' an existing product to save the research costs, development time, and special facilities involved in fashioning a totally new product or range of products, one for each country. (J. M. Blaut, 1967, 201–2)

Accordingly, this opening section is designed to avoid the charge of mere theory tropicalisation. But there is hardly space to discuss the problems of each country, and cross-reference between general theory and tropical facts will continue wherever that seems useful.

* As in Chapter 6, where a particular illustration of a general point is made elsewhere in another chapter, an italicised page number in square brackets gives the appropriate reference.

R. G. Williams, 1969, is optimistic about the world-wide spread of container traffic, whereas D. Hilling, 1969b, while not being pessimistic, is realistic about the problems in a West African context. It is over-simple to say that a debate has emerged over container spread, yet there does appear to be a gap between what is eventually possible in the long term and what is practical in the early 1970s. Perhaps these contrasts can be brought out by considering the topic from a succession of viewpoints—technical, economic, social, and political.

Many railroads of tropical countries are of insufficient gauge to take the eight-foot wide container; many roads are unsurfaced, becoming impassable in the rainy season. The past colonial history of some developing countries has left them with dual economies in which compact urban areas adjacent to the ports are backed by undeveloped inland areas, 'islands of modernity surrounded by a sea of traditional activity' (W. A. Hance, V. Kotschar, and R. J. Peterec, 1961, 495 ff.; and W. A. Hance, 1967, 5). Containerisation could be adapted to such a pattern but might further unbalance the areal spread of development throughout such a country, especially where B. S. Hoyle's model African *cityport* attains its final 'nothing succeeds like success' stage (1970b, 10 and 12–13). W. P. Hedden, 1967, 17, has pointed out that a container berth is basically an area of hard standing alongside deep water and could be used for bulk cargoes if container traffic does not materialise (see also R. A. Sandford, 1964; and A. H. Earley in *Conference on Unitisation*, 1967, 33). If the lifting appliances are mobile, they can be moved to another part of the port if necessary. Specialised fixed container handling appliances are costly mistakes if not regularly used. R. G. Williams, 1969, suggests a first stage for movement of containers in which they are shipped in conventional vessels. This was the case with the 'African Container Express', started in 1965 by a consortium of Elder Dempster Lines, the Nigerian National Line, and the Palm Line, serving several African ports and notably one of the berths of the Apapa Quay, Lagos, the first specialised container berth in Africa. Captain Williams sees the use of the roller-jack as an important factor in this stage since this device allows more containers to be stowed 'tween decks on conventional ships. He also points out that small module containers bonded within twenty-foot frames could be used on routes where cargo is generated in rather small consignments. Conventional vessels would first unload their containers at the port's heavy lift berth, and then proceed to a conventional berth to unload the rest of the non-containerised break-bulk cargo. D. Hilling, 1969b, 13, sees the barge-aboard-ship system [102] as avoiding these difficulties since the lift is incorporated in the ship, and the container in the form of the barge can float to small feeder ports along coasts or up rivers. Advice on all such technical points in the planning of port installations and services can be given to interested governments by the Technical Assistance Branch of the UN Development Programme.

Governments of developing countries have to consider the opportunity cost of port improvements for unit traffic, bearing in mind the commodity mix of their seaborne trade. Very often this is made up of non-containerisable exports: bulk minerals, packaged timber, and food crops, such as cocoa. Five-sixths of West Africa's exports are in the form of bulk cargoes. Most of the imports could arrive in containers, but as import substitution spreads, such a high proportion might diminish. On a long-term view, as developing countries become more industrialised their cargo generation for containers would increase. If containers became dominant, trade on a tariff basis of FAK (freight all kinds) might become the rule. In this situation where rates are charged per container rather than per commodity class, this is to the disadvantage of developing countries with exports of a much lower value per unit of weight than imports, and thus having to bear a higher value proportion of transport costs in total CIF [203]. The United Nations Conference on Trade and Development (UNCTAD, Geneva) is concerned that if a developing country makes improvement to its port or ports, so that faster turnround or berth through-puts are possible, then such benefits are retained within the country. In practice, the whole route receives the benefit of the cost reduction, including the ship operator; and conferences often average rates over a group of ports so that the reduced cost of serving one port is spread over many ports, some of which may be in a country that has not bothered to improve berth facilities (*Development of Ports*, 1969, 6) [213].

Under a social heading it may be noted that some ports in developing countries have labour-intensive port handling, and though turnround may be slow, labour costs are also low. Nevertheless, H. J. Molenaar, 1967, deduced that containerisation would spread very slowly to such ports [116]. Displacement of waterfront labour would be a problem with the introduction of unit loads since labour is with great difficulty absorbed elsewhere in economies of developing countries (*Symposium*, etc., 1966, 14, 41). This disadvantage would have to be traded off against cheaper imports and exports and a contribution to the balance of payments. The remaining manpower would have to be much more skilled, not only because of mechanical handling, but because of the higher tempo of work involving more dangerous lifts of twenty tons or more instead of literally manhand-

F*

ling cargo (J. Mudugi in *Conference on Unitisation*, 1967, para 22).
The political difficulties of developing countries in implementing
unit services derive from the proliferation of states, each wishing for
a place in the developmental sun. This has sometimes led to establishing a new national port, e.g. 'Aqaba for Jordan' (P. Hindle, 1966,
and B. Nagorski, 1968, 42–3), and some duplication of port facilities
such as the new ports of Cotonou in Dahomey, 1965, and Lomé for
Togo, 1967 (D. Hilling, 1969a) though rail connections to both
these new ports could not accept 20 ft containers. Where a number
of political boundaries lie transverse to the coast, a pattern often
inherited from a colonial system developed from port bridgeheads,
lateral connections are weakly developed compared with routes
directly inland. This also occurs in the 'developing yet developed'
continent of Australia (J. Bird, 1968, 177–8). Regional grouping of
states for regional planning of transport is therefore difficult,
although this is desirable to meet the concentration of port facilities
that containerisation often implies. An interesting yet isolated
example of such international cooperation is concerned with the
port of Pointe Noire where Congo-Brazzaville, Gabon, the Central
African Republic, and Chad have formed an autonomous international transport agency called *Agence Trans-Equatoriale des
Communications*, responsible for the management of the port and for
the hinterland serving the port. This seems a hopeful pointer to the
solution of some of the political problems of Africa where there are
no less than fourteen landlocked states, relying on seaboard gateways
in other nations (B. Nagorski, 1968, 42).

Recently, there has become available a valuable collection of fourteen essays on seaports and development in tropical Africa (B. S.
Hoyle and D. Hilling, eds., 1970). In their opening paper the editors
recognise certain common characteristics of tropical African ports—
a period of colonial control, and a highly imbalanced trade, both in
cargo kind and in the manner that exports far outweighed imports.
Hinterland transport nets were built not primarily to serve this unbalanced trade but generally to serve administrative convenience so
that the fragmented political pattern of Africa is reflected in a fragmented transport network pattern. A particular example of this is
the excellent harbour of Freetown which has yet to reach full
economic potential because of its small economic hinterland restricted to the exiguous territory of Sierra Leone [227] (J. McKay, in
Hoyle and Hilling, op. cit.).

This general economic and political situation distinguishes port developments in the tropics from those in more advanced countries where port
growth generally takes the form of a gradual evolution [68] with the

result that the ports inherit centuries of experience and the advantage of hinterlands with a high technological level and relatively abundant supplies of capital for investment. . . . Developing countries must be prepared to break the vicious circle in which port developments are postponed until increased traffic provides an obvious economic justification [*88*] but traffic cannot be further increased until port facilities are extended. (Hoyle and Hilling, op. cit., 5)

B. Ogundana (1966 and in Hoyle and Hilling, op. cit.) adds a useful dimension to the changing relative status of ports, with special reference to Nigeria. He shows that port growth models which rely on a concentration of trade at fewer ports [*Fig. 14* and *132*] ought to be supplemented by an account of circumstances leading to what he calls *port diffusion*. This occurs when leading ports decline, absolutely or relatively, as new ports arise to serve new trades or part of an existing trade. He uses A. Hirschman's index of trade concentration to measure port concentration or diffusion. This technique was used in connection with the concentration of commodities in a single port's cargo make-up by J. N. H. Britton [*144*].

$$I = \sqrt{P_1{}^2 + P_2{}^2 + \ldots P_n{}^2}$$

where P_1 is the total trade handled by the port in question. Consistent decline in the value of the index through time gives statistical indication of port diffusion. The era of the impact of European colonisation on the West African coast was such a time; increasing technical efficiency may promote concentration [*132*]; while political fragmentation of hinterlands and the entry into seaborne trade of low value per unit of weight bulk cargoes may lead to port diffusion.

One last example from an emergent African country may be taken from the development of Tunis-La Goulette, a port which handles half of the seaborne trade of Tunisia, a country of 4 million people. This port exemplifies a fascinating interplay of site factors with increasing size of ships [*33*]. The entrance to the port from the Mediterranean is at La Goulette, not far from the ancient port of Carthage, and this was the port of sailing ships. But with the development of land communications, especially the railroad, the transport focus for government and commercial functions became established at Tunis, 10 km inland west of La Goulette. Accordingly, in 1893, a ship channel was dredged with a depth of 9 m, but it was difficult to maintain, and by 1962 the ruling draught was 7½ m with the banks subject to erosion by the wash of ships. The Tunis port basin is also subject to silting due to the inflow of storm sewers and is sited on soft plastic clay which makes the founding of heavy quay walls very difficult. A new quay, part of a Tunis port expansion programme, ruptured in 1950. These accumulated reasons lay behind the 1964 decision to develop La Goulette as the main area for deep-sea vessels aided by a World Bank loan. The modern development of Tunis– La Goulette is thus a reversal of the late nineteenth-century plan, dictated by the increased average size of vessels (W. P. Hedden, 1967, 240, 250).

After an example of interplay between components of an individual port, interplay between separate ports on the same coast may be briefly cited. The port of Haifa was built with British capital during the period of the Palestine mandate (B. Menzinger, 1966). When this new deep-water port was opened in 1933, the trade of Beirut suffered immediately, so this port was thereupon declared a free port in order to attract transit trade (R. C. d. Lega, 1957, 22–6). As far as the Mediterranean coast was concerned, the independent state of Israel found itself equipped with one deep-water port in the north and the shallow draught lighterage ports of Tel Aviv and Jaffa where, as at Haifa, built-up area presses close to the port area restricting upland development [72]. Most importantly, a new deep-water port was required to serve the developing south of the country, especially the citrus fruit exporting area with centre of production in the Rehovot district twenty kilometres south-east of Tel Aviv. Potash from the Dead Sea and phosphates mined from the Negev indicated that the bulk of mineral exports would also lie close to a point on the coast well south of Tel Aviv. The site chosen for the new port was the estuary of the River Lakish, some thirty kilometres south of Tel Aviv. But the site was chosen mainly for the flat area adjacent to the coast since the river is a dry wadi throughout most of the year. The coast is straight, like the rest of Israel's Mediterranean coast except for the embayment at Haifa. The sea bed was free from rock, but artificial protection had to be provided on the straight open coast. The location of Ashdod was thus first conditioned by features of land situation (the areas of origin of export cargoes), and then by the feature of land site (flat terrain alongside the coast). The water site (harbour) had to be constructed and protected. (For interplay of site and situation see [29] and *Ashdod*, etc., 1961.) This involved heavy capital expenditure, and W. P. Hedden (1967, 177–213) recommended that the interest charges at Ashdod should be supported by sharp increases in the port dues on the established trade of Haifa, where the capital cost had already largely been paid for by the British. Such cross-financing suggested the need for a national body to oversee the country's ports, and was a major reason for the foundation of the Israel Ports Authority. The first ships entered the harbour of Ashdod in 1966, and 11·5 m of water depth are available. Two other points may be noted. The seasonal nature of the fruit exports from Ashdod has led the Israel Ports Authority to formulate the concept of seasonal planning, or 'intermediate planning' [*218*], of a port's activities. Secondly, the extreme political segregation between Israel and the Arab States and the closure of the Suez Canal has resulted in many cargoes from Middle East countries being shipped overland via Saudi Arabia to Beirut to avoid the long haul around the Cape.

Asia and the Far East

The description ECAFE countries (UN Economic Commission for Asia and the Far East) covers the same area as included in this section, but also includes Australia and New Zealand. The highly developed maritime country of Japan is thus banded with several countries where maritime trade is very small. ECAFE countries are involved in about one-third of the world's seaborne trade, but possess only about one-eighth of the world merchant fleet, and nearly three-quarters of this one-eighth belongs to Japan (S. M. Husain, 1967). With the exception of this one country, there emerges a picture of a vast Asian area with ports and hinterlands repeating the pattern found in developing countries and mentioned with special reference to Africa. Long-distance container services first entered the ECAFE area from outside in 1969 with the inauguration of the Europe–Australia service, and within the area Japan has become the focus for trans-Pacific services. Sydney, Melbourne, and Yokohama have emerged as the first container pivot ports [*120*]. Further contenders for such a role appear to be Hong Kong, Singapore, and a port in Ceylon. The container vessels are largely owned by consortia based outside the area, and the selection of container bases is usually outside the control of the governments within the area. This exotic technological impulse merely mirrors the exotic proclaimed impulses that founded the majority of Asian port cities. As R. Murphey, 1964, 240, points out, the indigenous Asian city is usually to be found inland; Asian port cities were rare before the advent of Europeans who were the first to recognise the commercial opportunities of maritime outlets.

One result was that the new port cities which arose, of which Calcutta was the pioneer and prototype, were dominated by Western traders as in effect outposts of the booming world of commercial/industrial Europe . . . (loc. cit.)

The introduction in that preceding paragraph suggests a wide agenda, and this selective survey concentrates first on the India–Pakistan sub-continent, then on the particularly fascinating port of

Hong Kong, before attempting to deal briefly with the maritime phenomenon of Japan.

Many basic features of Indian seaports are revealed in the following table.

TABLE 20

ESTIMATED INCREASE IN TRAFFIC OF MAJOR INDIAN SEAPORTS
DURING THE FOURTH FIVE-YEAR PLAN

	Million tons	
	1967–8	*1973–4*
Bombay	16·75	21·30
Calcutta	8·99	17·43
Madras	5·84	11·69
Cochin	5·42	7·73
Visakhapatnam	6·61	14·08
Kandla	2·47	3·93
Marmugao	8·12	11·27
Paradip	0·90	4·43
Mangalore	—	2·24
Tuticorin	—	2·66
TOTAL	55·10	96·76*
		(70% bulk; 31% iron ore)

* In addition, another 3 million tons of foodgrains is expected to be handled by Indian ports.

Source: V. K. R. V. Rao, 1969, 14.

First, one notes the large number of ports dealing with more than one million tons of traffic, as might be expected given India's population and the very long coastline of 2,900 miles. Indeed there are no less than another 165 working ports. Secondly, there is the forecast large proportional rise in tonnage, symptomatic of emergent maritime nations, using that phrase to mean emerging fully into international currents of trade. Alongside the old-established major break-bulk ports, new ports are developed to deal with bulk cargoes, particularly iron ore. Such ports as Visakhapatnam and Paradip have been equipped with bulk-loading berths rated at 2,000 tons per hour compared with the minor ports' performance of 2,000 tons per day.

An international study team reported on Indian ports in 1968 (*Study Team Report on the Major Ports of India*). They noted that the largest class of tanker that could be berthed at Indian ports was 35,000 tons deadweight, and they suggested that the 'Shell' system should be investigated. This functions in a way somewhat similar to the so-called 'central terminal station' [90], where large super-tankers are discharged offshore into smaller tankers which have been equipped with a system of fenders, nose cradles, hoisting gear, and oil transfer hose. There are advantages for India in establishing such facilities for both the east and west coasts. At Bombay the team criticised the multi-functional nature of the Nhava Sheva port expansion scheme where bulk and break-bulk cargo-handling were planned in close proximity. The team thought the plan overly ambitious, no doubt realising that if container trade were to develop the principle of 'expansion [of trade] in reduction [of area]' [*119*] would be likely to apply. The team also noted that lessees of the port could not easily be displaced even when port areal expansion was vital, and this underlines the necessity for a port to be master in its own house [*199*] (op. cit., 117–21). At Calcutta, the team thought that the long-term problem of the Hooghly would involve development downstream, as at *Anyport* [*68*], to Haldia. But again there seemed to be a barrier to long-term expansion with a dry-dock and other non-cargo handling facilities, including even a port housing project, planned for areas in which future berth expansion might lie (op. cit., 130–1).

A major recommendation of the study team was to institute a degree of centralised planning (including a nationalised dredging fleet to save foreign exchange) to avoid proliferation of new berths with low occupancy factors. This advice seems to have been heeded.

While . . . [it] is undoubtedly true that the necessary infrastructure of port facilities and other equipment have to precede development of the country's trade and economy and all the ports on our long coastline will have to be ultimately developed, in the present stage of our developing economy and stringency of financial resources, on clearly practical considerations it would be more feasible that efforts are concentrated on provision of facilities at a few selected ports which have an already developed trade, inland transport and other facilities or which hold promise of such a development in the near future rather than disperse our limited resources over a wider range to meet the possible long-term requirements. These have to wait till the resources position improves or until the hinterland is adequately developed and adequate volume of trade is generated to warrant the extension of the facilities. (V. K. R. V. Rao, 1969, 17)

The area now known as East Pakistan vividly exemplifies the importance of political dictates in the choice of port outlet sites. The following bald summary (based on Q. H. Siddiqui, 1967) shows the contrasting power impingement on the Ganges delta.

16th century   Portuguese style Chittagong 'porte grand' in contradistinction to their port classification 'porte pequeno' (small port).

1690   English permanently establish their stronghold at

	Calcutta, and as they gain ascendancy the major part of East Bengal traffic flows through this port. (A typical example of a colonial *port* in contrast to an indigenous Asian regional centre established inland, R. Murphey, loc. cit.)
1947	Partition, and foundation of Pakistan. Chittagong the only East Pakistan port, and much of Pakistani jute forced to flow through the now Indian port of Calcutta.
Post-partition	Anchorages established on River Pussur, first at Chalna (100 km from the sea) and then at Mongla (10 km from the sea). An example of a port functioning without any permanent installations on shore [50].
1970	Permanent berthing installations at Chalna.

Hong Kong presents a puzzle that is deceptively simple. Since its hinterland is so small, one might be tempted to explain maritime success in terms of location in relation to foreland opportunities, formerly including mainland China and now in most other areas of south-east Asia. B. Boxer, 1961, acknowledges the importance of these 'seaward hinterlands' as he calls them but also reveals the importance of institutional factors [14] in the port's ability to survive amid very different trading conditions. Before the Second World War the seed of a future industrial role had already been sown with the establishment of Imperial Preference in 1935. But this role was overshadowed by the rise of Hong Kong to become one of the world's greatest entrepot or pivot ports in the late 1930s (B. Boxer, 1961, 28–36), buying, selling, and transhipping for the China market. One could argue that this was the destiny of a port with such a location, not requiring much of a diversion from the long-haul shipping routes from Europe to Japan, and making a useful Asian terminal in itself, with a position favourable to feeder coastal services to much of south China. But the weight attached to these locational advantages could also be applied to other port locations on the south China coast. The fact that foreland connections are not the whole story is revealed by the fact that Hong Kong survived and prospered when the foreland of China was cut off, and when its only locational advantage might seem to be merely as a staging post, now seemingly in a peripheral location and politically vulnerable.

The importance of the institutional factors in the case of Hong Kong is multi-faceted. A ground bass to the argument is the presence of a highly industrious manpower reserve of some three millions. The efficiency of banking, insurance, and warehousing have always been much above the standard normally achieved in south-east Asia. The colonial government has been stable and dedicated to the principles of *laissez-faire* capitalism in which the private sector has been allowed to operate with few political shackles. This governmental climate favoured investment in Hong Kong by emigré Chinese who found their status in their adopted countries somewhat tenuous. Hong Kong continued to attract ships by reason of its bunkering, ship-repair and ship-breaking services. Its role as a pivot port for areas of south-east Asia, other than mainland China, was increased with the loss of competition from such ports as Swatow, Amoy, and Foochow on the China mainland. The Hong Kong–Straits run developed as a flourishing trade, though many European-owned shipping companies that operated out of Hong Kong found their share of this route, compensating for the loss of pivot mainland China trade, threatened by long-haul carriers, and this made the Hong Kong maritime interests very ready to service Hong Kong as an industrial centre in its own right. This competition between various shipping interests in a *laissez-faire* environment 'enabled the Colony to rapidly assume the significant role of consumer and producer so soon after her traditional economic base was forcibly altered' (B. Boxer, 1961, 87). The relationship between break-bulk trade and industry at Hong Kong could become quite close because of the absence of any hope of primary industry. The lesson to be drawn from this potted account of Hong Kong is that the locational advantages only come into play when a favourable institutional climate allows them to do so; or qualities of site and situation can only be understood by attempting to look through the lenses of those that appraise them [24].

Any aspect of Japan's recent economic growth presents a concave curve, of course steeply upward in recent years. From a point of time on such a steep slope, it is difficult to show the rapidly changing scene in perspective. The fact that only a limited space is here available demands generalisations, and it is to be hoped that Japanese correspondents will be quick to point out errors of emphasis or of fact. If port functions are to be crudely classified into bulk handling and break-bulk handling, the Japanese advance has been most notable in the first sector, for two main reasons. The first reason is that most of Japanese heavy industry has always been sited in seaboard locations, which for complicated reasons stated elsewhere [81 ff] are able to take immediate advantage of the economies opened up by the coming of the super bulk carriers. Secondly, the Japanese played a major role in this advent of gigantism in ships. Until 1950 Japan was prevented from undertaking shipbuilding, although the great yards that had built the capital ships of the Imperial Navy were waiting unscathed. Shipbuilding managerial and technical staffs turned their bottled initiative to looking afresh at shipbuilding problems, and to hand was the remarkable example of the American D. K. Ludwig. He had obtained a lease of the former naval shipyard at Kure, and in the port's huge building dock the first of the large bulk carriers began to take shape using new systems of applied technology in manpower and assembly. This experience and pent-up Japanese initiative was allowed full play in the early 1950s, accelerated by the Suez boom in ordering ships that came in 1956. Thereafter the familiar advantages of energy, relative cheap and docile labour came into play, but rather post hoc than as prime stimuli.

Sharpening the focus on seaports of Japan, the theme taken here is the contrasting objectives that Japanese decision-makers have chosen for their ports, and following D. Takase, 1969, Table 22 sets out four distinct periods since the nineteenth century, with the changing objective pursued.

This table shows that the 1967 port law was a great turning point for Japanese ports when the idea of the Port Development Authority was born, and J. Hasegawa, 1969b, has called this the concept of megaloport. For the first time, Japan contemplated the exclusive use of certain berths. Kobe may illustrate the traditional method of berth assignments which was a first-come-first-served arrangement for the public wharves. As a result the ships that were berthed at the public piers did not correspond to the cargo in the sheds. In 1967 some 80% of Kobe's break-bulk cargo was transhipped between ship and lighter, both exports and imports. The imports were conveyed to private warehouses. The *Ports and Harbours Act* of 1950 set a strict restriction on the sphere of action of port managers (Article 13). The 'fair and just activities' of private sectors in the port must not be impeded or interfered with, and this clause was inserted as a result of active lobbying by the Japan Warehouses Association, among other organisations. As a result it was cheaper in Kobe to convey goods by lighter to a private warehouse than direct loading and unloading from a public wharf (K. Yomota, 1967). This philosophy of treating ports as public services was altered with the financial policy included in the Act setting up Port Development Authorities in 1967, whereby a principle of 'a port development paying its way' was built in [204]. Table 22 summarises the plans for the seven-year period 1967–74.

There appear to be three main reasons for the necessity to establish such authorities (after D. Takase, 1969). (1) The volume of foreign trade cargoes will increase from 32 million tons in 1966 to 70 millions

TABLE 21

JAPANESE PORT PLANNING PHILOSOPHIES

Period	Port Planning Authority	Major aim(s)	Charges
1890–1939	National government	To serve public interest	Free or low

Second World War

1950 (*Ports and Harbours Act*)	National government in conjunction with local autonomous bodies	To serve public interest	Low

⎧ 1955–65   3⅓ increase in tonnage handled by Japanese ports

⎨ 1961–1965 1st Five-year ⎩ Plan)	,,	To relieve congestion at ports	Low

⎡ 1965–1969 (2nd Five-year Plan) ⎨	,,	To increase port facilities for bulk carriers and to increase length of berths for specialised ships	Low

⎣ 2nd Five-year Plan's 1969 projected tonnage achieved in 1967

1967   *Law concerning Port Development Authorities*

1968–1972 (3rd Five-year Plan)	Port Development Authorities in parallel with above system	To consolidate, expand and modernise the port facilities in the metropolises	See Table 23

Based on D. Takase, loc. cit.

TABLE 22

Keihin (*Tokyo Bay*) *Port Development Authority*	*Tokyo*	*Yokohama*
Container wharves	11 berths	6 berths
Conventional-type ocean liner wharves	26 berths	0 berth
Hanshin (*Osaka Bay*) *Port Development Authority*	*Osaka*	*Kobe*
Container wharves	7 berths	9 berths
Conventional-type ocean liner wharves	0 berth	26 berths
*Ise Bay Port Development Company**	*Nagoya*	*Yokkaichi*
Container wharves	4 berths	2 berths

* Outside the control of the Ministry of Transport; liner companies and local authorities have holdings, and central government holds 10% of shares.

in 1975. (2) Provision for container services on all deep-sea routes is envisaged. (3) It is necessary to have an administrative framework separate from the central and local government, and the autonomous port bodies set up under the 1950 Act, in order to allow new methods of financing the great cost of these developments (see below).

TABLE 23

JAPANESE PORT DEVELOPMENT AUTHORITY: METHOD OF FINANCING
(30-year period)

	Percentage
Central Government and Local Autonomous Board (10% each, including interest)	20
Raised by government-guaranteed loans, with interest rate of 7·4% (on the basis of yields accruing to lenders)	40
Loans* to be obtained from shipping companies and licensed port and terminal operators to whom the facilities are to be leased at an annual interest rate* of 7·6%	40

* To be paid or repaid from proceeds arising from charges collected from private users to whom port facilities are leased for their exclusive use.

Southern continents

Recently there appeared a survey of Australian seaports (J. Bird, 1968), and from it three themes are selected which may have a wider interest beyond the context of Australia. The chapter numbers indicate where the topics are principally treated in the 1968 study: the dominance of the seaport capital cities (Chapters 2 and 10); industrial terminals (Chapters 7 and 8); and developmental problems (Chapter 10).

Perhaps one of the most fascinating and rewarding features of studying ports in a relatively new country lies in the reasons for the foundation of ports being often available in the words of the original decision maker. The proclaimed impulse [24] of the establishment of governors' residences and legal ports of entry was the initiator of the great dominance of the seaport capitals in the demography of Australia. Other maritime factors contributory to the dominance of seaport capitals are the peripheral distribution of some important resources. This applies particularly in the cases of water and coal, including of course opportunities for linkages by water transport. In the case of minerals, peripheral dominance may be weakened by future discoveries as the continent becomes more completely explored; but a resource on the coast may be more economic than an interior source with cheaper on-site exploitation because of the former's cheaper transport to an export shipping port. Inland traffic has concentrated upon large ports because they offer greater ranges of sailings and more frequent sailing dates. This has been reinforced by the fact that Sydney and Melbourne have become pivot container ports, natural bases for feeder services to outlying areas, though 90% of the first container cargoes were destined for the Sydney and Melbourne metropolitan areas (J. Reeves, 1969, 6). These factors combine with social, political, psychological, and other economic factors to promote centralisation of population within the large seaport cities.

The existence of six states in the federated Commonwealth, each with diverse economic policies, has greatly affected the development of ports in a country without a national port policy. Four state boundaries transverse to the coast have interfered with the boundaries between major port hinterlands. Some ports are autonomous and financially self-contained, but there are very diverse forms of port administration, and some ports are at the mercy of a state consolidated fund. The existence of six states implies that they should each receive some developmental funds for their own port plans, whereas the greatest need is to co-ordinate port development to serve what has been called the 'fertile crescent' of south-east Australia. Australia grew as a series of areas expanded from port bridgeheads, and the existence of six states confirming those early hinterlands has acted as a brake on the full force of concentration as developed in the port hinterland model [130], although the concentration induced by deep-sea container services is a step in this direction. But two other factors promote port diffusion as B. Ogundana, 1970, see above, p. 171, would term it. First, the ability of a port to attract ships, notably through the presence of some local magnet within the port area itself, such as the provision of a new installation, or the establishment of a local industry with the necessity of tide-water access for raw material supply. Secondly, the presence of an accessible raw material or fuel source will promote an export port [132]. These two reasons explain the burgeoning of mineral exporting ports on the northern coast of Western Australia and why Newcastle and Port Kembla have thrived within the economic shadow of Sydney.

The seaport industrial machine of Australia was described as a great coastwise wheel encircling the continent (J. Bird, op. cit., Fig. 40), with radial lines of transport transverse to the coast. Where such a radius meets the rim of coastwise routes, a port functions. Newcastle and Port Kembla have the busiest marine industrial terminals where steel works are located at the point where the New South Wales coalfield outcrops close to the coast. The cargoes handled by

Port Kembla are almost exclusively raw materials and fuel. Even many of the industrial products of the steel works are shipped via Sydney because of its greater number of sailings by break-bulk cargo vessels. Though wool from New South Wales can be shipped from Port Kembla, with the same inland transport rate as to Sydney, little wool has in fact been so exported because shipowners are reluctant to service the port for a part cargo.

The table opposite shows how repercussions of heavy industry have spread to every state of the Commonwealth of Australia, and it is the ship that has carried these repercussions of basic industry—another example of the ship being the active agent and developments at the port taking place as a reaction to shipping initiatives and industrial opportunities [195].

The Republic of South Africa is a rail-dominated transport universe, since long-distance carriage of goods by road is curtailed by government decree. N. M. Shaffer, 1965, in his study of the competitive position of Durban and other southern African ports could thus avoid the usual difficulty of obtaining comprehensive data for road transport [126]. He was therefore able to compare actual hinterlands based on rail origin and destination data with theoretically derived hinterlands based on three different criteria:

(1) hinterlands based on rail mileage from ports;
(2) hinterlands based on break-even points of rail tariffs to competing ports;
(3) hinterlands based on a version of the gravity model [136], using the tonnages of imports received by ports and allowed to decline with the square of the rail distance.

The correlation coefficients (r^2) of the hinterland boundaries thrown up by these methods with the actual hinterlands measured by rail origin and destination data were respectively: 0·81, 0·56, and 0·90; and the mean deviations from the actual boundaries were, again respectively: 139, 112, and 85 km.

One would expect a gravity model to give a better result than rail tariffs since these reveal only the inland leg of cargo movement and do not include statistics generated by the facilities of the port and the efficiency of cargo-handling and the regard in which these features are held by importers and exporters. In fact in the case of Durban there is

the inertia created by long and continued usage of the port by inland consumers and shippers who are reluctant to transfer their business to another port, and ... the desire of South Africans, both private individuals and government agencies, to use a national port. (N. M. Shaffer, 1965, 230)

TABLE 24

SOME SIGNIFICANT DATES IN THE AREAL SPREAD OF
SEABOARD INDUSTRY IN AUSTRALIA

Iron and steel

1888 Port Pirie (S. Australia), erection of lead smelting plant

1897 Report recommends Port Kembla (NSW) for southern NSW coal

1899 Broken Hill Proprietary Company (BHP) secure leases over Iron Knob ore reserves, S. Australia

1901 Whyalla (S. Australia). Opening of this port to supply iron ore as flux in Port Pirie smelter

1911 BHP announce decision to become a steel maker

1912 Choice of Newcastle (NSW) for steel works based on ore exported from Whyalla

1928 Port Kembla (NSW). First blast furnace blown in by Australian Iron and Steel Ltd (AI and S)

1935 AI and S become part of BHP group

1937 BHP secure further 50-year lease over South Australian iron ore, provided blast furnace erected at Whyalla

1939 BHP decide to begin shipbuilding at Whyalla

1942 Rapid Bay (S. Australia) begins to supply Newcastle and Whyalla with limestone for flux

1948 Ardrossan (S. Australia) begins to supply all steel-making centres with dolomite

1957 Kwinana, Western Australia. BHP establishes a rolling mill supplied with billets from Port Kembla

1963 Commonwealth Government waives restriction on export of iron ore from certain areas in view of very large proven reserves, resulting in iron ore exporting ports and associated pelletising plants in north-west Western Australia post 1966

1967 BHP agrees with Commonwealth Government to establish a blast furnace at Kwinana

Bauxite—Alumina

1963 Weipa (Queensland), bauxite export

1964 Bauxite refinery, Kwinana, shipping to alumina refinery, Point Henry, Geelong (Victoria)

1967 Gladstone (Queensland) and Bell Bay (Tasmania), alumina refineries using Weipa ore

Fig. 19 shows a remarkable correspondence between the actual and gravity model boundaries in the cases of Port Elizabeth and East London, whereas Durban's hinterland has been extended at the expense of Lourenço Marques. Note how Durban's hinterland is expanding away from the coast [*134*]. N. M. Shaffer concludes that another of Durban's chief advantages is that it has a very vigorous primary hinterland [*125*], and this causes the port to be successful in general hinterland expansion. South African hinterland patterns will change with the entry into service of new bulk berths (W. L. Speight, 1970), and the provision of the first container berths at Durban and Cape Town (*Report*, etc., 1970).

In the late 1960s there seemed to be many obstacles to containerisation of South African trade: the difficulty faced by narrow gauge railways (1·07 m, 3 ft 6 ins) in transporting the ISO container, the reluctance to write off investments in pre-cooling stores for fruit exports, and the faith in palletisation and pre-slung loads. But the Republican railways use the same rolling stock as in Britain; ISO containers will just have to be transported a little more slowly on the South African tracks. Experience with conventional ships in the UK–South Africa trade showed that only a maximum of half the cargo of conventional vessels can be converted into unit loads by palletisation and pre-slinging of cargo. No savings are forthcoming; these unit methods merely halt the rise in handling costs. Economies on such a route of H. J. Molenaar's type 2 [*116*] can only come with a fully containerised service, and like decimalisation of coinage, the longer it is put off the more it costs; and when it happens it has to do so overnight, with all legs of the route able to handle the new technique. The 1970 *Report* (op. cit.) includes perhaps the most powerful reason for containerisation, the 'band-wagon' effect of a successful innovation and the accompanying fear of being left behind [*104*].

Fig.19 Comparison of actual and derived hinterlands in South Africa

Top: hinterland divides based on actual despatches and receipts to and from indicated ports by railroad stations.

Middle: divides drawn at equidistant points along the shortest rail routes from indicated ports.

Bottom: divides based on a gravity model comprising the actual import tonnages handled at ports and the square of the distance along relevant railroads.

'. . . it is suggested that a better estimate of the hinterland of a port can be made using selected characteristics of the port itself rather than equidistant points along a transport route or using tariff divides.' (N. M. Shaffer, 1965, 227)
Source: ibid., Figs.5, 6, and 50.

See also J. A. Coetzee, 1963, The Transvaal competitive area and the distribution of its sea-borne imports via the ports of South Africa and Lourenço Marques, *Tijdschrift voor economische en sociale geografie*, **54**, 186–92.

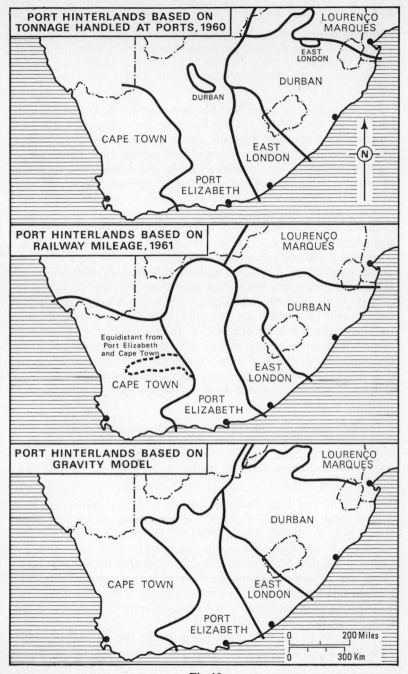

Fig. 19

In the last resort, however, the Republic has little choice. The rest of the world, and in particular the industrially advanced and leading nations, are containerising at a rapid rate; and if it desires to maintain, let alone improve, its export position, a country with such a high foreign trade dependence as South Africa must of necessity follow suit.

Finally, it may be noted that the passenger traffic between South-ampton and South Africa is still buoyant. The voyage lasts the con-venient period of eleven days and 80 % is always fine weather sailing. Thus once again sea passenger travel and pleasure are intermixed.

Latin America from Mexico to Chile and Argentina consists of twenty-one separate political units, only two of which are land-locked. This continent is on the periphery of world economy, and there is a continuous struggle to obtain higher prices for the primary products that enter world trade to match the ever-increasing cost of manufactured imports. This has prompted various ideas of Latin American economic groupings including the Latin American Free Trade Association (LAFTA) under the Treaty of Montevideo in 1961, culminating in a Latin American Common Market, optimisti-cally by 1985. Efficient transport is the key to this integration, and it appears that the sea will play the role taken by the railroad in nine-teenth-century North America (R. T. Brown, 1966, 114). Land com-munications across boundaries lie through population deserts. Thus the exogenous network of water transport, circa-continental, would most effectively weld the area together for intra-continental trade, and this development would have an impact on port planning in a continental context.

The deficiencies and difficulties of transportation will make necessary close cooperation between members of the free-trade area. More important than the lack of means are the inadequacy and high operational cost of many ports and the absence of regular service on some routes. (V. L. Urquidi, 1964, 112)

These features of high transport costs and an incomplete network will be considered in the light of a shipping and port model devel-oped by R. T. Brown, 1968. Secondly, two countries will be con-sidered: one manifests a fascinating interplay between port water and land site situation problems (Trinidad); in another there is the case of an apogee of centralisation upon the capital city port (Uruguay). Finally, the ironic case of the port of Pelotas is brought forward as an example of a declining port in the developing province of Rio Grande do Sul, southern Brazil.

The linear programme model erected by R. T. Brown, 1966, Appendix D, is designed to select shipping routes within South

America so that shipping capacity is adjusted to transport requirements. The model has three basic ingredients: (1) the intra-South
American traffic flows in 1962; (2) the concept of a 'shipping route';
and (3) what is considered to be a cost. There are seven basic assumptions of the model:

(1) eight ports only are considered, one for each country;
(2) the cargo to be transported is taken as fixed rather than
varying with freight rates;
(3) a shipping route is defined so as to permit a vessel operating
over that route to make a round trip, returning to the port whence
she sailed from originally;
(4) all ships stop at all intermediate ports along their routes;
(5) all ships operate at the same average speed;
(6) the network is considered as closed upon the South American
continent;
(7) costs of transport are taken as navigation costs and inventory
costs incurred by the shipper.

With eight ports there are 128 shipping routes, but only 58 are independent $(R_n = P_n(P_n - 1) + 2$ where R_n is the number of independent shipping routes and P_n the number of ports).

The average carrier costs per ton transported (excluding cargo-
handling and port charges) generated by the model vary from $1·14
to $1·21, depending on whether or not it is specified that at least
5,000 tons must be carried between a pair of ports and whether or
not tramps are allowed to deal with the peak traffic involved in shift-
ing seasonal shipments of bulk wheat. The figures are incredibly low
when compared with the actual 1962 costs of $15 to $80 per ton
depending on the product and the route. However, the carrier cost
of the model has to be increased since a ship operating within the
LAFTA area spends 35–40% of her time in port [15] which would
give a model-generated figure of $3·35 per ton, to which must
be added $8 to $10 per ton for loading and unloading cargo. The
total model cost now appears as an average of $12 to $14 per ton,
compared with the actual cost range in 1962 of $15–$80. The difference represents the room for increased efficiency simply by planning
and programming cargo movements within South America, without
considering the cargo-handling savings that will be achieved by the
diffusion of unit cargo techniques under whatever system chosen.

Trinidad's west coast, facing the Gulf of Paria, presents great geo-
morphological contrasts. The folded mountains of the north meet
the coast obliquely and their drowned valley extensions, or rias [30],
give deep water offshore; this pattern is succeeded to the south by

shallow water offshore fringed by mangrove swamps, but a coastal
site immediately south of the mountains has easy east–west access
inland. In the early 1930s the question was whether to develop the
deep-water sites at Chaguaramas and Tembladora in the north and
face the expense of difficult land communications or dredge a long
channel to the waterfront of Port of Spain, the largest settlement on
the island partly because it commanded the east–west route axis.
Since dredging can be allied to reclamation [40], in 1935 a channel,
3·6 km by 9·75 m, was dredged to Port of Spain, and the spoil was
used to push forward the wharf line to reclaim 166 hectares of flat
land for the port area (W. P. Hedden, 1967, 151). Here is a fine
example of the dredge-reclamation extension of an existing port city
being preferred to the provision of lengthy land communications to

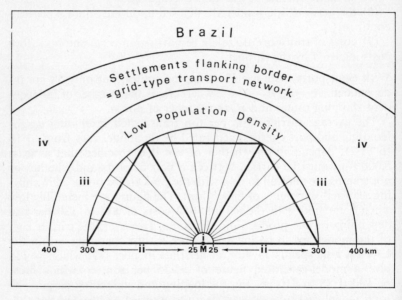

Fig. 20 Schematic diagram of the hinterland of Montevideo

   (i) immediate hinterland, up to 25 kms from Montevideo;
  (ii) hinterland where routes diverge at an average angle of 12°, so
      that five routes could be envisaged as covering one of three
      equilateral components of a semi-hexagonally shaped hinter-
      land [134 ff];
 (iii) zone of low population density;
 (iv) zone where transport network is independent of the radial pull
      of Montevideo.

Source: diagram derived from information in D. E. Snyder, 1962,
101 ff.

urban centres from isolated sites on rias, where by definition steep plunges of land offshore are continued by steep gradients inland [*30*].

Montevideo dominates Uruguay, being twenty times larger than the second-ranking city in the state, and some 35% of Uruguayans live in the capital city port. As might be expected, the reasons for this dominance are many. Below are tabulated those given by D. E. Snyder, 1962, and it can be seen that the port played a vital role in this concentration (italicised in the table), following the proclaimed impulse [*24*] of the foundation of the capital and the centralisation there of the Church. The summary makes an interesting comparison with that supplied for Australia (J. Bird, 1968, 225–9). The two major differences result from contrasts in the social setting, and these are emphasised by being preceded by double asterisks.

TABLE 25

SOME REASONS FOR THE DOMINANCE OF MONTEVIDEO IN URUGUAY

(1) *Water site factors of Bay of Montevideo in initiating port settlement.*

(2) Location of capital at M. focusses national administration and transport network.

(3) Unitary rather than federal political structure emphasises 2.

(4) **Roman Catholic church centred on M.

(5) Optimum location for expansion of government functions, because of 2.

(6) *Optimum location for export and import functions because of 1 and 5.*

(7) *Optimum location for industries processing exports because of 1 and 6.*

(8) Optimum location for consumer-oriented industries because of population engaged in above functions [*84*].

(9) **Political concessions to urban population by liberal politicians in a struggle against conservative rural landholders, so that the city became the source of 'economic opportunity for impoverished masses' (D. E. Snyder, 1962, 98).

(10) 'As a multiplier [*200*] of the success of established activities M. became the only rational choice of site for newer, more specialised activities. Hence existing inertia accelerated' (idem).

Three ports share the hinterland of Brazil's most southerly state, Rio Grande do Sul, and they are all located close to the 340-km-long ship channel through Lake Patos. Rio Grande is only 16 km from the sea whereas Porto Alegre is at the head of navigation on the ship channel, and Pelotas occupies a compromise location forty kilometres inland from Rio Grande. Porto Alegre occupies the typical head of navigation where *Anyport* began [*68*]. Today the largest ships, especially tankers, proceed no further than Rio Grande, yet

Porto Alegre has close access to the agricultural lands of the central part of the state with inland navigation on the Jaceui system, and has become an important regional centre as capital of the state. The port's trade is one of exporting agricultural produce and lumber, and importing fuel coastwise, apart from transhipment functions.

TABLE 26

A DECLINING PORT (PELOTAS) IN A DEVELOPING REGION
(RIO GRANDE DO SUL STATE, BRAZIL)

	Totals of imports and exports (*tons*)						Total of Rio Grande do Sul State*	
	Porto Alegre		*Pelotas*		*Rio Grande*			
1938	224,255	(38)†	42,064	(7)	203,459	(35)	582,674	(100)
1953	525,228	(90)	28,151	(5)	685,815	(118)	1,364,960	(234)
1958	452,125	(78)	22,493	(4)	1,250,095	(215)	1,837,783	(315)
1963	402,136	(69)	10,663	(2)	787,550	(135)	1,332,430	(229)
1968	1,441,078	(247)	3,382	(0·6)	1,014,307	(174)	2,815,839	(483)

* The trade of other ports which makes up the state total includes notably the river port of Livramento on the border with Uruguay.
† The index figures in brackets are relative to the state total of 1938 rendered as 100.

Source: *Anuário Estatístico do Brasil.*

Pelotas is not so centrally situated and has lost its fuel import trade (formerly coal, now oil) to Rio Grande. Now that much export trade is delivered by road, the lorries may as well continue beyond Pelotas to Rio Grande, the deep-water port. Pelotas has been sustained by possessing industrial premises like a rice mill and a wheat mill which have generated trade [*81*], but the port stands as an example of one that is neither on deep water, nor near the centre of important hinterland activity, and is consequently losing ground even though the state shows general economic advance [*139*].

Finally, Fig. 21 shows the places in South America with the first container depots. The correlation with the more populous areas of the continent is obvious, just as the container revolution began in the more developed parts of the world which this lightning tour of all the continents began to consider two chapters ago.

Fig. 21 First ports or depots able to handle containers in South America

Ashdod: the New Modern Deep Seawater Port in Israel under Construction (1961) Lisbon: Israel Marine Insurers' Association.

Awad, S. (1967) *The Situation in Africa*. Paper submitted to Interregional Seminar on Containerisation etc., organised by United Nations in cooperation with UK government, London, 1–12 May.

Bird, J. (1968) *Seaport Gateways of Australia*. London: Oxford University Press.

Blaut, J. M. (1967) Geography and the development of peasant agriculture, *Problems and Trends in American Geography*, Ed. S. B. Cohen, 200–20. New York: Basic Books.

Boxer, B. (1961) *Ocean Shipping in the Evolution of Hong Kong*. University of Chicago: Department of Geography Research Paper no. 72.

Brown, R. T. (1966) *Transport and the Economic Integration of South America*. Washington: Brookings Institution.

Conference on Unitisation, Mombasa, 23 and 24 November 1967 (1967). Mombasa: East African Cargo Handling Services.

d. Lega, R. C. (1957) *La zone franche du port de Beyrouth*. Beirut, Faculté de Droit.

Development of Ports: Improvement of Port Operations and Connected Facilities (1969). New York: United Nations [Preliminary report by UNCTAD Secretariat] TD/B/C.4/42/Rev. 1.

Hance, W. A. (1967) *African Economic Development*. New York: Praeger.

Hance, W. A., Kotschar, V., and Peterec, R. J. (1961) Source areas of export production in tropical Africa, *Geographical Review*, **51**, 487–99.

Hasegawa, J. (1969a) The ports of Japan, *The PLA Monthly*, **44**, 270–7.

——(1969b) The megaloport concept in Japan, *The PLA Monthly*, **44**, 404–9.

Hedden, W. P. (1967) *Mission: Port Development—with Case Studies*. Washington: American Association of Port Authorities.

Hilling, D. (1965) The new port of Cotonou, *Fairplay Shipping Journal: Cargo Handling Supplement*, October, xlii–xlv.

——(1967) UN container seminar (a report), *The Dock and Harbour Authority*, **48**, 121–4.

——(1969a) Togoport—the new port of Lomé, *The Dock and Harbour Authority*, **49**, 423–4.

——(1969b) Container potential of West African ports, *The Dock and Harbour Authority*, **50**, 9–13.

——(1969c) The evolution of the major ports of West Africa, *Geographical Journal*, **135**, 365–78.

Hindle, P. (1966) 'Aqaba: an old port revived, *Geographical Journal*, **132** (1966), 64–8.

Hirschman, A. O. (1958) *The Strategy of Economic Development*. New Haven: Yale Studies in Economics, vol. 10.

Hoyle, B. S. (1967) *The Seaports of East Africa*. Nairobi: East African Publishing House.

——(1968) East African Seaports: an application of the concept of 'Anyport', *Transactions of the Institute of British Geographers*, **44**, 163–83.

——(1970a) Transport and economic growth in developing countries: the case of East Africa, *Geographical Essays in Honour of Professor K. C. Edwards*. Nottingham: University Department of Geography, 187–96.

——(1970b) *The Port Function in the Urban Development of Tropical Africa*. Paris: Colloques Internationaux du Centre National de la Recherche Scientifique.

—— and D. Hilling, Eds. (1970) *Seaports and Development in Tropical Africa*. London: Macmillan.

Husain, S. M. (1967) *The Situation in Asia and the Far East*. Paper submitted to Interregional Seminar on Containerisation, etc., organised by United Nations in cooperation with UK Government, London, 1–12 May.

McKay, J. (1970) Physical potential and economic reality: the underdevelopment of the Port of Freetown, in Hoyle and Hilling, op. cit., ch. 5.

Menzinger, B. (1966) *Der Hafen von Haifa.* Tübingen: Mohr.

Milburn, K. (1969) The port of Hong Kong, *The PLA Monthly*, 44, 278–81.

Molenaar, H. J. (1967) *Basic Economics of Containerization and Unitization in Ocean Shipping.* Paper submitted to Interregional Seminar on Containerisation, etc., organised by United Nations in cooperation with UK Government, London, 1–12 May.

Murphey, R. (1964) The city in the swamp: aspects of the site and early growth of Calcutta, *Geographical Journal*, 130, 241–56.

Nagorski, B. (1968) Port problems in developing countries, *The Dock and Harbour Authority*, 49, 36–43.

New Zealand Overseas Trade: Report by the Container Cargo Handling Committee [Molyneux Report] (1967). Wellington.

Ogundana, B. (1966) *Some Elements of Changing Port Concentration in Nigeria.* University of London: unpublished M.Sc. thesis.

——(1970) Patterns and problems of seaport evolution in Nigeria, in B. S. Hoyle and D. Hilling, op. cit., ch. 10.

Rao, V. K. R. V. (1969) Port Development in the Fourth [Indian] Plan, *Indian Shipping*, 21, 21–7.

Reeves, J. (1969) The Australians take a close look at the container bug, *Containerisation International*, 7, 4–7.

Report on Cargo Handling and Packing Methods [Steenkamp Report] (1970). South African Department of Commerce, Johannesburg.

Sandford, R. A. (1964) Port improvement in developing countries, *ICHCA Journal*, 6, 16–17.

Siddiqui, Q. H. (1967) Major ports of Pakistan, *Port of Karachi Magazine* (November issue), 36–43.

Snyder, D. E. (1962) Commercial passenger linkages and the metropolitan nodality of Montevideo, *Economic Geography*, 38, 95–112.

Speight, W. L. (1970) Harbour developments in South Africa, *The Dock and Harbour Authority*, 50, 463.

Symposium on Palletisation (1966) Calcutta: Institute of Port Management, 22–3 August.

Study Team Report on the Major Ports of India (1968) Tokyo: International Association of Ports and Harbours.

Takase, D. (1969) Unprecedented growth rate brings big change in [Japanese] port policies, *Journal of Commerce*, 18 July, 3–4.

Tresselt, D. (1967) *The West African Shipping Range.* New York: United Nations.

Urquidi, V. L. (1964) *Free Trade and Economic Integration in Latin America.* Los Angeles: University of California Press.

Williams, G. R. (1969) Containerisation in developing countries, *The Dock and Harbour Authority*, 49, 348–52.

Yomota, K. (1967) On relationship between port management and in-port transport companies at Kobe, *Ten-minute Speeches.* Tokyo: International Association of Ports and Harbours Conference, 1967, 19–21.

G

8

PORTS AND PLANNING (1)

Perhaps the biggest problem faced by port administrators is that of planning for the future, and this subject comprehends planning at different scales in two dimensions. On the time scale, the topic extends from the day-to-day programme of port activity through intermediate range planning to cope with uneven loads of traffic month-by-month, perhaps due to seasonal factors in the hinterland. This involves the problem of peaking. Then there is the longer range planning of facilities that may take four years or more to come into operation. Finally, the subject extends away into the time distance, perhaps involving forecasting over a period of a quarter of a century. On the spatial scale, the port planner may be concerned with an individual installation, the future of a berthing complex, or the relationships between a port and its approach channel on the one hand and with its hinterland on the other. Preoccupation with the hinterland is port planning at the regional scale, but the ports of a country need planning on a national scale so that they function together harmoniously in the most economic service of the territorial unit. If there is an economic grouping of states, ports are easily led into the international realm, which is also their natural milieu by reason of the international trade links of a deep-sea port *ipso facto*. A way of approaching this large subject is to repeat that traffic demand is served by ships which in turn make demands that ports struggle to fulfil, in a way that is compatible with their responsibilities to land transport and with the nature of the physical sites they have available for development.

Ports as servants of shipping
The most obvious impact of shipping developments upon ports has

been the increasing size of vessels (F. Posthuma, 1967), but as the last chapter showed, new types of ships with different methods of cargo-handling can also have profound repercussions not only upon port lay-outs but also upon the ability of a port to retain or advance its relative position in a national league table. The increasing size of vessels notably the bulk carrier, has been a feature of shipping developments since the Second World War, and ports have struggled to be able to berth these ever-larger ships. This is a master-servant relationship, but good masters study their servants; and there are some brake factors on the economies of scale that naval architects delight to indulge. As ships grow larger, their flexibility of operation may well decrease as fewer ports can handle giants, and the largest bulk carriers have even overrun the draught available in seas covering the continental shelves. There is also the difficulty of the step function of capital outlay if the units of investment are very large. This has not inhibited oil companies, but it may be a factor limiting the capacity of container ships. For a large ship to maintain the same schedule as a smaller ship, the cargo-handling rate must increase, and cargo must be collected from a wider area, encouraging port concentration (E. C. Emerson, 1968, 107). A ceiling in such areas and those mentioned in Table 3 (p. 37) would pose a limitation for optimal ship size.

A most important point to remember when designing a berth is the lowest *total* costs of operation. A quotation is repeated:

The basic economic concept to be applied when planning material handling centres is the balancing of costs of delays against the cost of providing the service. (F. G. Culbert and F. C. Leighton, 1963, 23)

Z. Pelcynski, 1964, also pointed out that if a port management plans for maximum profits, its charges should be fixed at such a level as will ensure the lowest possible joint costs of cargo-handling and ship's time. But the minimum of cargo-handling costs and the minimum of the joint costs will occur at a stage of berth occupancy below the maximum degree of berth utilisation of which the port is capable (see also *1970 Outlook*, etc., 1967, 44; and *A Study of Port Operations*, etc., 1967, 3 and 11). W. J. Daniels, 1966, demonstrated that designers of bulk terminal facilities base their calculations on the assumption that no control can be exercised by ports over the rate at which vessels are presented for discharge, nor over the times of arrival, making it necessary to plan for efficiencies of about 50%. This is the master-servant relationship with a vengeance, for it implies that half the cost of such port undertakings are beyond the control of port managements. There is another set of circumstances that give ship operators greater freedom of action than port administrators. Suppose a 'shipping development planner' is imagined as a counterpart to a 'port planner'. In real life the latter may be one man or one management; at widest, a group of ports in the same land area may be planned together, perhaps even on a national basis. But the 'shipping planner' is in reality the decision maker of a wide number of shipping companies and consortia and bulk fleet operators—functional sectors of the international fleet; and each of these may control resources far in excess of the individual port, or likely to be allotted to one port. While the port may have a monopoly of location like a tree, the ship is a mobile animal that can be tethered elsewhere if need be.

In door-to-door deep-sea transport, the ocean freight charges are the largest single item and explain why the ocean carriers have been the innovators of through systems. While ocean freight includes sea transport, ship's time, loading and discharging costs, and port expenses paid by the carrier, it does not include port charges which are a relatively minor item of the total cost (see Table 27). Thus ports

TABLE 27

NORTH ATLANTIC TRADE: RESULTS OF PILOT SURVEY

	% of total transport cost (inland origin to inland destination)
Ocean freight (transport, loading and discharging, and port expenses paid by the carrier)	62**
Inland freight	28
Port charges and other costs	10*
**Estimated survey over-weighting of ocean freight, giving estimated share of ocean freight for all north Atlantic trade	55–60
Ocean transport (transport, excluding loading and discharging, and port charges paid by the carrier, but including cost of ship's time in port-wages and amortisation)	33†

* Confirmed by *Containerization: the Key to Low-Cost Transportation* (Report by McKinsey and Company, Inc. for the British Transport Docks Board, 1967, 12).

† Confirmed by *Investigation of Ocean Rate Structures in the Trade between United States North Atlantic Ports and Ports in the United Kingdom and Eire* (US Federal Maritime Commission Publication no. 65–45, 1968, 33).

Source: *Ocean Freight Rates as Part of Total Transport Costs* (Paris: OECD, 1968, 8).

cannot compete with each other by adjusting their charges, but rather by adjusting their efficiency which means in effect adjusting to the ships which present themselves for loading and discharge.

Finally, shipping operators have been getting bigger and more powerful by combining one with the other, so that the scope of the planning of even one 'shipowner' may transcend not only that of individual ports but even groups of ports on whom they make demands. The deputy chairman of the Cunard Steamship Company Ltd. once stated that association with other lines was not sufficient. The company wanted to cooperate in a business, and a business had to have a management (P. H. Shirley, 1968, 18). The managements of these shipping consortia and the managements of the world's bulk fleets (including oil and steel firms) are those whose decisions are the foundation upon which port planners have to build.

Port administration

Types of port administration vary widely, and so many writers have commented on the differences, desiderata, and difficulties, that a special list of references on this topic alone is provided at the end of this chapter (References B). While a discussion of the differences resembles a catalogue and is therefore consigned to Table 28, the difficulties emerge in considering what should be the aims pursued in structuring the port administration. On this topic there is a surprising degree of agreement between the majority of those writers who are not involved in defending some *status quo*.

Many of the studies quoted come to the conclusion that autonomous port trusts are the best form of port authority for major multi-functional ports. Trusts have the characteristic of independent, non-political administration, jurisdiction over an area regardless of local government boundaries, and a constitution that can be varied to suit different local conditions. The advantages are unity of administration within the port, and an independent financial status gives no chance of a financial policy being confounded with a political policy, or of one port being favoured at the expense of another, as is possible when a group of widely separated ports is under one administration. The following clause of the *Mersey Docks and Harbour Act* (1857) is a model of the excellent safeguards available when a large port is operated as an autonomous public trust:

No moneys receivable by the [Mersey Docks and Harbour] Board shall be applied to any purpose unless the same conduces to the safety or convenience of ships frequenting the Port of Liverpool or facilitates the shipping or unshipping of goods; or is concerned in discharging the debt contracted for the above purposes.

The disadvantage of such a port authority is a possible insufficiency of capital funds. Port public trusts can usually borrow from the public only with government consent and only by means of port stock carrying fixed rates of interest. They cannot raise share capital or adjust dividends. Their income is dependent on past successes in attracting traffic. Unless there is some coordination, it is difficult for a series of autonomous major ports to work together for national ends. Sometimes, as a result of an effort to make a fair port constitution, the executive committee may be too large. The executive members are elected in those countries where many of the payers of dues (shipowners) are likely to be nationals of the country wherein the port is situated. Where this is not the case, the members of the port trust are appointed by the government, but this need not circumscribe their freedom of action if the port trust constitution is framed with adequate safeguards.

An autonomous public trust seems best for the general direction of a port with many different installations within it, where break-bulk cargo berths have to be allocated among a number of users, and where a compromise decision has to be made in the matter of the approach channel and berth capacities. Such an authority combines control by men of local experience with freedom from local political or financial restrictions. For a small port where most of the trade is carried on at one or two specialised installations, some other form of port administration may well be acceptable, with industries perhaps owning their adjacent port terminals. Where a major port embraces a number of such installations, the private operators may be tenants of the port authority or subject in some way to its control so that all ships may use the port as compatibly as possible.

Port authorities need not have uniform constitutions, but at least those of the larger ports should be comparable in style throughout one country, so that each would be on the same footing in the search for capital and the bearing of responsibility. Each port of a country is a competitor of the others in the search for development funds. The ultimate arbiter of choices for major capital development must be the central government. Ports cannot of themselves increase the total of national trade which is dependent upon national effort reflected in economic and trade policies. Undue development of one port may rob another. The success of port trusts to lobby in their own cause depends very much on their relationship with the major cities of the country, and upon how many ports there are. Where there are few major ports, and those adjacent to the largest cities, as in Belgium and the Netherlands, then there is little chance of the central government being unaware of the needs of the port. Where there are very many ports such as in the United Kingdom, France, the United States, and Australia, the lobbying influence cannot focus so easily upon the councils of the capital.

TABLE 28

TYPES OF PORT ADMINISTRATION WITH EXAMPLES*

Types, with brief notes on advantages and disadvantages	Examples
National state authority: adv. national port policy possible with adequate funds and regularisation of charges; disadv. political influences, absentee direction, possibility of number of ministerial departments involved	Argentine; Canada (eight major ports); Italy (excl. Genoa, Trieste); Portugal; British Transport Docks Board (former railway operated ports)†
Municipal, with some private firms as tenants: adv. local administration and enthusiasm adapted to the special needs of each port; disadv. local politics, port may need to outgrow the municipal territory, port may be taxed to help city, insufficiency of local funds	Antwerp, Baltimore, Bremen, Bristol, Ghent, Hamburg, Kobe, Osaka, Rotterdam, Yokohama
Autonomous public trust: adv. unified functional administration over functionally defined area; disadv. possible insufficiency of funds and lobbying power in its own cause, national port policy impossible unless some surrender of authority	Barcelona, Calcutta, Copenhagen, London, Liverpool, Melbourne, New York, Rio de Janiero
Private: adv. run as a commercial enterprise, with flexible administration geared to maximising profits of port or associated enterprise; disadv. may not be operated to public advantage	Felixstowe, Port Arthur, Port Lyautey, Port Sunlight, Rapid Bay
In conjunction with a canal: adv. if administration is one of the above, *vide supra*, functional cohesion with inland transport; disadv. may be run for the benefit of the canal rather than for deep-sea vessels which may outrun canal dimensions	Brussels, Manchester
In conjunction with a railway: adv. very commercial criteria employed, functional cohesion with inland transport; disadv. may discriminate against road transport	Alexandretta, Bahia Blanca, Parkeston Quay (Harwich)

* This table owes much to L. Baudez (op. cit.).
† If nationalisation ever takes place, several of the British examples will have to be moved to the first category.

Many ports in developing countries may have begun as colonial bridgeheads, with concessions to foreign nationals either as shipowners or railway companies. Once such ports become 'nationalised' they are administered according to the policy of the state in which they are situated; though if that state wishes to borrow from the World Bank in order to develop its ports, the following remarks of a vice-president of that institution are worth quoting:

> One recurrent problem . . . is the unnecessary and sometimes misdirected intervention in port affairs by a national government reluctant to leave the day-to-day operations of the port to those in authority over the port . . . In general, it has been our experience at the [World] Bank that the problems involved in achieving adequate standards of management and reasonable operating efficiency are usually of greater complexity and more difficult to solve than those involved in the carrying out of the physical improvement projects. [Reason: project execution is a one-shot operation; running a port is a continuous operation.] . . . It is the Bank's view that ports should be operated by an entity subject to government control in respect to general policy, investment planning, tariffs and budget, otherwise enjoying a high degree of independence in the day-to-day operations of the port facility. In many instances, the best solution may be to establish a port authority. (S. Alderwereld, 1967, 4, 5, and 10)

Ports as multipliers

The regional planner is interested in the benefits that a port brings to a city or region, and the difficulty resides in quantifying the benefits. These are the direct income and what may be termed the multiplier effects. The direct income is easy to understand, but not so easy to measure. E. Schenker, 1967, 129–30, lists fifty items of community income directly generated by port operations, ranging through items like marine services, such as tug hire, through wages earned on the waterfront, to profit on ship supplies and other port services. The Delaware River Authority, as a result of a detailed questionnaire survey, has actually estimated the direct port expenditures for goods and services according to each ton of cargo handled by the Port of Philadelphia, broken down by commodities (*The Value of a Ton of Cargo*, etc., 1953 and later; see also *The Economic Impact*, etc., 1958). Applying these figures, with some modification, to Milwaukee in 1963, E. Schenker found that break-bulk cargo generated about seven times greater direct income than bulk cargo, but this was before containerisation (op. cit., 131–5).

The multiplier effects can be understood when the direct effects are treated as 'basic' income, in the sense of basic industries (see p. 84 above), the income arising exogenously to the port. Then indirect effects of this basic income on personal income and general investment are the multiplier effects. I. Hoch, 1959, 230, calculated from input-output tables of labour statistics a multiplier effect on household activity in the Chicago area of 2·905 for the 'water transport industry'. A multiplier was calculated for Milwaukee by K. J. Schlager (on the same basis as the calculation of a regional multiplier,* see E. Schenker, Appendix F) of 2·33. This represented the multiplier effect of the basic port income (see above) on local income. A further calculation by K. J. Schlager (E. Schenker, op. cit., 137, *n.* 22) gave a figure of 2·55 as the effect of port investment on the community. Obviously, more studies of this type need to be made, but would require the availability of detailed input-output analyses. However, one can suggest that for both direct income generated and for the amount invested in ports, the consequent multiplier effect on the associated city community may be between 2·00 and 3·00. The net benefit conferred by this multiplier is the amount by which it exceeds the multiplier resulting from similar amounts of investment elsewhere in non-port locations.

Port finances

There are three main sources of income for a port: dues on ships, dues on goods, and charges for services rendered either to ships or to importers and exporters of goods. Perhaps the most common basis for port charges on ships is net tonnage. The cost of berthing a ship is often closely related to the cost of building the quay involved; and a rough and ready calculation is that such a cost increases with the square of the depth provided alongside. E. P. J. Lunch, 1966, agreed with this, but added that the length of the vessel is also important; and if this is multiplied by the depth squared, a volume is obtained. Net registered tonnage is in fact a volume, and there is a good correlation between it and the square of the depth. Basing port charges on net registered tonnage seems sound psychologically, for it no doubt appears the fairest basis to shipowners, and so it is the easiest tariff rule to sell to them as customers. Many occasions for reductions of shipping dues occur: for ships that import or export only a limited tonnage of goods at a port of call; for coastwise vessels; for ships that need only specialised services—bunkering, repairs, passenger embarcation, or ship provisioning. Services to vessels, such as pilotage, towage, locking in and out, are subject to special charges, either by the port authority itself, if it performs these services, or by private enterprises operating within the port. Nevertheless, more could be done by ports to make their charges reflect the cost of the service, especially scheduling charges on a time basis.

Charges on goods vary, according to whether they are imports or exports. Sometimes tariffs on exports are much reduced or they are

* The regional multiplier $= \dfrac{\text{change in total employment}}{\text{change in basic employment}}$

even exempted to stimulate trade. Customs exemption is a feature of the free port or the foreign trade zone within a port. These features may stimulate re-export goods which can be processed or even manufactured within the protected area. By its nature such a zone has defined limits, and this may raise the cost of establishing an enterprise there, besides the cost of enclosing and guarding this frontier within a frontier (R. S. Thoman, 1956). Bonding is a device whereby a merchant enters into a bond that goods placed in customs-approved warehouses, with private and state locks upon them, shall not have the duty paid until the goods are removed for internal use. In Britain this practice began with an Act in 1685, and an Act in 1832 gave H.M. Customs wide discretion in appointing sufferance wharves with bonded privileges (J. Bird, 1957, 126–8). This method has been preferred in Britain to the erection of free zones, because the number of interests within British ports would make it difficult for them all to be fairly represented. A more serious difficulty for many ports is that of finding a suitable isolated site where all classes of shipping could be received. Dispersed linear patterns of ports based on estuaries may be a disadvantage in this respect.

Charges on goods may also vary according to the length of voyage, and, above all, according to their value per unit of weight. This latter feature is an example of the transport principle of charging what the traffic will bear. For goods of high value per unit of weight, the cost of transport is only a small proportion of the total CIF of the delivered goods; and therefore the charges for their passage through the port can be proportionately higher per unit of weight than for low value goods. This feature is annulled by goods in containers where the complexity of tariff rates induced by the 'charging what the traffic will bear' principle may be reduced by the 'freight any kind' principle, where rates are based on the movement of containers from point to point, regardless of the type of goods inside. The only distinction in the value of goods that then becomes valid is the one that destines low value per unit of weight cargoes to be shipped in bulk. Delivered prices for break-bulk cargo may become the rule where the buyer knows in advance the total cost, and the seller is made aware of the total transport costs.

Port charges do not seem to be an important feature in routeing cargo since they are only a small part of total transport costs. But such influence as they have is likely to be more important in the sphere of charges on goods rather than the dues on ships. The effect of changing charges on goods handled is direct and immediate. Varying dues on ships is a less sensitive tool, since shipowners may absorb the costs or savings, and there may be many ways of passing

TABLE 29

TYPES OF SALES CONTRACT

C & F (cost and freight)—named point of destination

CIF (cost, insurance, freight)—named point of destination

Ex (point of origin as ex factory, ex mill, ex plantation, ex warehouse, ex works) —named point of origin

Ex dock (or ex quay)—named port of importation

FAS (free alongside, also FAS vessel)—named port of shipment

FOB (free on board; FOB plus specification of inland carrier or vessel in specific port)

Delivered price (CIF to buyer)

Source: H. D. Tabak, 1970, 369 ff., for amplification and other variations. See also *Incoterms 1953* (1967).

the changes on to the shipper who may not be able to identify that the increase or savings were originally due to the changes in the tariff of the port through which his goods pass.

It is rather difficult to estimate the proportion occupied by port charges within total transport costs (see Table 27). The majority of overseas shipments are made on liner terms under which sea freight includes the cost of loading and stowage aboard ship, and discharge, and port charges borne by the vessel. In 1966 an OECD study of *Ocean Freight Rates as Part of Total Transport Costs* (published 1968), port charges had to be defined as mainly costs for handling and lightering, loading and discharge of inland carriers, and customs fees. On this basis, the incidence of port charges appeared to be one-third that of the inland freight, and roughly one-sixth on the sea freight for the sample studied. For the break-bulk cargo trade between Britain and North America, it was estimated that ocean freight accounted for 55–60% of the total transport costs. This would indicate that port charges as defined above would constitute 10% of the total transport cost, but to this would have to be added a figure for the port charges absorbed in the shipping rate. The chief factors which cause the percentage to vary are the volume/weight of the shipment, the unit value of the shipment, the inland transport distance and the applicable tariff. It seems unlikely that total port charges would amount to more than 15–20% of total transport costs, and for large shipments over long distances they would fall well below this figure. For the shipowner the cost of strikes or go-slows and the savings resulting from quick turn-round are generally of a much higher order of cost than variations in port charges. Where ports are required to pay their way, the national government may also stipulate that their charges shall be 'reasonable', as in the British *Harbours Act* of 1964, section 27. It has been pointed out that when a charge is required to be reasonable, the reasonableness may be challenged in a court of law (T. A. McLoughlin and E. Eden, 1964).

Every country ought to consider what should be the broad financial programme for its seaports. The Rochdale Report (*Report of the Committee of Inquiry*, etc., 1962) recommended that British ports should pay their way. These ideas first found explicit expression in the 1961 British Government White Paper, *The Financial and Economic Obligations of the Nationalized Industries* (later rewritten as *Nationalized Industries*, 1967). According to the Rochdale Report, port charges should be fixed at a level to meet the following financial objective:

. . . ports should aim at providing, out of revenue, for (a) working expenses; (b) interest on loans; (c) depreciation of assets on a replacement cost basis; (d) taxation. We think that ports should also provide out of revenue some margin for reserves to meet unforeseen contingencies (e.g. premature obsolescence) and to help finance minor improvements, but that major new developments should be financed largely by new capital raised on the market on normal commercial terms. (loc. cit., para 167)

The 1961 White Paper had shown that from 1955–61 in Britain the rate of return on capital in private enterprise was around 15%, whereas only two of the nationalised industries achieved 8%. By 1967 targets had been set for nationalised industries ranging from breaking even to achieving $12\frac{1}{2}\%$. The Rochdale targets imply a rate of return on capital invested in ports at the lowest target for public or private industry, and this in turn implies a recognition of the external economies generated by seaports (E. H. M. Price, 1966). This idea that ports should pay their way is comparatively recent, and W. P. Heddon (1967) believed that it is derived from the frequent separation of responsibility of port administration from the administrative and budget-making activities of a tax-supported government. Israel and Trinidad (1961) and Tunisia (1965) each laid down that port authorities should be 'self-supporting'. The quotation marks are necessary because all kinds of subsidies may be present such as: tax and real estate rate reliefs, state-aided borrowings, special low rates of interest, and even donation of state land or water areas. A useful comparison of costs of (subsidised European) continental ports and (unsubsidised) United Kingdom ports is to be found in a report with that title published in 1970.

Three principles of port charging may be set out. (1) There should be a statutory obligation to present port accounts on a replacement cost rather than a historic cost basis. If the finances of a port are depressed because of a failure to take into account the full impact of inflation on long-lived capital assets, not only are the services of that port depressed, resulting in diseconomics, but the whole system of national ports may be affected by the creeping disease. (2) The charges should reflect the cost of the service provided. If some services are provided below cost, to the detriment of the port's general finances, these uneconomic services may grow at the expense of the encouragement of those services that make a profit. Cross-subsidisation is taking place, although this may be justified if one service faces a more inelastic demand curve than another. Raising the cost in the inelastic sector and lowering it in the more elastic market may increase total revenue (C. O'Loughlin, 1967, 180). (3) All ports that are in competition for development funds, from a nation state or from an international agency, should present their accounts in the same way. This also applies to evidence presented to agencies of regional and national planning.

The problems of determining tariff systems for transport services and a charging policy for the use of infrastructures are highly complex. The principal criterion used throughout the Allais Report to the Commission of the European Economic Community was the theory of the optimum allocation of resources (*Options in Transport Tariff Policy*, 1965). Distinction was made between infrastructure and transport services because the former belong to a differentiated sector, characterised by a concave function (increasing returns) and marked indivisibility; transport services have the opposite features (20, paras 78–83). The authors argued that the correct charging policy for infrastructure is one that leads to optimum utilisation, but that this would lead to a deficit. After other systems had been reviewed and found wanting (46–50; ch. 3, 119–31), the Allais Report recommended that there should be a mixed policy based on budgetary equilibrium, with and without the possibility of borrowing according to circumstances. Two quotations from the report are significant for later conclusions in the next chapter.

In the last analysis . . . , the final choice will be a political one and inevitably based on a certain weighting of the various possible objectives of transport policy (para 15).

Decisions regarding investment in infrastructure, particularly where large indivisible projects are concerned, should be co-ordinated centrally for all modes of transport, such centralisation being carried out at regional, national or Community level as necessary (para 921).

Port investment appraisal

This section links the foregoing brief survey of port finances and the discussion of port planning at various scales in Chapter 9. Methods of investment appraisal have to be built into port planning procedures, inserting a financial yardstick. The costs that the methods reveal should be reflected in the subsequent charging policy for use of the project appraised and approved. Until quite recently, the decision to extend or deepen a port was largely a matter of experience or intuition on the part of the decision maker, partaking more or less of the nature of the gambler's hunch (T. Thorburn, 1960, 140). Sometimes a person with a 'monopolistic advisory position' was able to persuade a port to produce a facility far in advance of its time. John Macaulay, general manager of the Alexandra Dock and Railway Company, Newport, Wales, was able to decide on an entrance lock 305 m long in 1914, then the longest entrance lock in the world. Sir Frederick Palmer, first chief engineer of the Port of London Authority in 1909, and engineering consultant to many ports between the wars, especially Southampton and Calcutta, showed much foresight in his planning of long straight quays capable of easy adaptation and of berthing long and short ships together if necessary. But there was never any attempt to measure how plans that would prove far-sighted to later generations might prove a burden in the short term by reason of the over-provision of facilities. This is an ever-present difficulty in port infrastructure works because of the indivisibility of most projects. In economic terms there was little attempt to measure the opportunity cost of the money invested. Generally, ports were expanded piecemeal, *ad hoc*, as trade expanded; often shackles were placed on future developments, either by the nature of the port works themselves or because other land use functions were allowed to pre-empt precious waterfront sites.

The problem of large-scale investment is of course not confined to port expansion projects, and so several techniques have been moved sideways from their use in other investment sectors. An early paper that confronted the problem was by R. T. Eddison and D. T. Owen, 1953, and consisted basically of an exercise in operational research. Port development was there seen as increasing tonnage through the port on the x-axis with cost per ton of ore on the y-axis. Conditioning the shape of the resultant curves were the number of berths, the number and type of unloading appliances, and the berth occupancy factor. The problem was to optimise the operation by balancing the cost of provision of berths and appliances against the cost of delays to shipping. A development of this type of operational research was the simulation technique employed by P. Omtvedt (1963).

In few words the simulations carried out during this study are nothing more than an attempt at calculating the costs incurred at each operational phase for each ton of cargo passing through a port during a period of time, at the same time registering the costs as either costs of ships' time or costs of handling in port.

By changing the relevant parameters, one by one or several together, one would reach an indication of the effects on transportation costs caused by port developments in various forms. The parameters would comprise length of quays, number of cranes, prevailing working hours, loading and discharging rate and a number of other capacity elements. (23–4)

P. Omtvedt gave an example of the results obtained in applying the simulation technique to Port Harcourt in 1963. The lowest total cost is seen to be achieved with a quay length of about 1,200 m. With increased tonnages, the minimum is pushed further to the right, but bear in mind that quayage can usually be provided only in blocks because of the step function of capital investment in projects that are most economically built in large units. In other words, it is hardly practical to make a metre-by-metre addition to quays to match the ton-by-ton increase of trade.

In recent years increases of traffic have been so rapid at many ports that very large extensions of facilities or deepening of port approaches have had to be considered, particularly where the traffic has been of a new kind that cannot be handled in the older parts of ports for one reason or another. The opportunity cost of the capital required must be borne in mind, using techniques of investment appraisal. The discounted cash flow (dcf) technique involves calculating year by year over the expected life of the project the net cash flow (cash receipts minus capital expenditure) (*Investment Appraisal*, 1967). In the first few years the cash flows may be negative because of the heavy capital expenditure; at the end of the project's life there may be some residual capital value. There are some difficulties in assigning a duration for the life of a port installation. The technical life of a wharf, for instance, may not be the actual life which eventuates, as A. Hendrup, 1966, has pointed out. New developments may make existing structures obsolescent, and the older parts of ports are threatened by the expanding central functions of cities. Changes in commodity mix may make specialised facilities redundant, oil terminals replacing coal staiths; and maybe a change-over to atomic power will in turn prevent those very oil terminals reaching the end of their technical lives.

The net present value of the project appraised is the sum of the present values of each of the years of the project's life, discounted at the agreed rate of discount to be employed (see L. H. Klaassen and

N. Vanhove, 1970, 30 *n.*; and M. H. Peston and R. Rees, 1970, Appendix i). The discounting is necessary because £100 today is worth £110 in a year's time, so that cash flows in the future must be discounted backwards to obtain the net present value. (R. O. Goss, 1968, quotes a formula, 183; see also R. O. Goss, 1967.) Such a technique can be used to compare investments in alternative port projects, and a variant of it, using discounted costs, was employed to select the optimum type of iron ore terminal for South Wales (*Iron Ore Imports into South Wales*, 1963). If a project has an NPV greater than O, it is economically viable; between alternative projects, the one with the higher NPV is selected. Such an alternative might comprise comparing a port expansion with some other capital investment in another sector of a country's economy. Where alternative port projects are in question, the revenue over the life of the projects may be considered as identical, and then discounting the costs alone may be consider justifiable.

L. H. Klaassen and N. Vanhove, 1970, 50, have pointed out that the amount of capital involved in a project must be brought into the calculations, and if $\dfrac{B}{C}$ is the benefit-cost ratio and R the ratio of dcf to total present value of costs, then

$$\frac{\text{dcf}}{C}=R=\frac{B-C}{C}=\frac{B}{C}-1$$

This paper by a Dutch economist and a Belgian economist is cast in macro-economic terms.

> The objective of this report is to indicate those elements which must be taken into consideration when making a macro-economic evaluation of port investments. . . . Everyone who is reasonably familiar with port investments knows that, if port projects are considered from a micro-economic point of view, then in most cases they do not give an acceptable return. (op. cit., 3)

The paper is exceedingly interesting, even historic, because it appears to be the first expression from within the European Economic Community of the conclusion that the 'optimal degree of subsidisation of a port is zero' (24). This is a brave statement to make in countries where millions of public dollars have been poured into Rotterdam and Amsterdam and down the throat of the Scheldt.

However, economists rarely conclude in favour of subsidies. (For a detailed analysis of a subsidy programme for a merchant marine with a conclusion that it makes 'no substantial net contribution to

TABLE 30

SCHEMA OF POSSIBLE COSTS AND POSSIBLE BENEFITS
TO BE CHARGED IN THE CASE OF A PORT INVESTMENT

Costs	Benefits
Net profit foregone of the private investor.	Consumers' surplus* of the users of the port.
The surplus by which the expenditure of the private investor on factors of production surpasses the alternative product of these factors.	Receipts of the public sector from the sale of industrial sites.
The consumers' surplus* resulting from private investment.	Receipts of the public sector resulting from the sale or the renting out of new transhipment sites.
The extra receipts of complementary enterprises less additional use of factors of production. Less the diminution in welfare contribution of competing activities pursuant to private investment.	Receipts of the public sector from the running of port installations.
	Expenditures rendered superfluous in consequence of the port investment.
Total cost of infrastructure of the port investment.	Increase in welfare of complementary activities.
Expenditures of the public sector for the running of the port. Less the amount by which the expenditure on the port investment surpasses the alternative product of the factors of production.	Other possible benefits: (a) the eventual creation of recreation zones and housing estates, eventual creation of beaches; (b) favourable influence on international liquidity and balance of payments; (c) national independence of supplies;
Diminution in welfare of competing activities.	(d) the regional spreading of prosperity by the distribution of improved incomes;† (e) the cost of avoiding pollution (air and water and through the risks attendant on the transport inland of toxic substances).

* Consumers' surplus is the excess between the price that a consumer actually pays and the price that he would be willing to pay rather than forego the commodity.
† See also *Le projet Zeestad*, Analyse des coûts et gains, Appendix VIII (1969).
Source: L. H. Klaassen and N. Vanhove, 1970, 29–41, esp. 36, 38, and 51, except 'other possible benefits'.

the economy' see A. R. Ferguson *et al.*, 1961.) Governments frequently use subsidy allocations as part of policy, and this is just as frequently a source of noise between economic models and real life decision-making.

A paper by M. H. Peston and R. Rees, 1970, on the feasibility of
H

a cost-benefit study of MIDAS (maritime industrial development areas) for the United Kingdom raises some very interesting issues. A feature of the Peston–Rees approach is that the viability of MIDAS must be compared one with another, and also with developments elsewhere (inland, and around airports for example); and there must also be comparison of *ab initio* port development with expansion of existing ports. The authors recognise that there are two 'sets' of industry: one is closely dependent on tidewater transport; and there is a second set which is dependent on the first (see also *The Greater Delta Region*, 1968, 33). Three gaps in an admirably clear analysis appear to be: (1) the locational pull of the overseas raw material source and the export market making the port site increasingly attractive as raw material supplies increase (most efficiently carried in bulk by water) and provided there is elasticity of demand in the export market. These locational advantages are unique to the coast or inland waterway bank, for low value per unit of weight raw materials cannot be carried by land transport as cheaply as by bulk carrier, except at present in the case of oil in pipelines. (2) New MIDA sites are likely to be on reclaimed land so that the cost is likely to be an engineering sum rather than a result of bidding between competitive land uses (cf. the case of most airport sites). (3) Industrial land-use planning permission is more likely to be granted for newly-reclaimed coastal sites, especially if the area is separated from existing settlement and on a lee shore to the prevailing wind. It certainly seems likely that a MIDA built as a logical extension to an existing port or estuarine port complex would be economically more attractive than one built on a 'bluecoast site' (a term analogous to that of 'greenfield site' for industry). The former case could profit from existing investment in transport links, availability of labour and services, and the proximity of a market and industrial linkages in the extant port itself.

The Peston–Rees comments on cost-benefit techniques seem to sum up the present position very well:

A cost-benefit analysis may rule out certain possibilities on objective grounds, but may also leave sufficient possibilities on which subjective judgements will have to be made. (22, para 25)

In sum, the relevant alternatives are specified, the relevant flows of costs and benefits are itemised, and the form in which they will be relevant to decision making is laid out. Equally the multi-dimensional nature of the problem is indicated so that it will always be apparent to the decision maker which cost and benefit flows have been quantified and evaluated and which have not. (36, para 64)

The authors distinguish between direct and indirect benefits of a port project and introduce the concept of a cost difference which is

equal to the difference in port and other costs of using the facilities between the old and the new ports plus the transport saving to the new port plus the transport saving from the new port plus the change in the costs of handling, storage and wastage. Not all these elements need be positive. Some may be negative but be offset by larger positive savings elsewhere. (27, para 39)

If as price varies by one unit, the use of the facilities varies by a, 'the total gain in net benefit is equal to the cost difference, c, times the quantity change, $\dfrac{c}{a}$, divided by 2, i.e. $\dfrac{c^2}{2a}$'.

Indirect benefits accruing to the second set of industries are manifested by rises in land values, and there are rises in employment opportunities (multiplier effect), although these latter two features may be a benefit switched from another area where they are cancelled out as a cost. A step-by-step investigation is recommended. The first phase would deal with port costs and the costs and benefits accruing to the first set of industries. The locational problem of industries and the detailed investigation of the second industrial set, together with the amenity problem, would receive greater emphasis in stage two of the exercise.

Finally, Professor Peston and Mr Rees raise the chicken and egg question of whether ports generate large-scale industry or whether 'location plans and trade independently considered and determined by other factors give rise to demand for new port development'. This author would argue that the second case is nearer the truth, but there is the important factor of what may be termed industrial latency. The demand may exist but the locational opportunities may not because coastal sites by definition are not ubiquitous, and suitable coastal sites probably have to be constructed. It is this sequence of events that give port projects the superficial appearance of industrial stimuli. In other words the hen (industrial decision-maker) wants to lay an egg (obtain a seaboard industrial site) but cannot do so. Hen food is provided (port industrial infrastructure), and the hen lays the egg (seaboard industrial implantation), and lays the egg, moreover, at relatively short notice. But the hen must have the latent ability to lay the egg in the first place. These ideas chime in with the 'infrastructure-superstructure construction time differential' emanating from Rotterdam's practical experience (see p. 87 ff., above, and Fig. 22).

Professors Klaassen and Vanhove do allow a weighting for a port project in an underdeveloped region, 'the revaluation being the result of an economic-political option' (op. cit., 29), but in the framework of a European port policy (46). This problem was once looked at (J. Bird, 1967, 318–19) in the light of J. K. Galbraith's theory of countervailing power. In this theory the growth of concentration in industry is counterbalanced by the increasing power of the suppliers and customers. But this countervailing power will not arise so readily against seaports because customers and suppliers will themselves foster seaport concentration to a large extent. The tendency in non-bulk deep-sea shipping economics is to concentrate on the largest ports, and in a European context the economic integration of the hinterland will tend to cause land carriers to focus on the largest ports with the best long-distance communications. Professor Galbraith has declared that the support of countervailing power has become perhaps the major domestic peacetime function of government (J. K. Galbraith, 1957, 136). But in seaport terms this would be extremely difficult, since it would mean the assistance of carriers to ports. In Europe such assistance would run counter to the Commission's transport policy. On the sea such assistance would be available to EEC 'nationals' and non-nationals (foreign shipowners) alike. Consideration of countervailing power leads to the conclusion that, if it cannot be operated, the best substitute would be the subsidisation of competition—the support of smaller ports against those deriving greatest benefit from the economic union of the hinterland. Of course, it might be decided merely to pursue the principle of comparative advantage to the full, and L. Rodwin has an interesting comment on this:

. . . one might argue that there is no need for criteria or decision rules for regional development. Presumably, the optimum pattern would emerge from traditional market behaviour. But this rule wouldn't be of much help in deciding where to invest overhead capital unless one assumed that these public decisions were to be made after the private investment decisions occurred, which after all would be equivalent to following the dictates of the market. (L. Rodwin, 1964, 41; see also H. Juergensen, 1970)

The weight of evidence seems to suggest that for the foreseeable future port investment appraisal will include a weighting for governmental intervention. But it is most important that the economic exercises be first carried out as rigorously as the techniques and data availability permit, so that decision-makers are aware of the dimensions of the weighting subsequently applied. One of the considerations involved will be a judgement of the risks attached to various projects, and L. H. Klaassen and N. Vanhove suggest that cost-benefit ratios might be provided with associated probability distributions (op. cit., 51). Finally, on this subject of cost-benefit analysis, a possible difficulty with such an assessment technique in establishing criteria for port improvements has been pointed out by R. O. Goss,

1968, 172, and derives from the international linkages of ports. While the costs of port investments are borne by one country 'the benefits may accrue to that country and to a variety of trading partners in proportions depending on the elasticities of supply and demand' (R. O. Goss, in correspondence to the author, 14 April 1970); see also the problems of developing nations in this connection, p. 169 above).

For such appraisal exercises to be meaningful, port charges must be related to costs, preferably marginal costs, and the question arises as to whether these costs should be short-run marginal costs or long-run marginal costs. J. O. Jansson, 1969, has suggested that the basis of long-run marginal costing is preferable where there is a dynamic situation of growing traffic, but that short-run marginal costing is preferable to smooth out peaks and troughs of traffic flows. It would appear that port charges would have to be assessed on the long-run to carry out dcf exercises, which in themselves would have been necessitated by a desire to increase infrastructures in a dynamic situation of rising trade. R. O. Goss, 1968, 181, has pointed out that because a non-optimal system of port pricing is common, optimal results by dcf methods cannot be achieved. Benefits are difficult to measure but are included in the 'shadow values' of ships using the installation. A shadow price includes all the normal costs of operating the vessel, the rate of return in the long run, plus any specific variation in these figures, such as lower turn-round cost, brought about by the project in question. G. H. Peters, 1968, 49–50, in a comment on these ideas, points out that there are few externalities in the sphere of port pricing, or direct group wants. Such application of investment appraisal on the basis of marginal social cost pricing is here being introduced not because commercial and social interests conflict, but because the costs do not truly reflect the benefits. In economic terms this is therefore an argument for pricing according to the marginal costs involved in providing the service.

Investment appraisal involves not only a criterion for an optimal pricing policy, the subject of the preceding section above, but is also a tool in port planning. This discussion may seem to come off the page with an aura of the desk and the study, but it finds terse and practical support from a vice-president of the World Bank. Principles propounded from that source demand alert attention from those countries who seek international aid in developing their ports:

Another basic principle of Bank policy is that a port entity should be financially viable; charge rates should be related to the cost of the services provided and should produce an adequate return on the investment. (S. Alderwereld, 1967, 4)

(A) GENERAL REFERENCES FOR CHAPTER 8

Alderwereld, S. (1967) *Problems in the Development of Ports in the ECAFE Countries.* Tokyo: International Association of Ports and Harbours Conference, 1967.

Bird, J. (1957) *The Geography of the Port of London.* London: Hutchinson.

——(1967) Seaports and the European Economic Community, *Geographical Journal,* 133, 302–27.

Comparison of the Costs of Continental and United Kingdom Ports, A (1970) Report to the [British] National Ports Council by Touche Ross and Co.

Culbert, F. G., and Leighton, F. C. (1963) Application of a digital simulation model to the planning of a bulk commodity deep-sea marine terminal, *Canadian Transportation Research Forum,* 1–3 May, Vancouver.

Daniels, W. J. (1966) The economics of berth employment and carrier size, *The Dock and Harbour Authority,* 47, 251–3.

Economic Impact of the Delaware River Ports [The] (1959). Philadelphia: Alderson Associates Inc.

Eddison, R. T., and Owen, D. T. (1953) Discharging iron ore, *Operational Research Quarterly,* 4, 39–51.

Emerson, E. C. (1968) Aspects of container flows, *Proceedings of an International Container Symposium.* London: Chamber of Commerce, 104–11.

Ferguson, A. R. et al. (1961) *The Economic Value of the United States Merchant Marine.* Evanston: Northwestern University Transportation Center.

Galbraith, J. K. (1957) *American Capitalism: the Concept of Countervailing Power.* London: Hamilton.

Garnett, H. C. (1970) Competition between ports and investment planning, *Scottish Journal of Political Economy,* 17, 411–24.

Greater Delta Region: an Evaluation of Development and Administration [The] (1968). Rotterdam: Municipality.

Goss, R. O. (1967) The economics of dredging, *Dredging.* Proceedings of the Symposium organised by the Institution of Civil Engineers 18 October, 17–21, 23.

——(1968) *Studies in Maritime Economics.* Cambridge: University Press.

Hendrup, A. (1966) Some remarks on the rules of depreciation for new harbour construction, *Ports and Harbours,* 11, 5 and 15.

Hoch, I. (1959) A comparison of alternative inter-industry forecasts for the Chicago Region, *Papers and Proceedings of the Regional Science Association,* 5, 217–35.

Incoterms 1953, International Rules for the Interpretation of Trade Terms (1967). Paris: International Chamber of Commerce.

Investment Appraisal (1967) London: National Economic Development Council, 2nd ed.

Iron Ore Imports into South Wales (1963). London: HMSO, Cmnd. 2706.

Jansson, J. D. (1969) *Some Aspects of the Theory of Pricing and Investment in the Transport Infrastructure, using a Sea-port as an Illustrative Example.* London: ICHCA, mimeographed project MS.

Juergensen, H. (1970) *The Investment Policy of European Maritime Ports with regard to Regional Implications.* Paper delivered at Semaine de Bruges, April. Bruges: College of Europe.

Klaassen, L. H., and Vanhove, N. (1970) *Macro-economic Evaluation of Port Investments.* Paper delivered at Semaine de Bruges, April. Bruges: College of Europe.

Lunch, E. P. J. (1966) Comment (p. 85) on A. S. Svendsen (1966), see below.

McLoughlin, T. A., and Eden, E. (1964) *The Harbours Act 1964 with Annotations.* London: Dock and Harbour Authorities' Association.

Nationalised Industries (1967) London: HMSO, Cmnd. 3437.

1970 Outlook for Deep Sea Container Services (1967) Report to [British] National Ports Council by Arthur D. Little Ltd.

Ocean Freight Rates as Part of Total Transport Costs (1968) Paris: OECD.

O'Loughlin, C. (1967) *The Economics of Sea Transport.* London: Pergamon.

Omtvedt, P. (1963) *Report on the Profitability of Port Investments.* Oslo: mimeographed.

Option in Transport Tariff Policy (1965) [Allais Report] EEC Transport Series I, Brussels.

Pelcynski, Z. (1964) *The Influence of General Cargo Quay Facilities on the Costs of Transport.* Gdansk.

Peston, M. H., and Rees, R. (1970) *Feasibility Study of a Cost Benefit Assessment of Maritime Industrial Areas.* London: National Ports Council.

Peters, G. H. (1968) *Cost-Benefit Analysis and Public Expenditure.* Eaton Paper no. 8. London: Institute of Economic Affairs.

Posthuma, F. (1967) *Impact on Port Development of Modern Trends in Ship Design.* Tokyo: International Association of Ports and Harbours.

Price, E. H. M. (1966) Port economics, *The Dock and Harbour Authority*, **46**, 367–8.

Projet Zeestad, Le: analyse de ses possibilités techniques de réalisation et de son interêt économique (1969). Brussels: Banque de Paris et des Pays Bas.

Report of the Committee of Enquiry into the Major Ports of Great Britain [Rochdale Report] (1962). London: HMSO, Cmnd. 1824.

Rodwin, L. (1964) Choosing regions for development, *Regional Development and Planning*, J. Friedmann and W. Alonso (Eds.), 37–580. MIT.

Schenker, E. (1967) *The Port of Milwaukee.* Milwaukee: University of Wisconsin Press.

Shirley, P. H. (1968) Why do we use containers? *Proceedings of an International Container Symposium.* London: Chamber of Commerce, 18–20.

Study of Port Operations [A]: *Part A—The Total Port System* (1967). University of Lancaster: Department of Operational Research.

Svendsen, A. S. (1966) Does the traditional set-up of port charges favour old and unmodern ships? *Papers read at the Oslo Conference of the Ship Research Institute of Norway*, 67–79a.

Tabak, H. D. (1970) *Cargo Containers: their Storage, Handling, and Movement.* Cambridge Md.: Cornell Maritime Press.

Thoman, R. S. (1956) *Free Ports and Foreign Trade Zones.* Cambridge, Md.: Cornell Maritime Press.

Thorburn, T. (1960) *Supply and Demand of Water Transport.* Stockholm: School of Economics.

Value of a Ton of Cargo to the Area's Economy [The] (1953 and later). Philadelphia: Delaware River Port Authority.

(B) DISCUSSION OF TYPES OF PORT ADMINISTRATION

Basten, H. (1952) *Report on the Turn-round of Ships in Australian Ports.* Canberra: Commonwealth Government, 4 January.

Baudelaire, J. A. (1966) Ideal port organisation, *The Dock and Harbour Authority*, **47**, 90–2, 111–14.

Baudez, L. (nd) *Economie portuaire.* Antwerp: Lloyd Anversois, pp. 71–93.

Bird, J. (1963) *The Major Seaports of the United Kingdom.* London: Hutchinson, 423–5.

——(1968) *Seaport Gateways of Australia.* Oxford: University Press, pp. 218–20.

Buchanan, Sir George (1926–8) *Report on Transport in Australia with Special Reference to Port and Harbour Facilities.* Canberra: Commonwealth Parliamentary Papers, V (Session 1926–27–25) [vol. I] 81–239 and [vol. II] 241–99.

Chapon, J. P. (1966) The recent changes in French port administration, *The Dock and Harbour Authority,* **46** (1966), 345–8.

Delwaide, L. (1964) Systems of port administration and management, *The Dock and Harbour Authority,* **44** (1964), 348–50.

Gordon, L. (1937) The Port of London Authority, *Public Enterprise.* London: Allen and Unwin.

Hedden, W. P. (1967) *Mission: Port Development—with Case Studies.* Washington: American Association of Port Authorities.

Morgan, F. W. (1958) *Ports and Harbours.* 2nd ed. London: Hutchinson, 22–5.

Nagorski, B. (1955) Administration of the ideal port, *Progress in Cargo Handling,* **1**, 25–33.

——(1960) The operation and administration of ports: comparisons of various systems of management, *The Dock and Harbour Authority,* **40**, 371–3.

——(1968) Port problems in developing countries, *The Dock and Harbour Authority,* **49**, 36–43, 39.

Report of the Committee of Inquiry into the Major Ports of Great Britain [Rochdale Report] (1962) London: HMSO, Cmnd. 1824, 36–43.

Szczepaniak, T. (1968) The Polish model of port administration and organisation of the port services, *Fifth International Harbour Congress,* 2–8 June. Antwerp. Paper 8.1.

9

PORTS AND PLANNING (II)

Port planning and the time scale

Transport is not only carriage of an item from one place to another, but also a synthesis of space and time. The space is that occupied by the routes and nodes of a transport network. The time element is involved in the schedule of movement through the network and the planning of such movement over short, intermediate, and long periods of time ahead. A port is manifestly a node within a network, and for the sake of exposition the time element in port planning is considered before a survey of the spatial effect at different scales.

Short-term port planning concerns periods of up to only a few days ahead. One of the basic difficulties has resulted from the fact that the sea carrier has always had a larger capacity than the contemporary land carriers, and so matching of cargo quantities between carriers has always been a prime function of ports, storing cargo in transit sheds or container parks for short periods, or in warehouses for longer periods, of say more than ten days. Before the advent of radio, ships appeared in port approaches with little notice, and precise times of arrival are still affected by weather hazards, although the influence of these has decreased while the incidence of strikes and labour go-slows has increased. The *ad hoc* arrival and departure of the sailing ship was the prime reason for the growth of casual employment on the waterfront—men themselves engaged *ad hoc* for the irregular work load. Many factors have helped to reduce the uncertainties of ship movement: ship's speed being independent of weather; radar aids in fog; bigger, faster, and fewer ships make for easier programming; and the homogenisation of cargo in bulk or in containers makes for speedier cargo-handling once the ship has arrived. Each port or terminal maintains a berthing programme so that ships may use the installations as compatibly as possible. But the role of the harbourmaster with his local authority over port operations has declined in importance compared with the traffic officer who is in touch not only with ships in the port and its approaches but also on the oceans, and even overseas before the voyage relevant to that particular port has even begun. Essentially, short-term planning is an attempt to cope with short-term peaks and troughs, attendant on the arrival and departure of ships.

Peaks and troughs may also occur seasonally because of the periodic harvest of agricultural crops or perhaps the winter freeze-up of port approaches. If the product is not perishable, port stores can even out the flow. For example, Queensland sugar mills feed port terminals only during the crushing season which is the latter half of the year, and so port storage sheds have a capacity which is enough for six months' loading of ships at the end of the crushing season. The Israel Ports Authority was forced to define the duration of different time periods of port planning owing to the seasonal irregularity in the volume of citrus fruit shipments, with a December–April peak. Short-term planning is defined as covering the period of one to three days ahead, while intermediate planning covers future periods up to one month or a year. Long range planning is held to cover periods longer than one year. The necessity for the concept of intermediate planning arose in the 1963–4 citrus fruit season, when shipping bottlenecks occurred, with delays of up to five days. The main problem was the organisation of the labour force to cope with the uneven work-load, and this would have been easier if peaks of traffic could have been foreseen. Accordingly, among the tasks of intermediate range planning are:

(1) recruiting and training a suitable labour force;

(2) increasing the work rate prior to the date of peak loads, so as to enter the peak with a smaller back-log;

(3) reducing the amount of cargo handled manually during the peak period, as this contributes to congestion;

(4) encouraging shipment direct from land carrier during peak periods;

(5) providing a port information service warning shipowners of peaks of traffic at ports (in the case of Israel, at Haifa and Ashdod); and

(6) planning maintenance of equipment and leave of labour to coincide with the slack period (*Intermediate Range Planning*, 1968).

The Israel experience shows that it is necessary to issue a monthly forecast every fortnight, since as soon as one enters the period covered by intermediate planning, the information about ships becomes less reliable as Table 31 shows.

TABLE 31

INFORMATION FOR PORT PLANNING AND THE TIME ELEMENT

	Information during planned month		
Item of information	*Days 1 to 10*	*Days 11 to 20*	*Days 21–30*
Name of ship	Always known	Usually known	Sometimes known
Date of arrival/departure	Always known, with accuracy	Variances of ± 2 days common	Average variance ±3 days
Type and quantity of cargo	Known in most cases with accuracy	Only known in certain circumstances	Usually unknown and only general indications can be deduced

Source: *Intermediate Port Planning*, op. cit.

A year makes a good division between intermediate and long range planning because many of the figures that require to be projected into the future exist in time series erected on an annual basis. The planned or hoped-for growth in a country's gross national product (GNP) is often used as a basis for projecting the growth of seaborne trade; and a model can be constructed to distribute trade between ports in the future as it has been in the past (see pp. 138–9), with local implications for the provision of installations. Two forecast exercises carried out for the Greater Delta Region of Rotterdam will illustrate the techniques used to deal with the complicated interrelated factors. (*The Greater Delta Region*, 1968, and *Rotterdam–Rijnmond Land Use and Transportation Study*, 1969.) Consider Table 32 which appears so simple and definite, and then working through the various cargoes mentioned therein, consider also the assumptions made in order to extrapolate from present figures to construct the table and the factors considered relevant.

The oil forecast assumed diversions from German ports as deeper draught becomes available to Europort, and also assumes that 25% will consist of transhipments to Great Britain. The ore tonnage assumes an average ore content of 45%; but producing countries may enrich their ore before shipment (benefication). If this makes average or content rise to 90%, then the forecast tonnage would have

TABLE 32

GREATER DELTA REGION OF ROTTERDAM:
FORECAST POTENTIAL TONNAGES

million tons

Year	Oil	Ore	Cereals	Fertilisers	Coal	Other bulk cargo	Break-bulk cargo	Total
1967	79	18	7	5	6	4	22	141
1980	278	68	15	6	12	13	38(7)	430
1990	398	100	17	6	16	22	55(14)	614
2000	545	128	19	6	20	35	75(23)	828

Figures in brackets represent potential diversion as air cargo.
Source: *The Greater Delta Region*, op. cit., 69.

to be reduced by 60%. Cereals also include an assumption that there would be transhipment to Great Britain, comprising half the tonnages quoted. The forecasters have noted that demand for cereals and fertilisers is much less elastic than for other cargoes (plus more 'home' production of fertilisers), and this causes their forecast growth to be much less than for other cargoes. The forecast for 'other bulk cargoes' is in line with the assumed industrial growth of the European Economic Community at 5% per year. Other assumptions are that break-bulk cargo will follow the forecast growth of the Community's GNP which is expected to decline from 4·6% to 3% in the year 2000. Finally, it is forecast that 60% of break-bulk cargo will be containerised in 1980, 80% in 2000; with 20% carried by air in 1980, rising to 30% in 2000 (*The Greater Delta Region*, op. cit., 71–7).

Assuming all the time series considered relevant have been assembled, the Rotterdam–Rijnmond study shows how to refine the forecast.

It would have seemed feasible, though not satisfactory, to extrapolate the trends apparent in these time series and arrive at a forecast in a straightforward manner. A much more convincing, but difficult, approach is to take each time series individually or in groups, and determine as far as possible the prime causes of change within them. In this way a number of 'explanatory' causes are determined for each variable to be forecast, all of which are best described in the form of other time series. (op. cit., 9)

Of course, special events that cannot be ascribed to economic causes, such as the Suez Canal closure, have to be given special treatment. It must also be admitted that if all port tariffs and facilities were

TABLE 33

FACTORS IN PORT TRAFFIC FLOW FORECASTING

Cargo diversions from other ports with increased size of ships and their
  consequent less flexible terminal operation
Changes in cargo content (benefication and containerisation)
Varying elasticities of demand
Growth of relevant GNPs
Competition from the air
Industrial growth
Relative demand at home and overseas for imported and exported products
Time series emanating from the past

Known facts*	Unknown factors
Port capacities	Political considerations affecting port investments
Hinterland linkages	Budget restraints
Location, size and type of hinterland industries	Industrial investment in the hinterland
	Changing policies of regional planning
	Technological innovations in transport and industry

* Based on R. Regul (1970, 38–9).

equal for all European ports, there would still be different tonnages
flowing through the ports of Europe simply because they are in
different places. And the physical ability of Rotterdam to take larger
vessels than some other North Sea ports gives this Dutch port a cost
advantage over those rivals. With these three points in mind, it
nevertheless proved possible to make equations for the flows of
traffic based on a fifteen-year time series of flows. Where the product
flow could be specified, the independent variables fell into the
following groups:

(1) where the demand or requirement for a particular flow could
sometimes be represented by the consumption minus the home production of the commodity, though more often the destination country
exports the same product group or imports it from more than a single
source, involving the addition of a variable to allow for elasticities of
substitution;

(2) where the tonnages of flow do not always indicate the utility of
the cargo (the mineral content of ores is different with different
origins);

(3) in the form of a constant term, denoting a residual preference
for the flow in question, including dormant variables (that have not
varied over the last fifteen years), masked variables, which do not act
as independent variables because they are counteracted by other

variables, and various psychological factors that go to make up the total reason for port preference.

An example of one of the equations is given below, referring in fact to the largest transit flow forecast by the model for the year 1990:

Freight flow Rotterdam–Rijnmond to Belgium–Luxembourg

$$\text{Economic Union} = 1457\ R_b{}^{0.01} \left(\frac{Z_h}{Z_f}\right)^{0.41} I_b{}^{1.77}$$

where

R_b = oil requirement in Belgian–Luxembourg Economic Union
Z_h = refinery capacity in the Netherlands
Z_f = refinery capacity in France
I_b = refinery capacity in Belgium–Luxembourg smoothing factor

The upper case letters denote the major variables, the lower case letters denote the destinations and products, and the numerical coefficients express the contribution made by the respective variables.

The Rotterdam–Rijnmond study also attempted a modal split forecast for the year 1990. 'Modal split' is a term referring to the proportion of traffic carried by different forms or modes of transport, and in the case of ports indicates the ways in which cargo is collected and dispersed by land transport. A modal split equation was derived from examination of past time series, and after some 250 regression equations had been analysed, it was found best to base the modal split equation on the estimated costs of various forms of transport, with a time-lag of one year built in so that transport users could have time to react to cost changes.

As time goes on, and more data and better basic information become available, it will be possible to make better forecasts. Forecasting should therefore be a continuous process; and in order to obtain the maximum benefit from the models that are being developed as part of this study, a regular system of updating and model refinement is essential. (op. cit., 34)

There seems to be a consensus on this type of continuous revision approach. Compare the above quotation with

Planning is a continuous process. New data are produced continually, on the basis of which conclusions must be reshaped. For this reason, the present study [dated 1963 and projected to 1980] will be kept under review by the Port [of New York] Authority during the years ahead and its findings modified to reflect changes in conditions, in experience and judgement. (*Metropolitan Transportation—1980*, 1963, vi) [and] . . . we need a general long-range plan . . . of a 'rolling' type . . . (*Nordtrans*, 1969, 187)

Port planning and the spatial scale

The spatial spheres of port planning may be conveniently analysed under five headings, with progressive areal increase of the field of action: the lay-out and functioning of a particular berth—the operational approach; within the perimeter of port and water conservancy area—the port management approach; the port with its hinterland—the regional approach; the port as one of a group of ports serving a national territory—the national approach; and the port as one of a group of ports serving states linked together economically—the international approach. These spheres of action interlock not only with each other but also with the various time scales.

The operational approach has already been covered, particularly in Chapters 3 and 4. Taking the port as a whole, management can plan for physical expansion if forecasts of future traffic are kept in trim and look good. Very often the key factor to port development is the depth of water in the port approaches. Where ports must maintain or capital dredge their approaches out of their own budgets, their future development is linked to their past successes in attracting traffic. Under circumstances of each port paying its way, inclusive of dredging bills, no new major multi-functional port is likely to arise in an area that may require heavy initial capital dredging costs in competition with established ports that have hauled themselves through the phase of capital dredging over many decades. Where ports have the dredging costs borne to a greater or lesser extent by the state, there is a risk that ports and ships may plan for depths in channels regardless of expense. Two examples of the safeguards necessary in such a situation are given from Western Germany and the US.

The following quotation is extracted from a treaty between the Bremen *Land* (a State government which administers the Port of Bremen) and the central Federal Government:

Bremen has continuously worked towards the deepening of the navigable channels from the sea to Bremen so that standard-sized cargo vessels in international trade [*Regelfrachtschiff im Weltverkehr*] can navigate between the high seas and the Port of Bremen. The [Federal] State will do the same. (*Zusatzvertrag mit Bremen*, etc. 1922, 224, paras 18 and 19)

The Corps of Engineers of the United States Army undertakes port approach dredging in the US which is thus financed by the national federal budget. The initial request for dredging is to formulate depth requirements which are authorised after public hearings and reports through successive levels within the Corps of Engineers, finally reported to Congress and, if approved, incorporated in a

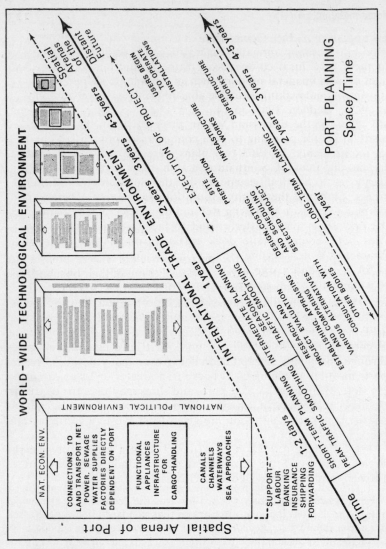

Fig. 22 Port planning over space and time

The rectangular blocks, retreating into the time distance, represent the spatial sphere of the port planner. The physical perimeter of the port is represented by the small rectangle, with the concern of the port planner becoming less direct, but still requiring to be active even off edges of the block, in the direction of the two arrows. In the time sequence the periods are approximate for major projects. Where a user plans and executes infrastructure works himself, the time span may well be shorter, i.e. moved towards the bottom left for each stage. See also *The Greater Delta Region*, etc., 1968, 136–52.

Rivers and Harbors Bill. Committees of Congress vote other 'appro-
priation bills', usually annually, for maintenance dredging, and very
often there is a 'local co-operation clause', requiring some small
amount of local financial support, such as a minimum shore terminal
improvement, and making available abutting land and spoil dumping
areas (W. P. Hedden, 1965, 35–6).

Still retaining the discussion within the port perimeter, another
necessity arises for planning to be a compromise between land and
water requirements. In 1963 two plans were put forward for the
future development of Southampton, but they were both based
primarily on a nautical viewpoint, by the Southampton Master
Mariners' Club and the Trinity House Pilotage Service. There is a
sound nautical reason in having wet and dry docks aligned parallel
to the prevailing south-westerly wind to facilitate easy entry; and
this led both bodies to site dock entrances on the west side of
Southampton Water, despite the fact that all landward communications for break-bulk cargo are focussed on the eastern side where
there is plenty of room to expand the existing docks. Thus it is unlikely that development on the shore opposite from the existing
docks will supervene until the extensions on the eastern side have
used up the available flat area, merely extending the existing landward links. In 1964 the author, commenting in this vein, went on to
adumbrate a four-step process in port planning, once an economic
demand via trade growth had been established:

Step A The drawing of plans based on a compromise of what appears
         best from *both* the nautical and landward appraisals of the sites.

Step B Engineers' plans to satisfy the basic requirements of Step A.

Step C Revision of Step A in the light of engineers' advice, particularly
         in regards to costs; reference back to all interested parties.

Step D Programme of development drawn up so that it can be con-
         structed in stages, later stages being implemented as the demands
         of future users justify.

All port planning demands foresight. This may be achieved by one plan
ab initio. But this is a gamble. 'Open-end' planning hedges the bet. Then
future planners, or even future generations, can bend or alter each stage
of the plan to suit the exigencies and technology of their day. (J. Bird,
1964)

This proved to be a description of the planning policy followed by
the port authority at Southampton (S. A. Finnis, 1964).

The fear expressed that a port plan today might shackle the port
planner tomorrow also found expression in a fascinating informal
discussion held at the Institution of Civil Engineers on 26 November

1964 (Design for Obsolescence, 1965), one speaker confining himself to lock entrances for break-bulk cargo ships. As far as he could see ahead, entrances might be limited to receiving ships of 30,000 or 35,000 tons deadweight. All engineers inherited structures from the past and, with more or less ingenuity, they had managed to do something with them at far less cost than providing something completely new on a derelict site. In Hull, it had been possible to make use of docks and maritime structures many years after their normal obsolescence by relegating them to other types of traffic, providing completely new structures for the most recent traffic. In practice, no one could distinguish sufficiently between 30 and 60 years of life to make any real difference in design. A distinction could be made between five years and 100 years, but not between 30 years and 60 years. The lesson drawn by the speaker was that engineers must take care, if designing a structure for this type of life, to build in some provision for its demolition without too much cost when one's great grandchildren had to deal with the structure. Such was a view in the 1960s. The 1970s reveal that the break-bulk ship strives to avoid lock entrances altogether to achieve fast turn-round whatever the tide. But the port engineer who provides ten hectares of hard-standing for containers that do not materialise can easily turn the area into a dump for bulk cargoes, moving the container cranes elsewhere for grandchildren to play with, unless they are clever enough to have out-invented the container ship. As far as depths to be provided are concerned, a 1969 view was that

The best provision for uncertainty about future requirements is to design initially for greater depths than the immediately foreseeable requirement but prepare the designs by the most modern methods and using the utmost ingenuity to keep down costs. (*Port Structures*, 1969, 35)

The regional planner faced with an area with included ports, naturally hopes that inputs and outputs of the region's economy would pass through the region's own ports. These desires burn with even greater fervour in local chambers of commerce, especially if an extra-regional major port seems to be draining traffic away to a distant coast 'when we have perfectly good harbours available'. The fact is that deep-sea break-bulk cargo ships have steadily concentrated on those ports where large amounts of cargo are steadily generated. The British National Ports Council once called this the 'snowball of success' (*Port Development*, etc., 1965, 34, para 81). This may be illustrated by the case of Antwerp where, briefly, the snowball of success has grown as follows: shipowners make FOB concessions because of rapidity of discharge and the abundance of return cargo which in turn has been attracted to the port by the number of shipping services and the concessions they have made to exporters (A. Vigarié, 1953, 2,410). And the coming of the container ship has merely emphasised a recognisable trend.

There is a role for small ships making short ferry journeys across narrow seas. A maximum number of such small ports function where two coasts, backed by highly-developed economies, face each other without notable indentations or promontories. If there are deep-penetrating estuaries, this is where the ferry ports will be sited. The first case occurs on the English Channel coast as far west as Portsmouth; Melbourne is an example of a long-established port on a great indentation dominating local ferry traffic (across the Bass Strait to Tasmania). Small ports will also thrive if they are able to provide the required dimensions of deep water and flat riparian land. But the regional planner cannot divert established currents of trade, as Sir George Buchanan pointed out to Australians as long ago as 1926 (J. Bird, 1968, 225 ff.). The main conclusion is that it is futile to think of deep-sea ports as primers of regional development. It would be tantamount to regarding major ports only from the landward point of view and not as nodes within integrated transport systems. Such a node within such a system may act as a local multiplier (see pp. 200–1 above).

Developing ports on a regional basis, or in isolation, may lead to 'robbing Peter to pay Paul'. Very often in order to promote a port, rings of incremental radius are drawn to show how much population or cargo-generating power is within range of the port; yet the outer rings might easily be turned another way to make them of shorter radius from a rival port. Only a national body has sufficient width of view to see that the ports of the territory are developed as harmoniously as possible. A ring-master is needed, using the term in a literal sense: inside the ring are dangers of under-investment, resulting in under-developed ports; outside the ring are the dangers of over-investment and wasteful duplication of effort, resulting in under-used ports. The ring of balance must be held—a difficult feat since circumstances change and need a standing body to keep them under review.

National planning of port development is more difficult when the major ports are numerous. The number of ports serving a national territory depends not only upon the size of the country and on its density of population but upon the volume of its international trade, including transit trade. One may recall there is a distinction between a long 'centrifugal' coastline, which may give rise to many ports, and a short length of 'centripetal' coastline. Good examples of the former are islands or island continents, or squat peninsulas (e.g. Great Britain, Japan, Australia, Spain, India); and centripetal coastlines are where the territory of the country is rather pear-shaped with the coast being represented by the exposed part of the pear when cut off towards the top of the fruit (e.g. Belgium, Western Germany, Poland, Algeria, Gambia, Kenya, East Pakistan, Thailand, Cambodia). A mathematical way of investigating these relationships would be to calculate ratios of area to length of coastline for economic areas (often nation states). One would expect that the lower such a ratio, the greater would be the tendency to match a rank-size rule in which the second port had half the trade of the prime port, the third port one-third of the trade, and so on. Such a ranking is broadly found in the US with its long coastlines, four in number if the St Lawrence is included (G. H. Dury and R. S. Mathieson, 1970, 161).

Concentration sometimes occurs naturally because of the originally outstanding sites for harbours, or through other factors that may be political (as in Uruguay and Victoria, Australia). But where a number of ports of comparable size has grown organically over the centuries, the problem of the central government is often one of at least rationalisation of traffic, if not the advocacy of concentrating traffic at the most successful ports and running others down as far as their commercial trade is concerned. Unfortunately, the influence of many governments in ports is divided into separate agencies—concerned with shipping, customs, industrial development, inland transport, and even state real estate reclaimed by the port.

Many of these problems are avoided in centrally planned countries, although the application of state powers may err on the side of rigidity. In Poland for instance short-term and intermediate planning is in the hands of local port authorities who handle all the services within each port. A chief port dispatcher who controls all the dock labour and technical assistance in the port coordinates these during traffic peaks when he makes decisions on priority. However, the long-term plans are formulated by a central board of Polish ports, supervised by the Minister of Shipping. He lays down the role for each port authority under a national investment plan (G. Szczepaniak, 1968).

When states become economically grouped together, there would seem to be necessity for a unified port policy. The only mention of sea transport the Treaty of Rome setting up the European Economic Community occurs in Article 84, para 2:

The Council [of Ministers] may unanimously decide whether, to what extent and by what procedure appropriate provisions shall be made in respect of sea and air transport.

The vagueness of Article 84 (2) probably results from the inability of the Treaty signatories to agree on anything more definite (J. Bird, 1967a). The Treaty phrase 'sea transport' (*navigation maritime*) obviously includes the merchant marines of the Six which are bound by agreements wider in scope than the EEC, and any special rules imposed upon them might hinder their world competitive position. In addition, many of the cargoes imported and exported into and from the EEC are carried in 'third-country' ships, and indeed such carriers are important even in the intra-Community coastwise trade. These features were recognised by the Brussels Commission in the Memorandum on the general lines of the common transport policy, 1961.

Obviously sea and air transport have their own distinctive features and are (to a much greater extent than inland types of transport) closely connected with and dependent on the world economy. It is in the Community's own interest to take this into account and not to call into question the competitive position of sea and air transport outside the sphere of the Treaty of Rome. (op. cit., sec. 62)

In contrast, since seaports are manifestly upon the territory of the EEC, some commentators have declared that their component installations, if not the ships, fall under the rules of the Treaty (A. Reinarz, 1967), perhaps indirectly or 'par le biais' (Situation juridique . . . etc., 1962). But one document presented to the European Parliament by the Commission for Transport, and usually known as the Kapteyn Report of 1962, did consider the possibility of a European port policy. This document covered the whole question of a common European transport policy, and the following paragraph is a summary of the section concerning seaports, beginning with some general statements.

The EEC is not merely a common market but also a customs union with a common trade policy. If transport is the circulation of the blood, ports are the lungs of a continent. Ports are indissolubly linked to maritime transport. The trade of ports will increase not only because of European trade expansion but also because of the growth of trade in the developing countries. Thereafter comes the enunciation of a principle: there should be complete equality for seaports of all member states; none ought to be favoured, and all ought to have equal chances. But there are two special circumstances that might be considered: first, there are those ports where the hinterland has been restricted by the Iron Curtain, notably referring to Hamburg and Trieste [aid would be compatible with the Treaty of Rome, Article 92, para 2(c)]; secondly, there are those ports that have been handicapped by a loss of colonial trade, especially Amsterdam, Antwerp, and Marseilles [aid compatible with Article 92, para 2(b)]. The report recognises the need for concentration of port investments where the berthing of big ships is in question, though one must beware of creating monopolistic positions.

If the weight of expenditure necessitates a concentration of expenditure on a particular port for the berthing of 100,000-ton vessels, it would suffice that this concentration should be made in the context of a national plan.

Any inland transport rates favouring certain ports are contrary to the Treaty of Rome (Article 80), and it would enhance proper port competition if all ports were to be linked to the major inland waterways, presumably those waterways able to take 1,350-ton barges. Port charges play a small role in inter-port competition, but all port dues ought to be placed on the same footing. There can be no guarantee that shipping conference charges will include all Community ports in the same range, but if there are bilateral trade agreements, the ports to be used must not be stipulated, because this would again be contrary to the Treaty.

L. Schaus does not subscribe to the view in the Kapteyn Report that one can legally define a port policy under the Treaty.

For my part, I do not believe that one can thus circumscribe the port problem and consider the port as an activity in itself. In fact, with the exception of agriculture and transport, the Treaty did not envisage achieving economic integration sector by sector: the rules which it instituted aimed at individual enterprises and not at particular economic sectors. In such circumstances should a particular set of rules be drawn up for ports, simply because one is faced with a group of installations and services localised in their geographical site, and more particularly, simply because they are linked to the function of sea transport? (L. Schaus, 1963, 1462; 1965, 23)

L. Schaus goes on to argue that the harmonisation of inland transport will allow ports to exercise their proper function in a hinterland dependent upon their geographical position and their naturally competing capacities. Certain port traffics can be developed when this can be justified by economic or social necessity. The Commission cannot institute tariffs to help ports but can authorise their application. The Commission can orient the planning of major transport routes to improve the relation of certain ports with their hinterlands. Beyond this, L. Schaus does not see how one can have a Community port policy (*un régime portuaire*) within the framework of the rules of the Treaty (J. Bird, 1967b).

An interim report to the European Parliament (*Interim Report on the Common Port Tariff Policy*, 1967) compared national developments in the federation of the USA and the EEC. It pointed out that the line of separation between subsidy for a port and promotional inducement was a difficult one to draw—the ingenuity of developmental agencies always keeping one step ahead of legislative restraints. Nevertheless, it appeared in the US that the basic locational industrial patterns were not much affected by local state subsidies, although this was less likely to be the case where the rapidly growing seaboard complexes of western Europe were in question. The report saw the dangers of putting shackles on such seaboard growth poles since 'the economic growth process works concentrically outwards from the industrial areas to the less developed regions'.

In Fig. 22 the rectangular blocks representing the spatial spheres of port planning retreat into the time distance, but floating in two world-wide environments. Ports obviously enter the international realm by virtue of their shipping connections, but maritime technical improvements invented anywhere in the world are likely to become diffused through the whole system. P. H. Sinclare, research director of the British National Ports Council, once pointed out that while we commonly regard a port and its hinterland as a 'set', or symbiotic pair, a port also forms a no less important set with other ports overseas with which it is regularly linked by a sector of the world-wide fleet. The sets may be at different levels, between major ports or pivot ports, and between pivot ports and their feeder ports (*Nordtrans*, 1969, Figs. 3.2 and 3.3). A technical development in the world fleet, or implemented at the other terminal overseas, may impose a technical development at a port in order that an integrated service may be maintained. Yet it is not certain that all the benefits of an improvement in the facilities of a particular port will be retained in its home country. These benefits may be spread over the ship operator, ports and traders in countries at the other end of the route, port industries with international share capital, or even over rival ports which are lumped together in a conference rate that reflects the cost of turn-round for each member of the port group (*Development of Ports*, 1969, 6).

The agency that plans the long-term strategy of port development must be at least national in scope, to avoid the 'robbing Peter to pay Paul' form of planning, but also international in outlook to keep abreast of current developments world-wide. The next development in long-term port planning will be an agency that plans the strategic development of ports on an international basis. There is no continent where more integrated port planning would not bring important

important economic benefits, but at the moment only in the ante-rooms of the European Parliament does one discern the first stumbling moves in this direction, and the goal is still a long way off.

Bird, J. (1964) Development of the Port of Southampton. *The Dock and Harbour Authority*, **44**, 328.
——(1967a) Further debate on the Treaty of Rome, Article 84 paragraph 2 as it may affect maritime transport, *European Transport Law*, **1**, 24–47.
——(1967b) Seaports and the European Economic Community, *Geographical Journal,* **133**, 302–27.
——(1968) *Seaport Gateways of Australia.* Oxford: University Press.
Design for obsolescence in maritime works: extracts from an informal discussion [held at the Institution of Civil Engineers, 26 November] (1965) *The Dock and Harbour Authority*, **45**, 309–14.
Development of Ports: Improvement of Port Operations and Connected Facilities (1969) New York: United Nations [Preliminary Report by UNCTAD Secretariat] TD/B/C.4/42/Rev. 1.
Dury, G. H., and Mathieson, R. S. (1970) *The United States and Canada.* London: Heinemann.
Eddison, R. (1967) *Port Development.* Paper read to the Operational Research Society, 10 March. [For abstract see *Operational Research Quarterly*, **18** (1967), 187–8].
Finnis, S. A. (1964) Development of the Port of Southampton, *The Dock and Harbour Authority*, **44**, 365.
Greater Delta Region, The: an Evaluation of Development and Administration (1968). Rotterdam: Municipality.
Hedden, W. P. (1967) *Mission: Port Development—with Case Studies.* Washington: American Association of Port Authorities.
Interim Report on the Common Port Tariff Policy: Working Document of the European Parliament (1967) 24 November.
Intermediate Range Planning (1968). Israel Ports Authority.
Kapteyn, P. J. (1962) *Rapport fait au nom de la Commission des Transports sur des problèmes concernant la politique commune des transports dans le cadre de la Communauté économique europééne.* European Parliamentary Assembly. Document 126.
Metropolitan Transportation—1980: a framework for the Long-range Planning of Transportation Facilities to serve the New York–New Jersey Metropolitan Region (1963). New York: Port of New York Authority.
Nordtrans (1969) [*Norden as a Region for Coordinated Location and Transportation:* Summary in English]. Stockholm: Kungl.
Ordman, N. N. B. (1967) Port planning—some basic considerations, *Proceedings of the Institution of Civil Engineers*, **37**, 257–75; with discussion, 505–26.
Port Development: an Interim Plan (1965). London: National Ports Council.
Port Structures: an Analysis of Costs and Design of Quay Walls, Locks and Transit Sheds (1969) 2 vols. London: Report to the National Ports Council by Bertlin and Partners.
Price, E. H. M. (1967) *Port Development in the Context of National Planning.* Institution of Civil Engineers, London, Transportation Engineering Group. Unpublished paper and informal discussion, 14 December.

Regul, R. (1970) *Future Development of Maritime Transports and Its Implications on Harbour Facilities in Western Europe.* Paper delivered at Semaine de Bruges, April. Bruges: College of Europe.

Reinarz, A. (1967) *Transport Policy in the EEC.* Author's MS notes of a discussion held under the auspices of the Federal Trust, London, 23 February.

Rotterdam–Rijnmond: Land Use and Transportation Study Technical Report. Vol. II *Economic Analyses and Forecasts of Port Traffic Flows* (1969). Rotterdam: Municipality.

Schaus, L. (1963) La politique commune des transports de la CEE et la marine marchande, *Journal de la Marine Marchande*, **45**, 1,459–62.

——(1965) La CEE et les ports de mer, *Hinterland: Revue trimestrielle du Port (d'Anvers)*, **14**, 23–6.

Situation juridique de la navigation maritime et des ports dans le Traité de Rome (1962), *Revue mensuelle de Chambre de Commerce et d'Industrie de Marseille*, 737, 615–21.

Szczepaniak, G. (1968) The Polish model of port administration and organisation of the port services, *Fifth International Harbour Congress*, Antwerp 2–8 June 1968. Paper 8.1.

Vigarié, A. (1953) Anvers et l'européanisation des transports intérieurs, *Journal de la Marine Marchande*, **35**, 2,405–11, 2,417–19.

Zusatzvertrag mit Bremen (1922) Berlin: Reichsgesetzblatt.

INDEX

Bold figures indicate main references

Entries preceded by an asterisk refer to concepts, ideas, etc.

Note: Names of shipping lines, industrial firms, etc., are often abbreviated